TWAYNE'S WORLD AUTHORS SERIES

A Survey of the World's Literature

Sylvia E. Bowman, Indiana University

GENERAL EDITOR

SPAIN

Gerald E. Wade, Vanderbilt University

EDITOR

Vicente Aleixandre

(TWAS 85)

TWAYNE'S WORLD AUTHORS SERIES (TWAS)

The purpose of TWAS is to survey the major writers—novelists, dramatists, historians, poets, philosophers, and critics—of the nations of the world. Among the national literatures covered are those of Australia, Canada, China, Eastern Europe, France, Germany, Greece, India, Italy, Japan, Latin America, New Zealand, Poland, Russia, Scandinavia, Spain, and the African nations, as well as Hebrew, Yiddish, and Latin Classical literatures. This survey is complemented by Twayne's United States Authors Series and English Authors Series.

The intent of each volume in these series is to present a critical-analytical study of the works of the writer; to include biographical and historical material that may be necessary for understanding, appreciation, and critical appraisal of the writer; and to present all material in clear, concise English—but not to vitiate the scholarly content of the work by doing so.

Vicente Aleixandre

By KESSEL SCHWARTZ

University of Miami

Twayne Publishers, Inc. :: New York

Preface

Along with Jorge Guillén and Federico García Lorca, the most important and influential member of the Generation of 1925, which is often compared favorably with those of the Spanish Golden Age, Aleixandre shared with his fellow members their first exposure to pure poetry, surrealism, and intellectual poetry. He preferred suggestion to precise statement, and used subconscious and hermetic themes, free verse, visionary images and symbols. Aleixandre and his fellow poets inherited the pantheistic and impressionistic poetry of Juan Ramón Jiménez along with the temporal and historical projections of Antonio Machado. If Jiménez influenced the early Aleixandre, it was Antonio Machado who influenced the mature poet. In turn Aleixandre had a profound influence on following generations of poets such as Miguel Hernández, the Generations of 1936 and 1950, and, indeed, the most famous names of the poetic world in Spain.

In his erotic poetry, Aleixandre sought, through a fusion with the flesh of his loved one, to capture the light of unattainable passion and happiness; he broadened his psychoanalytic and surrealistic base for more human and social themes in his later work. Most critics recognize at least two stages in the poetry of Aleixandre. Starting off with a highly individualistic and irrational view of the cosmos, the poet makes of love the beginning and end of all things. In love with the cosmos, the stars, the sea, and the moon, Aleixandre seeks to fuse with his loved one because the only perfect love possible is a complete identification with the universe. Aleixandre equates thanatos with eros, for only through death and a return to the earth can one destroy the bodily limits which keep one from his love. Thus the final perfect love must be death. In his early works man, for Aleixandre, ranked last in the mineral, vegetable and animal universe. Later, from his own present, the poet tried to escape from the cruelties of civilization by returning to a kind of Paradise before the creation of man, a primitive world of innocence in which, of course, he could not permanently reside. The poet, in his universal love, which formerly put man on the periphery, concentrates in his second period, whose first real high point is *Historia del corazón* (1954), on man's existential and social problems, views man as a historical and temporal being, and feels a communion with all of humanity. Turning his eyes from cosmic love to that of man, Aleixandre sings for everybody and not just for the telluric elemental creatures. If Aleixandre's poetry of the thirties stressed the idea of cosmic fusion with the material universe through love, and in the forties and fifties examined humans, their childhood, their fleeting existence and the poet's own identification with the many, finally in 1962, with the publication of *En un vasto dominio*, it achieved a final reconciliation of man and creation. *Historia del corazón* ended with a stoic acceptance of death. *En un vasto dominio* also sorrows at man's demise but at the same time sees the universe, composed of one single material which may undergo temporal and physical changes, as eternal. A formless creation awaits fruition in the flux of time through the shaping and order of love, Aleixandre adds a new dimension to the poetry of the day, as did his destructive love and provocative Paradise, and preaches the universal communion of all matter.

Contents

VICENTE ALEIXANDRE

Chronology

1898   April 28 Vicente Aleixandre born at Seville. Had one sister. Grandfather military superintendent of the district.

1900   His father, an engineer, transferred to Málaga. Family spent summers at a house a few kilometers from the city at the beach of Pedregalejo.
Aleixandre attended school run by nuns.

1905   Attended classes of don Buenaventura Barranco. Read fairy tales of Andersen and Grimm.

1909-1913   Moved to Madrid. Entered the Colegio Teresiano for study, a school based on disciplinary approach. Read Conan Doyle, the Iliad, Schiller's dramas, and many other works found in his grandfather's library.

1913   Obtained his high school degree.

1914   Studied law and mercantile management in the Escuela Superior de Comercio. Took first course in Spanish literature and read intensively, in the National Library, nineteenth-century novels by Galdós and others.

1917   Vacationed in a little town near Avila, Las Navas del Marqués. Met Dámaso Alonso and discovered the poetry of Rubén Darío.

1920   Finished his studies and entered the School of Mercantile Management of Madrid as Assistant Professor.

1920-1922   Taught mercantile law and helped edit *Economics Review*.

1921   Published several articles on railroads. Employed by railroad. Discovered Bécquer and the Romantic world. Read the Mystics, Góngora, and continued his interest in Machado, Jiménez, Herrera y Reissig, Uruguayan poet, and Amado Nervo, Mexican poet.

1924-1927   Wrote poems for *Ambito* (*Ambit*), his first collection.

1925   Became ill in April and had to retire to the countryside outside Madrid, at Miraflores de la Sierra.

1926   August issue of *Revista de Occidente* contained his first published poems.

1926-1928   Published poetry in the reviews *Litoral* of Málaga, *Carmen* of Gijón, *Mediodía* of Seville and *Verso y Prosa* of Murcia.

1927   Returned to Madrid at Velintonia Street on the outskirts of the city.

1928   *Ambito* (*Ambit*) published.

1928-1929 Composed second book, *Pasión de la tierra* (*Passion of the Earth*), first announced under the titles *Evasión hacia el fondo* (*Evasion Toward the Deep*) and *Hombre de tierra* (*Man of Earth*).

1929   Discovered the works of Freud, Joyce and Rimbaud, and read Quevedo, Lope and Unamuno. Traveled to Málaga to meet Altolaguirre and Prados, publishers of *Litoral*.

1930-1931 Wrote *Espadas como labios* (*Swords Like Lips*).

1932   *Swords Like Lips* published. Suffered new illness, had a kidney removed. Convalesced in Miraflores.

1933   Returned to Madrid. Wrote *La destrucción o el amor* (*Destruction or Love*). Won National Prize for Literature for *Destruction or Love*.

1934   March: Mother died. Aleixandre traveled in England, France, Switzerland.

1934-1935 Wrote poetry of *Mundo a solas* (*World Alone*), announced under title of *Destino del hombre* (*Man's Destiny*).

1935   *Destruction or Love* published in Spain. *Passion of the Earth* published in Mexico.

1936   Finished *World Alone* in June.

1936-1939 Became ill once more. Enforced rest during the war years.

1939   Father died. At end of war young poets began to visit Aleixandre for poetry readings and consultations.

1941   Wrote *Nacimiento último* (*Final Birth*), originally announced as *Desamor* (*Lack of Love*).

1944   *Sombra del paraíso* (*Shadow of Paradise*) acclaimed as the Bible of the new generation of poets, published.

1945-1953 Wrote *Historia del corazón* (*History of the Heart*).

1949   Elected to the Royal Academy.

1950   *World Alone* published.

1952   *Poemas paradisíacos* (*Paradise Poems*), selections from *Shadow of Paradise*, published.

1953   *Final Birth* published.

1954   *History of the Heart* published.

1956   *Mis poemas mejores* (*My Best Poems*) published.

1958   *Los encuentros* (*The Encounters*) published.

1960   *Poesías completas* (*Complete Poems*) and *Poemas amorosos* (*Amorous Poems*) published.

1961   *Picasso* published. Also *Antigua casa madrileña* (*Ancient Madrid House*), later a part of *En un vasto dominio* (*In a Vast Dominion*).

1962   *In a Vast Dominion* published.

1965   *Presencias* (*Presences*), an anthology, published. Also *Retratos con nombre* (*Portraits With a Name*).

CHAPTER 1

Twentieth Century Spanish Poetry

I Modernism

WHILE the immediate impetus for twentieth-century poetic innovations undoubtedly came from the movement known as Modernism, a nineteenth-century poet, Gustavo Adolfo Bécquer, influenced the king of the Modernists, Rubén Darío, and a great number of other contemporary poets. Juan Ramón Jiménez felt that a fundamental relationship existed between Miguel de Unamuno and Bécquer, and Dámaso Alonso saw Bécquer's hand in the best of Rafael Alberti, Federico García Lorca, and Manuel Altolaguirre. Jorge Guillén admits Béquer's influence, and Vicente Aleixandre is perhaps Bécquer's most obvious heir as the poet of love.

In 1936, the anniversary of Bécquer's death, many special studies were dedicated to him by Luis Cernuda and others. Bécquer's fame as a lyric poet rests on one small volume called *Rimas* (*Rhymes*), love poems which some consider the spiritual autobiography of the poet. He sees his love in nature and in an imaginery muse in the form of a woman. He loved vainly a flesh-and-blood woman, Julia Espín y Guillén, who was also a factor in his seventy-six little poems (some say seventy-nine or eighty, for no authentic edition exists). Bécquer was deeply subjective and sentimental, musical, and melancholy. He deals in half shadows, uncertain shapes, suggestion, tenderness, and the intangible. His is a poetry of sighs, smoke, spider webs and wispy fog through which run the constant notes of resignation and tenderness. One can find Bécquer's melancholy in Antonio Machado, and in much of twentieth-century poetry his mystic, intangible, musical world. Dámaso Alonso, referring to the magic of his words, finds him the "point of departure for all contemporary Spanish poetry."[1] Although Darío briefly influenced a number of twentieth-century poets, they soon rejected him for Bécquer.

The Modernist movement has countless interpreters who define it in dozens of different ways. Listed as among its poetic procedures one finds brevity, intensity, rare mysterious melancholy, vague, intangible and musical themes, renovation of form, and in its initial stages, an overemphasis on escapist, evasive aestheticism. Like the Romantics, some poets sought inspiration in the Middle Ages. Others, reacting against the hated bourgeois society, sought inspiration in the French Symbolists and Parnassians, and lacking a public, decided to write for art's sake. Other adjectives applied to the movement might include individualistic, libertarian, subjective, aristocratic, refined, skeptical, exotic, and mythological. Many of the poets sought a geographical exoticism in China and Japan, looked to pre-Columbian civilization, and became interested in the great dualisms of life and death, sin and virtue, the flesh and the soul.

Most critics agree that Modernism was a revolt against everything represented by nineteenth-century prosaism which the poets felt had buried beauty under bourgeois poetry. They wanted to start afresh. In spite of the fact that they reacted against Romanticism, in a sense the Modernist poets were Romanticists in their rebellion and insistence on absolute artistic liberty. The Modernists were skeptical and pessimistic, and thus united only in a negative way against aspects of the past. They formed no real school and, indeed, lasted only a fairly short time as a movement. Federico de Onís, among others, found that Modernism reached its peak in 1896 and was already dead by 1905. He defined the movement as the Hispanic form of the universal crisis of letters and spirit which about 1885 initiated the dissolution of the nineteenth century.

Many theories are given as to the origin of Modernism. Some find that it started in America with the poetry of the Cuban, José Martí, around 1882; they see its developers as Manuel Gutiérrez Nájera of Mexico, José Asunción Silva of Colombia, and Rubén Darío, the Nicaraguan who inherited the mantle of leadership of the movement. Others feel that a parallel movement existed in Spain with the poetry of authors like Salvador Rueda Santos (1857-1933), whom they consider the true creator of Modernism in Spain, for he dominated Spanish poetry, and it was he who introduced Darío to the young poets of Spain. Some confusion has existed between the terms Modernism, which implemented a literary and poetical revolution in technique, and the "Generation of Ninety-Eight," which began a revolution in ideology. Some poets belonged to both movements. Unamuno, for example, rejected Verlaine's idea of *De la musique avant toute chose* to cry out that only that which is not music is poetry, rejecting beauty for ideas, while Antonio Machado followed realistic approximations of historical man and his social responsibility.

Rubén Darío (1867-1916), a Nicaraguan mestizo, learned French in El Salvador, worked as a journalist in Chile, and became a correspondent for *La Nación* of Buenos Aires. He visited Spain twice, in 1892 and in 1898. It was during the latter voyage that he met the young poets of the day, such as the Machado brothers and Juan Ramón Jiménez. His great gift to Spanish poetry lay in his contributions to change in meter and rhythms. He helped reorient Spanish poetic style, following, at least in his early poems, the Modernist creed of sensations rather than ideas. Some consider him an innovator. Others feel he deserves more the title of renovator.

Darío had the rare gift of assimilating the delicate rhythms of the French Symbolists and grafting them flawlessly onto Spanish letters. He changed the accent on the alexandrine, juggled the stresses of his lines, and varied the number of his syllables. Whether he was an innovator or a renovator, his European and cosmopolitan experiences helped temper his Spanish and American heritage, although he was at times unsure of the latter. He indulged in great verbal experimentation, combined Catholic and pagan, aristocratic and bohemian, decadent and religious elements, but basically he was emotional and sensual. While he had a great immediate influence on many of the young poets, one reason they drew away from him was that they sought more than the exquisite and perfect formality which he represented. He wrote beautiful, ornate, elegant, and decorative poetry, although in some of his later poems, abandoning some of his brilliance and pyrotechnics, he indulges in oral musings on life, death, and eternity. Of his many collections, *Azul* (*Blue*), 1888, the first, was hailed by the nineteenth-century novelist Juan Valera as original in a sense which nobody until then had had. *Prosas profanas* (*Profane Prose*), 1896, is a sensual, musical resurrection of palaces and swans and eighteenth-century still-life scenes. *Cantos de vida y esperanza* (*Songs of Life and Hope*), 1905, contains moral and religious preoccupations as well as a fear of the fate which awaits us all. In the final analysis, nevertheless, it is the flexibility, color, music, experimentation, and devotion to beauty which will continue to be associated with Rubén Darío's poetry.

Miguel de Unamuno (1864-1936), essayist, thinker, novelist, brought a highly personal tone to his poetry. For him a poet was one who uncovers his soul in rhythmic language. In a sense his philosophical, religious, and nature poetry belong to no school. He writes human and warm as well as abstract and intellectual poetry. His work is filled with contradictions, but his quest for immortality and his love of Spain shine throughout as constants in his work. Among his many collections are *Poesía* (*Poetry*), 1907, his masterwork *El Cristo de Velásquez* (*The Christ of Velázquez*), 1920, and *Cancionero, diario poético* (*Song Book, Poetic Diary*), a posthumous publication of almost two thousand of his poems on varied themes. In *The Christ of Velásquez* he includes mythic cosmology, and views Jesus as the granter of immortality. Unamuno's anguish, fear of loss of being, struggle to believe, and conceit are easily apparent. Without being highly preoccupied with form or poetic grace, his rough-tongued poems achieved great effect through their very nakedness. He once said that in his poetry he gave pieces of his heart. He rejected the refined verse of the Modernists in his search for answers to universal and fundamental questions, refusing to bow to any doctrine or dogma. Thus he remained true to himself, continuing his meditation and spiritual struggle and relating his existential fears to all mankind.

Antonio Machado (1875-1939), perhaps the most influential poet of the twentieth century and one of Spain's all-time great lyric voices, longed for a rebirth of Spain. Both the Andalusia where he was born and the Castile he came to love are to be found in his poetry. He lived a life of solitude, although there were two important women in his life: Leonor, his wife, and years after her death, the mysterious Guiomar. He greatly admired Unamuno as well as Rubén Darío, but he could not follow the latter's sensualism and aestheticism. For Machado poetry consisted of more than pretty words or sound and color. He agreed with Bécquer that one should suppress unnecessary adornments and allow the soul to speak. Machado's two major poetic works are probably *Soledades, galerías y otros poemas* (*Solitudes, Galleries and Other Poems*), 1907, and *Campos de*

Castilla (*Fields of Castile*), 1912. The first volume is oriented toward Andalusia, but his later collections came to be imbued with Castilian spirit. *Fields of Castile,* the spiritual and telluric masterpiece or poetic breviary of the Generation of 1898, reveals through the melancholy, silent countryside, the compassion, existential anguish, and temporal considerations involving religious uncertainties which beset Machado. Land, landscape, country, man's solitude, mystery, and death are Machado's themes. Lacking in verbal pyrotechnics, although he uses a variety of poetic meters and experimentation, he is intimately sober, deep, and movingly human. His withdrawal and solitude are very much like the countryside he describes, full of sadness and anguish, in part, perhaps, stemming from nostalgia over happier days with his beloved wife, in part from his preoccupation with man as an unhappy historical being.

Antonio Machado was an inconspicuous, simple, humble, serene, noble, carelessly dressed, and somewhat timid man. He remained aloof from fashionable literary gatherings and avoided new literary fads. For Machado poetry is neither phonic value nor sensation, but rather a deep palpitation of spirit which involved also the everyday world and everyday people. Some compare him to Horace, others to Fray Luis de Léon, but his work contains metaphysical implications missing in almost all other Spanish poets. Almost all of his poetry meditates on the mystery of the secret places in man's soul, and in his concern with God, time, and existential despair he is typically a twentieth-century poet. Of all these concerns, time seems to preoccupy him the most. Recalling his studies with Bergson, he views time as a continuous unity, for the present in which we exist is but a part of time's totality. The past, the present, and the future form a unity, as the poet seeks this "word in time" and reflects on the human condition and the death which awaits us all.

As with Unamuno, it is difficult to fit Machado into the narrow confines of a school. He states his own creed thus:

. . . poetry is the essential word in time . . . the history of the great problem which confronts the poet with these two imperatives, in a certain way contradictory: essentiality and temporality. . . . I feel, thus, somewhat in disagreement with the poets of the day. They propose a distemporalization of poetry, not only through the disuse of the artifices of rhythm, but, especially, through the use of images more conceptual than emotional in function. . . . The poet professes, more or less consciously, an existentialist metaphysics, in which time achieves an absolute value. Restlessness, anguish, fear, resignation, hope, impatience . . . are signs of the time, and at the same time, revelations of human conscience and being.[2]

Contemporary poets still seek inspiration in the eternal verities of Antonio Machado, finding his poetry moving, intimate, sober, deep, simple, evocative, nostalgic, and passionate, and many of them consider him to be the greatest poet since the seventeenth century.

Juan Ramón Jiménez (1881-1958) was an early heir of French Symbolism and Modernism as represented by Rubén Darío. Together with Pérez de Ayala and others he helped publish Modernist literary reviews such as *Helios* (1902). Later, through his contacts at the Residencia de Estudiantes, and through reviews such as *Indice* (1921), he served as a bridge poet to unite Rubén Darío and more modern poets, influencing post-Modernists and many of the leading members of the Generation of 1925 to which Vicente Aleixandre belongs.

The author of almost forty books of poetry, Jiménez at various times shows the influence of Heine, Bécquer, Verlaine, Góngora, Shelley, Rimbaud, and José Asunción Silva. After his flirtation with the sonorities and flashing colors of the Darían manner, Jiménez began to achieve his own style of "interior music," although his evolutionary process was never to be complete. Jiménez was obsessed with the idea of perfection, and he constantly changed poetry he had written, seeking always a closer approach to absolute beauty. He felt that a "poem is never finished, only abandoned." Thus Juan Ramón Jiménez passed through various stages, Modernism, embellishment and crowded sensations, and purity. Depending on the period one reads, one may see in him Symbolism, Impressionism, color, music, or mysticism. A great mystic and lover of nature, Jiménez in his pantheistic projections involving a quest for serenity, God, and the meaning of human love, life and death, elaborates his earlier personification and joy in the world about him and conveys a sense of mystery and transcendental ineffable immediacy. His best poetry is delicate, refined, and sad, perhaps because he creates a world of the imagination more real to him than reality, a world that might have been. Beauty and the cult of perfection, involving a continuing emphasis on simplicity, came to be his overriding concern.

With so many collections of Jiménez's poetry, it is hard to cite only one or two. Strangely enough it is his earlier work which influenced following generations. Among his many volumes one might choose *Arias tristes* (*Sad Arias*), 1903, an attempt to find the spiritual significance of nature; *Sonetos espirituales* (*Spiritual Sonnets*), 1914-1915, baroque projections; *Piedra y cielo* (*Stone and Sky*), 1919, an example of his attempt at purified poetry; and *Animal de fondo* (*Animal of the Deep*), 1949, involving a search for God.

In his gossamer-like poems preoccupied with the mournful, he is a recondite poet, dreaming dreams of great sensibility. When one compares his themes of anguish, sadness and melancholy to those of Machado, they seem almost rhetorical refinements rather than sincere outpourings of a Spanish soul, but his imagery is not completely intellectual. His supposed scorn for the world does not disguise the fear, sickness, and weaknesses he shares with all mankind. In his last works Jiménez embarks upon a quest for God, and as he himself explained, after an emotional encounter with God, he underwent an intellectualized experience, and finally achieved an interiorization which produced in his conscience the emotion of God. In a sense, then, the poet became one with God in a mystic, aesthetic fusion, seeking to create through Him and for Him a world of everlasting beauty.

In any brief discussion of poetic periods, countless names must be omitted. Among many other Modernist poets were Manuel Machado, Francisco Villaespesa, Eduardo Marquina, Ramón María del Valle Inclán, and Ramón Pérez de Ayala.

II *Post-Modernism*

Most twentieth-century Spanish poets, as can be seen, fit no convenient category, as schools fuse into one another. Roughly between Modernism and the Generation of 1925 or Guillén-Lorca Generation, there appeared a transition group of poets who, for want of a better name, have been lumped under the innocuous label of post-Modernists. It is perhaps impossible to apply clear-cut distinctions to this transitional group, or indeed, to put convenient beginnings and ends on any of the generations of poets. In twentieth-century Spanish poetry at least three different generations seem to be operating at the same time. In any event, these transition poets, while partaking of and consolidating Modernist innovations to an extent, foreshadow more daring innovations of later groups. Among the many so-called post-Modernist poets are Enrique Díez-Canedo (1879-1944), José Moreno Villa (1887-1954), Ramón de Basterra, and the greatest of them all, León Felipe Camino y Galicia (1884-1968). Indeed, so varied is León Felipe's poetry that it may be misleading to put him into any classification, however temporary, and in him one can find traces of Jiménez, Machado, Unamuno, and many others, including his favorite Walt Whitman, whom he translated.

A man of many professions, to which he refers in some of his poetry, Felipe has published *Versos y oraciones del caminante* (*Verses and Prayers of the Traveler*), 1920, containing moral, religious, and nostalgic themes of a man who believes in peace; a series of collections about the tragedy of the Spanish Civil War such as *El payaso de las bofetadas y el pescador de caña* (*The Clown of Slaps and the Fisher of Reed*), 1938; *El hacha* (*The Axe*), 1939; *El español del éxodo y del llanto* (*The Spaniard of the Exodus and Tears*), 1939; *El gran responsable* (*The Great Responsible One*), 1940, which stresses his political, moral, and ethical responsibility to man and society; *Ganarás la luz* (*You Will Gain the Light*), 1943, his spiritual and poetic autobiography, and many others.

Léon Felipe wanted to write grave and solemn poetry, and in his search for God and the meaning of life he turned to humble and simple things. He sought inspiration in the Bible, but felt that man abandoned by God was adrift in a world without meaning. During the Civil War his poetry became savage as he considered man's inhumanity to man and searched for his lost country. He passed from harangue, vituperation, and blasphemy, to sorrow and tragedy. He believed man must maintain his conscience through his tears and a sense of responsibility for his fellow man. Like Unamuno he stresses salvation, but his existential anguish emphasizes social aspects of the Christian message more than theological or religious ones.

Believing in beauty, Felipe longs to find it in daily life. Not encountering either it or God fully, he nevertheless postulates the possibility of man's love for his fellow man, admitting the absence of absolute values in an absurd and irrational world. He is best remembered as a poet of existential anguish whose themes of time, history, dreams, myth, God, and death reveal him to be a deep and original artist of profound humanity.

III *The Generation of 1925*

Often called the Generation of 1927, the Generation of the Dictatorship, the Generation of the Republic, the Guillén-Lorca Generation, or the Generation of 1920 to 1936, Aleixandre's poetic generation did not wish to destroy the poetry of older masters to whom they were deeply indebted. Dámaso Alonso claimed: "The poets of my generation do not abominate the already famous masters (Unamuno, Machado, Juan Ramón Jiménez). Moreover, the affiliation which the new group has with Juan Ramón Jiménez . . . is evident."[3] He and others argue that the generation may represent a continuity rather than a rejection of previous traditions, even though many different poetic techniques existed within the group, from the intuitive, irregular meters of Salinas to the precise, almost mathematical arrangements of Jorge Guillén.

The poets, nevertheless, did not escape contact with the many violent post-World War I movements such as Ultraism, a new kind of Futurism which ignored both emotion and experience; Creationism, whose Spanish master, Gerardo Diego, sought, along with the Chilean Vicente Huidobro, "to create a poem as nature creates a tree"; and Surrealism, which employed Freudian symbolism and automatic writing, and represented a kind of cathartic sublimation of the traumatic shock which many had suffered as a result of the First World War. Many of the poets, among them Aleixandre, employed associative imagery whose elements at times had no apparent relationship to each other, while often the poets used special symbols, such as the sea, much as earlier the oak had served as Machado's telluric symbol. For Olmos García, "The Generation of '27 with some exceptions, exaggerated the irrational tendency to the point of ignoring in their work concrete realities, at least until 1936."[4]

The Generation concerned itself also with pure poetry, which earlier Juan Ramón Jiménez had attempted in his own way. This cerebral rebellion against anecdotal-conceptual imagery had also been influenced by Ortega y Gasset's ideas on the dehumanization of art. Around 1925 a great debate took place concerning the theories of Brémond and Valéry on pure poetry. The following year, in the November issue of the *Revista de*

Occidente, Fernando Vela called for further debate on the matter. Correspondence between him and Jorge Guillén also appeared in the second number of *Verso y Prosa* in 1927. Valéry claimed that intelligence and reason were all-important, whereas Brémond felt that the ineffable lay in the emotion and that a poet transmitted by means of his expression through a kind of magical process of transformation.

Guillén defended Valéry's point of view. For him, "Pure poetry is all that which remains in a poem after that which is not poetry has been eliminated. Pure equals simple, chemically speaking." On another occasion Guillén stated, ". . . we have always rejected realism and sentimentalism, and we have condemned the latter as the worst of obscenities. For us poetry could be neither description nor effusion."[5] Yet this dehumanized poetry gave way to one of human and social concern, even for Guillén. Lorca substituted the poor Negro of New York for the colorful Andalusian gypsy; Guillén, human preoccupations for his songs to the joy of life; Salinas, a political and social conscience for a refined intellectualism. Dámaso Alonso, differing to a degree with Guillén, states that the formalistic, aesthetic and intellectualized poetry of exterior perfection and purity, lasting only briefly, ended as poetry "passionate, full of tenderness and not a few times frantic."[6] Guillén, Salinas, Gerardo Diego, and Alberti, among others, worked toward the revitalization of Góngora on the three-hundredth anniversary of his death. Finally, as with the poets of earlier generations, the Generation of 1925 was, according to José Olivio Jiménez, preoccupied with time, the great organic theme of all contemporary poetry.[7]

The Generation had its own reviews, among them *Verso y Prosa* in Murcia, *La Gaceta Literaria* of Ernesto Giménez Caballero, *Carmen,* and its supplement, *Lola,* and *Litoral* in whose supplements the editors Manuel Altolaguirre and Emilio Prados first published Aleixandre's *Ambito.* The poets of '25 had contributed their first poetry to magazines as early as 1921, although most did not publish a complete volume until some years later. Pedro Salinas, the oldest member, was born in 1891, and Manuel Altolaguirre, the youngest, in 1905. Luis Cernuda claims that his generation was the first to incorporate Spanish poetry into the European literature of the time, and further states that his fellow poets were primarily interested in "special cultivation of metaphor, a poetic cultivation which the group appropriates to itself and which signifies, among other things, a first approximation to Mallarmé and to Valéry."[8]

Although what unites the Generation far outweighs the differences among them, each poet has his own definition of poetry. Pedro Salinas felt limited by exterior reality but saw in it also a measure of the tragic and significant. He thought poetry was indefinable. "Poetry explains itself; if not, it is not explained. All commentary on poetry refers to surrounding elements such as style, language, sentiment, or aspiration but not to poetry itself. Poetry is an adventure toward the absolute. One comes more or less close, one travels more or less road; that is all."[9] Gerardo Diego thought that poetry "makes the lightning bolt, and the poet remains with astonished thunder in his hands. . . . In all poems poetry 'has been' but is no longer . . . To believe what we did not see, . . . is faith. To believe what we shall never see, . . . is Poetry."[10] Dámaso Alonso stated that "Poetry is a fervor and a clarity. A fervor, an intimate and strong desire for union with the great gusts of the world and its first cause. And a clarity through which the world itself is understood in an intense and unusual way. . . . Poetry is a nexus between two mysteries, that of the poet and that of the reader."[11] García Lorca said: "You will understand that a poet can say nothing about Poetry. Leave that to the critics and professors. . . . Here it is: look. I have the fire in my hands. I understand it and work with it perfectly, but I cannot speak of it without literature."[12]

Each poet offered a different aspect of poetry in his works. Salinas inherited the label of pure poet. His poetry is often subtle and intellectual, and he uses words carefully to convey their conceptual values. Skeptical of reality, he desires the essence hiding behind reality. *Presagios* (*Presages*), 1923, his first volume, meditates on nature, love, and interior reality. In it one finds the joy of youth. His later poetry is more intense and complex, as he continues to seek the loved one whose subtle presence is more felt than seen. In *La voz a ti debida* (*Voice Owed to You*), 1933, Salinas seeks the mysterious and ineffable. At times he seems sensual, at others a Platonic idealist, at still others a mystic. Everywhere love's power is affirmed. *Razón de amor* (*Reason of Love*), 1936, is intensely anguished poetry, but the poet seeks still for his interior reality where he may find happiness and love. *Todo más claro* (*All Most Clear*), 1949, seeks God and hopes that divine providence may save man from himself. *El contemplado* (*The Contemplated*), 1946, is a colloquy with his beloved sea. Other collections have similar themes. Starting as a refined intellectual, Salinas later longed for the possibility of idealism and faith in a loveless world.

Jorge Guillén (b. 1893) started as an exponent of pure poetry and a follower of Valéry. His first major work, which he constantly expanded through four editions between 1928 and 1950, is *Cántico* (*Canticle*), a paean to life and the world around him. Its varied meter and short poetic forms exude harmony, beauty, and perfection. The poet exposes us to momentary joy, light, and formal beauty as he expresses his ecstatic pleasure in being alive. Even in his early work which many found intellectual, cold, and impersonal, his harmonious and beautiful imagery contained a subdued passion, at least for some critics, who saw in his theme that life is the supreme happiness a reflection of an ordered and understandable universe which conveys emotion as well as formal beauty. A great number of critics, nevertheless, still consider him to have been in this work the most classical and intellectual poet of his generation. While Guillén's metaphoric artistry resembles that of Góngora, whom he admired, his poems represent substantive reality in the moment of artistic perception, suggesting an indefinite and personal reality instead of the obvious one. His second major collection, *Clamor*, stresses the need for a rebirth and renewal, and harmony in a universe threatened with despair and suffering. Its three parts, *Maremagnum* (*Miscellany*), 1957, *Que van a dar en la mar* (*Which Wind to the Sea*), 1960, and *A la altura de las circunstancias* (*At the Height of Circumstances*), 1963, do not reflect the optimism, vitality and formal perfection of *Cántico*. The poet still exalts life and love, but he sees the basic rhythm of things and knows of an approaching death, in the face of which one needs humanity and courage.

Gerardo Diego (b. 1896) was active in the Ultraist and Creationist movements as well as in editing and criticizing the poetry of the day. Often labeled an eclectic, he wrote both refined and primitive, intricate and simple poetry. His *Manual de espumas* (*Manual of Foams*), 1924, rebels against logic in a cubistic fashion and is probably the best sample of *ultraísmo*. *Versos humanos* (*Human Verses*), 1925, a more human work, shared the National Prize of Literature with Rafael Alberti's work, *Marinero en tierra* (*Sailor on Land*). Through the years he continued writing prize-winning poetry on everything from Beethoven to the bullfights.

Federico García Lorca (1898-1936), perhaps the most famous twentieth-century poet of Spain, from his earliest moments was a poet of inspiration who combined the real and the poetic world in such a skillful fusion that it is hard to know where the visual leaves off and the supernatural begins. His odd sensory combinations offer a vision of a world acquired with a primitive and almost childlike directness, combined, nevertheless, with a kind of sophistication. From its earliest moments, his work revealed this double reality as he talked of death, life, blood, and sex. His poetic world is full of subtle shades, presentiments, and melancholy at the passing of the human hour, marked by his favorite images such as flowing blood or a measuring clock.

In his *Libro de poemas* (*Book of Poems*), 1921, he treats a variety of subjects with tenderness; *Canciones* (*Songs*), 1927, brings out brilliant and unusual harmonies; *Romancero gitano* (*Gypsy Ballads*), 1928, which for many is the most influential work of poetry of the entire century, deals with the gypsy, driven by cruelty, love, violence, and beauty, paralleling in his primitive way the religious, philosophical, and daily lives of supposedly more sophisticated civilizations. Each little poem portrays a dramatic scene in which we suffer along with the protagonist. The work is filled with striking imagery: "The beaks of the roosters dig looking for dawn"; "When he bows his head on his chest of aspers, the night looks for a plain to kneel and worship"; "When all the roof-tops are nothing but furrows on the earth, dawn shrugs her shoulders in a vast profile of stone." Everywhere there is color and ryhthm, as the child, still present in the adult poet, seeks in a frustrated and abandoned world of pain and despair the simple and good life of a more primitive world.

Yet this primitive directness accompanies a strange sophistication, as the poet senses death at every crossing and in every tick of the clock, and feels the anguish of men who must suffer and die. *Llanto por la muerte de Ignacio Sánchez Mejías* (*Lament for the Death of Ignacio Sánchez Mejías*), 1935, the greatest elegy in modern Spanish literature, mourns the death of a friend killed in the bullring the previous year. Lorca turns from his friend's death to the meaning of death and fatality in general. *Poeta en Nueva York* (*Poet in New York*), written in 1929 and 1930 but not published until 1940, offers us a nightmarish and surrealistic world where Dionysian and Apollonian forces clash. Lorca uses new metaphors and symbols to proclaim his anguish at the sight of abandoned children and unhappy Negroes, victims of a cruel and violent civilization. Over everything lies a brooding concern with death. He continues to use unusual imagery and metaphorical ambiguities, adding other symbols to former ones of blood, the bull, the horse, and the moon, as saliva swords threaten to pierce and rivers of oil to drown. Lorca, in his folkloric elements, his paganism, color, music, harmony, rhythm, clarity, mystery, pride, innocence, Catholicism, and multileveled symbolism, but for his tragic execution in 1936, might have matured to be the greatest Spanish poet of all time.[13]

Dámaso Alonso (b. 1898), Aleixandre's most intimate friend, began with *Poemas puros* (*Innocent Poems*) in 1920. In other collections he radiates joy and meditates on death and the anguish of being human. His most famous collection, *Hijos de la ira* (*Children of Wrath*), 1944, contains sincere religious and metaphysical poems involving the individual's essence and the pain, death, cruelty, and ugliness of an unjust world. The poet hopes for belief in a life beyond death. Emilio Prados (1899-1962), along with Aleixandre the most direct practitioner of the surrealistic mode, spent most of his life in exile as a result of the Civil War. His poetry offers musicality, color, and a religious and anguished search for God. Luis Cernuda (1904-1963) wrote sad and disillusioned poetry which in his early stages resembled that of Bécquer. Almost all of his poetry was collected over a period of years into a kind of poetic anthology, *La realidad y el deseo* (*Reality and Desire*), containing themes of solitude, love, and often neo-Garcilaso themes to be found in the next generation of poets. In some poems he considers destruction, war, and death, shows the abyss between man and society and the struggle between the soul and body, as his sensual and poetic desires remain unassuaged. Manuel Altolaguirre (1905-1959) used varied rhythms. Abandoning many of the themes of his generation, of which he was the youngest member, he helped recreate the great interest in Garcilaso's poetry in the 1930's.

The other poet of the generation who, along with Aleixandre, Lorca and Guillén, is usually considered a master poet is Rafael Alberti (b. 1902). Among his many volumes of poetry is *Marinero en tierra*, musical, tender, poignant and appealing in its yearning for the unknown. The poet finds himself a prisoner of the earth and longs for the sea which hides in its depths the gardens of his hopes and youthful dreams. Brilliant and controlled artistic imagery mark this work. In others Alberti flirted with a variety of Gongoristic and surrealistic themes. Many consider his masterpiece to be *Sobre los ángeles* (*Concerning Angels*), 1929, which resembles somewhat the work of Blake and Cocteau as well as that of T. S. Eliot. He seeks a lost love and religious faith, a lost paradise, and a way out from the darkness of a world of disintegrating values. His symbols have universal impact, as do his themes of pain, death, and destiny. In America, where he lived in exile, he published a series of works on liberty, love, painting, and his personal past. Like Felipe, for a time he wrote poetry of social protest; it is of uneven merit. A poet of the greatest technical virtuosity, he combines the popular and the cultural, an exuberant happiness of life, recalling that of Guillén, with bitter tears of a poet who has outlived the death of a country which was his.

IV *Post-Aleixandrian Generations*

Many fine poets appeared after the masters of the generation which some consider as forming a second Golden Age. Some of the new poets sought a return to the formal elegance of the sixteenth-century Garcilaso and reacted away from Góngora. Representative poetry is that by Luis Rosales, *Abril* (*April*), 1935; Luis Felipe Vivanco, *Cantos de primavera* (*Songs of Spring*), 1936; Germán Bleiberg, Dionisio Ridruejo and José García Nieto. This Garcilaso revolt, often labeled *neo-Garcilasismo*, insisted on graceful poetry of counted syllables and an occasional religious note. Often this group, along with the Panero brothers, has been called the Generation of 1936. Sometimes because of a connection with the review *Escorial*, they are known as the *Escorial* group. Still other critics label these poets the Generation of 1939.

Among the poets who began to write in the middle thirties is Luis Felipe Vivanco (b. 1907), who resembled Unamuno and felt that poetry must be real. Among his themes are humanity, existence, and religious warmth. Leopoldo Panero (1909-1962) is perhaps Spain's greatest modern Catholic poet. Existential aspirations concern him as man finds himself alone in this life, which he must face, searching always for God. In that search he will return to his childhood, his native hearth and his mother's arms. His *Escrito a cada instante* (*Written at Each Moment*), 1949, shows how the name of God is constantly revealed and yet removed and how poetry also reflects this ebbing and flowing of life as the poet receives or lacks the divine vision. Tender and passionate, Panero experiences God everywhere, but he cannot help feeling some horror at death. Perhaps his best-known poem is *España hasta los huesos* (*Spain to the Bones*), a kind of elegy to García Lorca. Luis Rosales (b. 1910) showed great technical virtuosity in his early work such as *Abril*. In later works his outstanding characteristics continue to be serenity and repose. *La casa encendida* (*The Burning House*), 1949, a kind of autobiographical poem, is full of memories of hearth and home, along with love poetry, supposedly of the human heart.

The greatest poet after the Generation of 1925 (he did not really belong to the Generation of 1936) was probably Miguel Hernández (1910-1942), tragically killed, as was Lorca, as a result of the Spanish Civil War. In his poetry are fused the two eternal currents of Spanish literature, the popular and the cultural. His most decisive influence in Spain was undoubtedly Vicente Aleixandre, but his Andalusian elegance combined with an overwhelming passion gives his verse a fire and verve all its own. *Perito en lunas* (*Expert on Moons*), 1933, more impersonal and Gongoristic than his later works, reveals the influences of Rafael Alberti and Jorge Guillén. Even in its somewhat dehumanized and artificial aspects, the moon is the moon of Orihuela where he worked as a goatherd in his youth. *El rayo que no cesa* (*The Never Ending Lightning*), 1936, shows his full power in sonnets of life and death. While like Rosales he uses the Garcilaso classical form, unlike his contemporaries' derivative and uninspiring aping, Hernández' poetry explodes with emotion, agony, and tormented love as well as sorrow at the thought of man's inevitable death.

Like Aleixandre, who seeks to identify with the animal and vegetable kindgdoms, Hernández exclaims in a mixture of existential despair, tenderness and violence, "I am called clay, although they call me Miguel." *Viento del pueblo* (*Winds of the People*), 1937, dedicated to Aleixandre, vital poems about the Civil War, are genuinely patriotic in their acknowledgement of poverty and pain which must clear the path for future freedom. Hernández insists that it is the little man, the representative of the people, who offers the best hope for that future. Along with descriptions of the Castilian landscape and the exuberant fertility of beautiful Alicante, in his poetry the constant note is one of nobility, passion, which makes one cry and rage at man's inhumanity to man, and tenderness toward the poor of Spain and the world. *El hombre acecha* (*Man in Ambush*), 1939, portrays a Spain of despair and sacrificed youth. Sorrow and death prevail. In much of his other poetry he exudes the same note of personal passion, tormented and fatal love, and finally he reveals the sufferings of his imprisonment, the intimate diary of a solitary soul who feels himself close to death.

Hernández restored to Spanish poetry the eclogue, without its insipid qualities. As he talks of love, nature and shepherds, his own sweat and hard work as a youth are everywhere apparent, for the poet knows the earth and loves it. He uses a variety of meters, popular and traditional poetry, fusing the simple and the baroque with his own burning passionate voice full of tragic beauty. In his spontaneous poetry, above all, he insists always on humanity and the necessity to achieve mankind's potential. A poet of the earth, he was a creative artist of extraordinary force and originality.

Victoriano Crémer Alonso (b. 1910), aided by Eugenio de Nora (b. 1923), edited the review *Espadaña* in León, opposing the neo-classic vein and pure poetry. José Luis Cano (b. 1912) wrote much of love, as did Dionisio Ridruejo (b. 1912), founder of the *Escorial* review with Laín Entralgo, whose change of political philosophy was not at all reflected in his poetry, perfect in technique, if not in human emotion. José García Nieto (b. 1914), founder of the review *Garcilaso*, wrote of elegance and beauty, and Germán Bleiberg (b. 1915) wrote light and graceful verse. Blas de Otero (b. 1916) sang of an uprooted generation, of God, Love, and Death. Politically motivated, too, he speaks of a sad and sorrowing Spain and defends freedom and justice.

In 1943 the review *Garcilaso* was founded by a group of young writers calling themselves *la juventud creadora* (*Creative Youth*), whose poetry largely reflected spiritual dejection. Undoubtedly the Spanish Civil War of 1936-1939 divides Spanish poetry into two chronological ages. After the war poets once more began to look beyond form to themes of substance, without completely abandoning virtuosity and formal perfection. Dámaso Alonso and Aleixandre rejected a shallow return to Classical poetry and in free verse wrote meaningful and often anguished works both existential and social in scope, which emphasized religion without conveying genuine faith. Many of the poets of the previous generation, as well as poets like Unamuno and Machado, had already shown this twentieth-century anguish of man and his problems in a changing world where life is ephemeral. Themes of lost youth, existential finality, faith in God, and the need for social works and the brotherhood of man came to the fore. The establishment of the Adonais Prize stimulated the production of new and vigorous poetry, much as the old *Litoral* collection had produced works of merit.

A number of poets, nevertheless, wanted tranquility of spirit after the war years, and it was hard for them to leave the safe, melodic, harmonic structures of untroubled times. About 1946 or 1947, poets like Eugenio de Nora and Gabriel Celaya became the leading proponents of a new realism in poetry. The review *Espadaña* adopted an anti-formalist tone and sought the rehumanization of poetry in polemical and political themes. Machado's objectivity, historical man, fraternal spirit, humility and eternal verities were cherished more than ever, and the youthful poets found in the "work of Machado an echo of the preoccupations of the world in which they live—an echo which does not sound in the work of Jiménez."[14] These poets combated the sterile despair of their fellow poets, for "the human essence of poetry was crying out for a new form, a supreme message of spiritual and collective salvation. . . . They initiated the new attitude which had had vague forerunners dating back to 1944 in the work of Vicente Aleixandre and especially Dámaso Alonso. . . ."[15] Around 1950 other poets rediscovered Machado as a temporal poet, and wrote what Castellet calls "A poetry of daily experience, narrative, biographical, existential, temporal, that is to say, tied to memory, to the temporally lived."[16] Later movements such as *pajarerismo,* from the review *El Pájaro de Paja* (*The Bird of Straw*), in the decade between 1950 and 1960, sought what they termed authenticity, and attenuated versions of other brief movements, such as the somewhat surrealistic *postismo* of Carlos Edmundo de Ory, continued. The new Spanish poetry centers largely on human and social realities, as can be seen in the poetry of the latest group of poets, Angel Crespo (b 1926), José Angel Valente (b. 1929), and Claudio Rodríguez (b. 1934).

Of the poets born around 1920, the most important undoubtedly is José Hierro (b. 1922). In 1951 he won more votes from the leading Spanish intellectuals than any other Spanish poet for inclusion in a special anthology of the ten best young poets who had written and published their first works after the close of the Spanish Civil War. Hierro labels himself "documentary poet," but he admits to two styles, one documentary and the other of "hallucinations." Even in his second type, which concerns itself more with aesthetic considerations, he rejects "isolated beauty." Hierro writes of love and tenderness, death and solitude, countryside, time, joy and sadness, social problems and politics. In his existential anguish and semi-narrative vein he resembles Unamuno at times. Temporal considerations tinge all his work, for he feels himself to be a fleeting being in a senseless world of death. Hierro, who has been considered a revolutionary poet, has often implied that very little written in Spain under the censorship is worthwhile. He becomes nostalgic as he reflects in bitterness on a lost world of hope, a world that might have been, and longs for ideals by which to live. Yet, as he writes of earth and man, he is consoled by the possibility of a better life, for even in countries obscured and isolated by fog, flowers are born and a better day may dawn, "for after the bitterness and after the pain, life tenders us its most beautiful colors."

The list of poets of some reputation is surprisingly large. Carlos Bousoño (b. 1923), who writes of patriotism, anguish, despair, God, and eternity; José María Valverde (b. 1926), a kind of classical mystic, who dwells on memories of the past, serenity and harmony, a Catholic search for God in a world he finds beautiful and well ordered in spite of an occasional fear of the future nothingness; the well-known women poets

Concha Zardoya (b. 1914), Carmen Conde (b. 1907), Susana March (b. 1918); and other well-known poets such as Gabriel Celaya (b. 1911), José Luis Hidalgo (1919-1947), Vicente Gaos (b. 1919), Rafael Morales (b. 1919), Eugenio de Nora (b. 1923), José Manuel Caballero Bonald (b. 1926), along with the previously mentioned newest poets José Angel Valente and Claudio Rodríguez, strive for a poetic excellence which to date falls short of that of previous poets like Machado, León Felipe, García Lorca, Guillén and Aleixandre.

Thus we have seen that twentieth-century lyric poetry has passed through the hands of many master poets, reflecting the increased tempo of modern life with short-lived literary schools and modes, a process which is still continuing. Beginning with Darían Modernism, which ended around 1905, a generation of poets like Juan Ramón Jiménez, himself a modernist, reacted away from the stridencies of Modernism to a simpler, more sober and austere poetry. In the 1920's the poets sought purity and beauty and wrote dehumanized and depersonalized works, although a few attempted the popular and folkloric. Almost all abandoned dehumanization for a more vibrant and intense poetry of human concern. In the years immediately before and after 1927, great interest was shown in Gongorism. In the early 1930's the neo-classical revival of Garcilaso contributed graceful poetry to offset the previously baroque influence of Góngora. After the despair of the Civil War, when spiritual dejection ruled the day, a dejection not cured by the *juventud creadora* group, Dámaso Alonso and Vicente Aleixandre stressed free verse and human and religious themes. Also Victoriano Crémer rejected the neo-classic poets for a return to a new kind of naturalism.

Along with a poetry of despair and religious emphasis, Eugenio de Nora and others returned to Antonio Machado for his historical and temporal perspectives. Religious poets continued to write, and preoccupation with Spain, the hearth, and home existed along with existential, romantic, and highly personal poetry. After the temporal, existential generation represented by José Hierro, some younger poets came under the influence of the great Peruvian poet César Vallejo, but poets such as José Angel Valente, although with subtle differences, largely followed the tendencies of previous generations as they considered the crisis of individualism, man, religion, and human solidarity, denouncing injustice, and deeply preoccupied with social and political reform.

CHAPTER 2

The Evolution of Aleixandre as a Major Poet

I Influences

A S for all poets, one is tempted to find "influences" which helped determine Aleixandre's poetry. Max Aub finds that "what unites Aleixandre to all previous poetry, from Modernism on, is the evident pantheism of which his poetry is possessed. Aleixandre is a 'mystic pantheist,' Dámaso Alonso assures us. In the fusion and in the transfusion of the body with nature, we find in him a perfect correspondence with Juan Ramón Jiménez and Jorge Guillén. All the poetry of Aleixandre is movement, transformation, change . . . he uses surrealistic mechanics; with time, aesthetic or moral preoccupations will not be absent from his . . . poetry."[1] If he is a mystic, it is nevertheless difficult, as Concha Zardoya points out, to find God in his works. "The problem of God is not stirred up . . . in any . . . work of Aleixandre."[2]

Aleixandre often recalls that he started his exposure to literature with a thorough reading of the Realistic novel of the nineteenth century when he was fifteen and sixteen. His favorite author was Benito Pérez Galdós. He states: "Of all the contemporary poets perhaps I am the one who knew best, with regards to live frequentation, the realistic novel of the nineteenth century."[3] Aleixandre read novels and plays, including the Classic theater of the seventeenth century, among whose authors he preferred Lope de Vega. He was interested in action, not language.

The fatal memory of my preceptive instruction made me skip over, for example, the monologue-sonnets. . . . I was thus at 18 years of age, a boy saturated with reading, enthusiastic to the point of obsession with literature and its world of fantasy and passion, and unknowing, avoiding poetry. The sudden arrival of the latter was then something virginal, . . . pure and burning propagator of a soul, mature already in a certain way through literary beauty, but innocent

31

still of the discharge which comes quickly and totally, of poetic illumination.

At the end of that summer I discovered Antonio Machado and somewhat later chronologically Juan Ramón Jiménez . . . although Darío was the revealer of my being, my first verses, some months later, were no longer rubendarian. Machado first and Juan Ramón Jiménez shortly afterward were the great shadows who, as in other boys of my generation watched over my first juvenile verses.[4]

Aleixandre elsewhere recalls walking under the pine trees on a windy day in Las Navas del Marqués, and his introduction to Rubén Darío by his friend Dámaso Alonso. "It was not Darío whom I knew, it was poetry, in a perfect service of revelation . . . but, among many things, the value of the word in the rhythm, the number, it was he without doubt who taught me."[5] The poet soon discovered Bécquer, whose imagery he admired so greatly, and then turned to the poets of the sixteenth and seventeenth centuries, especially San Juan de la Cruz, Luis de León, and Luis de Góngora.

Vicente Gaos, a fellow poet, finds that Luis de León is of major importance in the development of Aleixandre's poetry. "In my opinion, the proximity of Aleixandre to Fray Luis is much greater than to Góngora, from whom the author of *Destruction or Love* doubtless took the twists of language indicated by Bousoño."[6] He cites a variety of techniques to prove his contention, such as negation followed by an adjective, the frequency of synthetic or neologistic superlatives, similar favorite words, and syntactic moods of various kinds shared by the two poets.

II *Style*

Yet Aleixandre, it must be stated, is an extremely individual poet with a personal and original style. He makes intense use of symbols such as the sea and the forest, and metaphors which convey a feeling rather than a logical sequence. A master of free verse and internal monologues, he adapts contrasting elements, combining the real and the unreal and using a variety of interrelated and dependent images to give force to his poetry. He sometimes employs special techniques such as repeated negatives with affirmative force, and an accumulation of words, at times in chaotic conglomeration, which produces the effect of drunken vertigo. In his freedom of expression and great sentiment, he strives for a kind of transfiguration through the evocation of his beloved, human or cosmic, and at times reaches transcendent heights in his attempt to capture a blossoming ambience, an all-pervading light, an obscure happiness. At times he writes hermetic poetry, full of melancholy, inner stress, and existential agony.

Carlos Bousoño, who has written extensively on Aleixandre's style, divides the imagery of Aleixandre into three classes: the symbol, the continued visionary image, and the vision. The symbol is an allusive image, spiritual and intangible, and does not transpose a real sphere bit by bit. Visionary images differ from symbols because several aspects of the image in question are used as points of comparison throughout the poem. The vision is an attribution of unreal qualities or functions of an object.[7] Aleixandre's use of language has been almost universally praised, although his use of free verse leads him to the brink of rhetoric at times. Max Aub finds his adjectives "vulgar and stale"[8] because his hyenas are always yellow, tusks white, foam clear, life beautiful, and mountains rocky. Jorge Blajot agrees with Aleixandre, however, that words are not ugly or beautiful in themselves, nor are verse forms important. "Neither the ones nor the others are worth while without the profound, sincere truth, with which previously they trembled in the resonant breast of the writer . . . . We spoke intentionally of resonance and trembling. No message will manage to pulse in the most vital fibres of man if this cordial dimension is lacking. . . . For me the most happy result of poetry is not beauty, but emotion. . . . It is a question of an interior combustion in contact with possessed truth."[9] Leopoldo de Luis reflects the point of view of most critics that in Aleixandre, as in few others, there results an enrichment of "the treasure of the language. . . . But what results even more renovating and fecund is the syntactic play and alogical leap of the image. . . . Vicente Aleixandre has gained some rhythmic qualities which make of his ample verse and exceptional poetic talent, a perfect fitting between what is expressed and how it is expressed."[10]

Aleixandre's poetry has no specific message, for he thinks in terms of words, movement, image, connotations and not denotations. We see in him suggestions half glimpsed, the vision of a poet of human life and the universe, but at times the reader senses experiences which vaguely may have been one of his own. As Guillén points out, for Aleixandre words mean communication, "the sign of an idea, the communication of a state."[11] He thus admits the possibility of a kind of obscurity in Aleixandre which does not apply to other poets of the generation. "Little by little over the years, almost all this so-called obscurity has drifted away—an 'obscurity' more tolerated in poets of great delirium and free form like Vicente Aleixandre."[12]

Aleixandre states that the obscurity of a poem may be due to attempts by a youthful author to express haltingly something he has been groping for, or it may be a matter of the poem itself which complicates the theme. While he admits that the poet may be the product of certain human conditions of a certain period of time, he feels his poetry has been clear, in keeping with his constantly reiterated position that poetry is communication. "People who read La destrucción o el amor in 1935 when it appeared, and abandoned it, 'because of not understanding it,' have shown themselves surprised ten years later on picking it up again, to find that it was perfectly transparent."[13]

III Neo-Romanticism

Often called a Neo-Romantic, Aleixandre is interested in nature and the elemental forces of primitive life. José Luis Cano agrees with Dámaso Alonso that Aleixandre is a mystic pantheist,[14] whose romanticism involves passion and romantic frenzy. He feels Aleixandre's poetry is intimately linked to that of Shelley or Hölderlin[15] and views its romantic elements as freedom of lyrical expression, tremendous subjectivity, and great sensation. Aleixandre opposes the specter of civilization to the forceful life of nature, much as he contrasts and identifies death with love. For Aleixandre nature is the real life, the instinctive life, into which men introduced a divisive note. He later tempered or elaborated his cosmos to include man, as we shall see. The animal kingdom abounds in his poetry. He identifies constantly with the elemental particles of the world, for the substance of all things is one, and the universal constants are love and death. Through sensuality the physical may become spiritual, so Aleixandre seeks oneness with all life in a voluptuous, sensual, and passionate imagery.

A great number of critics have underlined Aleixandre's romanticism. "Aleixandre and Cernuda, preoccupied essentially by the destiny of the human being and his irreparable solitude, express in Spanish poetry what is most important and definitive in contemporary universal poetry: the Neo-Romantic attitude."[16] As part of that attitude Charry Lara cites the mystery of the universe in its greatness and fantasy, and the minute varieties of the world moved by energies which create or destroy. Pedro Salinas sees a new quality of romantic poetry in the profound connection of the poet with the world, as a current from the earth itself seems to come from his mouth. At other times "Aleixandre expresses a cosmic aspiration, a desire to embrace the earth with his arms, to live delivering himself to the universe. The human, animal, and vegetable limits then disappear and the total creature, which is the world, is born."[17] Aleixandre thus makes the presence of the world, in its anguish and glory, known, and through its presence seeks to find his own essence and meaning. Denying that he is a surrealistic poet, he states: "The romantic root is visible in my poetry and is conserved in all of it, until . . . that synthesis of romantic background and new expressive classicism . . . which is *Sombra del paraíso* (*Shadow of Paradise*)."[18]

Federico Carlos Sáinz de Robles, conceding that Aleixandre is a kind of surrealistic existentialist, says that "The lyricism of the ego connects him beautifully with the world, . . . romantically, . . . to feel himself fundamental, to note himself melancholy, non-conformist, always breaking decisively, proudly, with strophism, with the rhetorical image. . . . His poetic cosmos has only those rules of pressing necessity of existing and manifesting . . . original and not always explainable rules . . . the fears, the desires, the passions of Aleixandre do not fit into the free play of metaphor but in the most astonishing subtleties of the intention."[19] Díaz Plaja finds him very romantic because the poet sees the world as a quarry of love over which he exclaims.[20] Finally, Rodrigo Fernández Carvajal states that each of these "splendid symphonies of love which Vicente Aleixandre's books represent, is constructed according to a very specific and determined concept of time. In each one of his books a different formula of harmony between flight and eternity molds and forms the basin for the loving torrent."[21]

Not everybody accepts the term "Neo-Romantic." Alejandro

Busuioceanu prefers the word Epiphanism, for poetry is not literature but rather poetic knowledge, an attempt to escape the immediate reality, or rational logic, to achieve "the revealing liberty of the unreal, the irrational, or, if one prefers, that abstract . . . presence which one senses but which remains inaccessible to logical rational knowledge."[22] This revelation of poetry in its "epiphanistic" quality reveals not only metaphysical reason but also the emotion and the most intense sentiment of the poetry before the mystery of the unreal. For him, Vicente Aleixandre, a visionary living in both the real and abstract worlds, a world of light and shadows, writes poetry through revelation, and is thus "epiphanic."

IV *Aleixandrian Stages of Development*

Aleixandre recalls how he wrote his first verses furtively, not speaking of them to anybody for a number of years. ". . . I was not a poet conscious of his vocation who knows what he wants and intends to realize it, facing the future. I obeyed a primary and confused instinct, powerful and almost unconfessable. A delicious anguished pleasure shook me. I treasured my verses as a testament of a passionate but painful and unsatisfactory activity."[23] He was always afraid of being wounded by having his verses examined by eyes wiser than his which might prove destructive in their judgment. However, his awareness of poetry as a decided vocation, he says, "flowered with the change that years later a long and grave illness imposed on the direction of my existence. . . . Hours and a future of months which changed into years, which were now my total life, separated forever from a different road. This total change decided my life. I wrote my first book. It was published."[24]

Carlos Bousoño believes that the writings of Aleixandre combine two aspects of Spanish poetry which have been present since the Romantic movement, that is, irrationalism and individualism. Aleixandre, born in 1898, not only was enabled to partake of the movements of pure poetry and surrealism but lived long enough to undergo the intense change which affected Spanish poetry after 1947. Disputing the label of intellectual applied to Aleixandre's early works, Bousoño finds Aleixandre a great individualistic poet with original vision who after 1930 turned to an identification with the world of men. "Aleixandre proclaims himself poet not of what 'distinguishes in a refined way, but of what essentially unifies'; not a poet of minorities, but a poet of the majority, at least in his artistic will."[25] Bousoño sees two basic stages in the poetry of Aleixandre. At first Aleixandre views the elemental as the world's reality. In his second phase he concentrates on man's historical existence, his efforts to realize himself in a temporal dimension, and the ethical implications involved. Bousoño points out that as early as 1933 Aleixandre began stressing the conviction that poetry was communication with all. The first period stretched from *Ambit* to *Final Birth*; the second began with *History of the Heart*. In the first stage Aleixandre is interested in the physical world; in the second, in human life. But the basic key is "the amorous solidarity of the poet, of man with all creation."[26]

Another critic, a fellow poet, views his work as consisting of two poles, the first, the chaotic one of freedom, liberty, death as love, the elemental, the inexplicable, and free association. It is a kind of rebellion against the "Levitical bourgeoisie which hems him in, but he still does not consciously know that to save himself from that oppression he has to convert his blind and inoperative rebellion into an efficient and conscious rebellion."[27] The second pole, rejecting his negative posture toward reality, accepts it instead of the mythic world. The latter loaded down with oneiric imagery and the collective unconscious "little by little gives way to the concrete and dated."[28] Celaya views *Shadow of Paradise* as a kind of bridge between the two poles. On the one hand the poet takes refuge in myth to escape the horrible realities of the day, and on the other faces that reality as he recalls his father, his city, and his infancy. Aleixandre, then, is viewed as a man who seeks to remain aloof from the reality of the day, its history and politics, but discovers that he cannot and finds himself in people when they begin to believe in him. This new compromise, he states, begins with *History of the Heart,* "a book with which Vicente Aleixandre has compromised himself perhaps more than he knows."[29] Refining his classification further, Celaya recognizes four substages in Aleixandre's work: up to 1928 where the poet is interested in terrible mythic elements of nature without people; up to 1936 where he is chaotic, delirious, and grotesque; to 1945 when he is academic, literary, cultured, and decorative; and finally when he finds historical and telluric man, his own dialectic reality, and identifies with the public.

Other critics, while accepting a change in his work from solidarity with the cosmos to solidarity with human life, see the
two periods, not as distinct, but as rather a gradual evolution,
"the organic development and clear exposition of what previously
was, more or less, a larval dream which was sung as an aspiration."[30] The poet himself, as early as 1945, in referring to
poets who concern themselves with humanity as "radical poets
who speak to the primary and elemental humanity," states,
"They cannot feel themselves poets of the minority. Among them
I count myself."[31]

Thus, while all critics admit a change in Aleixandre's poetry,
some consider it as consisting of a definite dichotomy, and
others as a development. In his first poetry he constructs a primitive logic out of sensory qualities, employing animal symbols in
combination with psychological repressions which tend to confuse the logical symmetries. He contemplates the world in a new
relationship based on an emotion which, if it is not surrealistic
and Freudian, is not easily distinguished from these tendencies.
Aleixandre accepts man who, to survive, must maintain a special
relationship and identification with Nature. The unity of Nature,
a cosmic force conditioned by love which could create and destroy, became his central theme. In his second poetry, from his
chaotic maelstrom he drew a vision of perfection against which
human life, destined to joy, sorrow, and death, evolved. Accepting humanity as a part of Nature at first, he later sought to distinguish the latter from culture in determining man's relationship
to man. The poet became aware of historical man, the temporal
man, that is, man in time and space. The role of man in the universe exploits the old themes of love and death in a new dimension, for love for one's fellow man is created through the recognition of the inevitable death of all. He recalls a lost happiness,
the anguish of life, the sense that man is a fleeting creature, a
being lost in a universe, but his despair is tempered by a note
of resignation as he considers the ethical and moral implications
of being human. By 1959 Aleixandre agreed that while all new
poetry is not social, the poet must write from "his preoccupation
as a member of a society and whose theme is especially man as
a collective subject . . . the great theme of the new poetry is the
consideration of historical man, of flowing man, immersed in the
here and now."[32]

In a sense, the violence and anger of *Destruction or Love*, the majesty and serenity of *Shadow of Paradise*, the sobriety of *Final Birth*, and themes and emotions of the other volumes converge on the single point of cosmic creation in both its natural and human aspects, involving a communion and a kind of salvation, either through solidarity with nature or with humanity. Carlos Bousoño finds in his total production, in all its vast panorama, a central idea. Of that work he states: "All of it, in its wide manifestation, forms a unique body of vast proportions, where the distinct members are irrigated by a circulating common blood which gives life to the solid structure."[33]

V *The Poet Speaks*

Through the years Aleixandre has granted a variety of interviews through which he has made known his poetic creed. His first statement of significance along these lines appeared in the famous Gerardo Diego anthology of Spanish poetry first published in 1932. Aleixandre believes in observing rather than in feeling while recognizing the danger of being so objective that one ignores the individual. He identifies man with nature, and thus claims that one may call the wind "lips" or "sand." He finds poetry to be "clairvoyant fusion of man with the created, with what perhaps has no name . . . aspiration to unity, synthesis . . . profound mystery."[34] He denies that poetry is a question of words, for it would be quite easy, in an almost obscene delight with verbal dominion, to confuse the sparkle of the glass with a profound creative light. He rejects narrow limits for poetic genius and finds the creation of a poem a flight or destiny "toward a generous kingdom, plenitude or sovereign reality, a supersensible reality, an uncertain world where the enigma of poetry is pierced by the supreme categories, ultimate potencies which illuminate and point out the obscure revelation, for which words overturn their customary sense."[35] And summing up his poetic creed, he states: "I do not know what poetry is. And I distrust profoundly all judgments of poets on the always unexplainable."[36]

In 1950 he stated that Andalusia was a constant in his work, especially the quality of Mediterranean light, that he had never felt himself to be a poet of minorities, that he was interested in poetry is its communicability. "Poetry more than beauty, seems what was fundamentally human, and that the essential truth of a thing of communication. . . . Poetry is a profound truth communicated. Beauty is like a light which is lit up in the message."[37] The poet accepts the anguish of man in a changing world and the possibility of religious affirmation and hope in our age of crisis as profound parts of "poetry which shows us vulnerable man in his anxiety of salvation or simply in his desperate existence."[38]

In that same year he reiterated that poetry is communication more than it is beauty. "The bad poet uses the same words as the good one; he says: death; he says: love. But, unintentionally he lies. . . . No, a word is not poetic of itself. There are no 'non-poetic' words and 'poetic' words. . . . It is their magnetization . . . which decides their qualification in the act of faithful creation. . . . Poetry is a profound communicated truth and this communication . . . heard where it can awake whole a mass of life communicated . . . poetry . . . a form of loving knowledge."[39] He came to feel, apparently, that there may be a correlation between the value of a work and the size of its audience.

In 1959 Aleixandre, in a poem called "Cumpleaños" ("Birthday"), traced his life along the iron links of years. In spite of a faltering physical stamina, his heart still beat, and his soul, stained with life as all must be "within the breast, placed in front like a/ life, rounded like the universe . . ."[40]

In an interview granted the famous Cuban essayist Jorge Mañach in 1960, Aleixandre commented on his illness which had remained with him always as a kind of second nature and created in him sedentary habits. He thought of himself as a timid man, fearful of his own nature, a product of his Mediterranean years, which like an undercurrent affected his life and work. Repeating a statement he had made often in the past, he commented that "I have always tried to sing not that which separates in a refined way but rather that which essentially unites. . . . To write of complicated matter with arduous words, perhaps is a condition of youth; to treat with simple words complex material, is perhaps a situation of maturity . . . poetry consists not so much in offering beauty as in reaching propagation, a profound link with the souls of men, establishing thus a human community."[41]

Aleixandre has constantly reiterated his message about poetry: ". . . each time I have come to feel it more firmly; it does not consist so much in offering beauty as in achieving

propagation, profound communication of the soul of men."[42]
Looking back over his total work, he found that the theme of
the majority of his works was creation, the unity of nature,
man as an element of nature. At first man was peripheral; later,
he was the protagonist and nature the background against
which human history ebbs and flows. At first Aleixandre viewed
the poet as a telluric expression of the forces of the earth, but
always beneath it all lay one unifying force, that of love, a
love which extends to the difficult human life in an infinite and
yet limited universe.

VI *Aleixandre's Significance and Contribution*

As early as 1950 Dámaso Alonso had commented that
Aleixandre's poetry was "perhaps with the exception of that of
García Lorca, and in a certain sense that of Guillén, the most
studied and commented of all the poetry of the last twenty
years."[43] Aleixandre's most frequent visitors were José Suárez
Carreño, José Luis Cano, Rafael Morales, and above all Carlos Bousoño. Poets from the provinces such as José Luis Hidalgo and Eugenio de Nora also went to see him when visiting
Madrid.[44] As we shall perceive later in this chapter, his influence upon them and other poets of the day was acknowledged
as perhaps the most important of all. An early issue of the
poetic review *Corcel*, in 1944, dedicated a special number in
praise of Aleixandre. Juan Ramón Jiménez stated that he confused Vicente Aleixandre with an "ocher turret . . . also with
a solitary tree . . . tree man tower reflects in the water of his
sea, the sky of his sierra."[45]

Dámaso Alonso compares him to a river like the Nile moving with its own mythology of monsters of the deep. "Like the
great rivers which have crossed the twilight of many battles
and which, impatient steeds, have finally broken . . . toward
death or exile, you also, you also drag tears and blood, so many
tears and so much blood of so much humanity, of so much
pain."[46] He views Aleixandre as a father of the Nile surrounded
by young poets who represent his juvenile currents. Concha Zardoya dedicated a poem to him, José Suárez Carreño saw his
poetry as like a lightning flash "furious and without sense, which
is inclined,/ mysterious, toward the depth of death."[47] Vicente
Gaos dedicated an Ode to Aleixandre protesting his love and
friendship, and Bousoño, in a poem, exclaimed: "Oh, to follow

you, to follow you losing myself/ in your kingdom of unend-
ing fire."[48] And Jorge Campos raises the possibility that Aleixandre could be a popular poet, of his "strong human value, his
cordiality, his capacity for friendship. . . ."[49]

Fourteen years later, another more famous journal, *Papeles
de Son Armadans,* dedicated two numbers of its Volume 11 to
Aleixandre. Included were poems dedicated to him by Angel
Crespo, José Angel Valente, and Claudio Rodríguez, all stressing
his influence. As the last-mentioned poet states: "For he is, and
he comes/ with us and sings, and leads us/ his wise youthful
hand . . ."[50] In the same issue Jaime Gil de Biedma praises
the exquisite quality of his attention as a guide to young poets,
as does Jaime Ferrán, who recalls the Sundays he spent at
Velintonia, No. 3, Aleixandre's house. He calls Aleixandre
"Father of poetry,/ extended and fluvial."[51] Finally José Hierro,
although at first not impressed by the poetry of Aleixandre,
joins Julio Maruri, Carlos Salmón, Ricardo Blasco, José Luis
Hidalgo and other disciples of Aleixandre in offering a testament to his poetry.[52]

In addition to simple homage and dedication, many sought
to analyse the effect his poetry achieved. In his anthology Juan
José Domenchina hears the poetry of Vicente Aleixandre as a
sob, "a virile sob without end . . . he does not overwhelm us
with tears. . . . But he suffers. . . . And he makes us participants,
not of his weakness, but of his heroic perseverance without
surrender."[53]

Gonzalo Torrente Ballester finds Aleixandre an authentic
poet who expresses himself through a vital necessity. He views
him as neither philosophic nor didactic, but as one who has a
constructive contribution to make through communication in
his poetry of intimate experience. He concludes that "the authenticity of Aleixandre and his excellent formal quality are
unquestionable."[54] Carlos Sáinz de Robles encounters simplicity, subdued light, and confusion at times in his work. He
states that the poetic greatness of Aleixandre is ". . . much beyond expression. That is to say, in a boundary and in a climate
and in a spiritual journey which not all can approach. . . .
Vicente Aleixandre is a deep poet and in his depth is obscurity
and its impossible limits."[55] Aleixandre was the only one in the
struggle between himself and existence, sharp desire and timidity of action who could touch the extremes of his created world.

Few poets, he felt, wrote as Vicente Aleixandre did or gave the impression of writing exclusively for themselves. Jorge Mañach considered Aleixandre "perhaps the most revolutionary of all . . . he raised a poetic voice unused in the Spanish language: a voice almost violent, challenging easy comprehension but of chilling and shaking eloquence as if arriving in it to the very limit in which the word, when not overwhelmed by mystic ecstasy, becomes desperate."[56]

It is surprising to find how many critics and poets consider the influence of Vicente Aleixandre to be, if not the most important, one of the basic influences in the development of all contemporary twentieth-century poetry. ". . . from the most difficult moments, the war really over, he was the master around whom many young poets congregated to receive advice and encouragement."[57] Dámaso Alonso states that the one poet the following generations followed with most enthusiasm was Aleixandre because of the constant juvenile youthful nature, the irrepressible eternal force of the beauty of youth and love he represented, and also the "radical renovation of expressive means"[58] found in his poetry. Eugenio de Nora insists that the poet's influence on the poets who come after is "much more profound than that of any other poet of his generation."[59] Among other critics who comment on his great prestige among the youth, and the debt of gratitude for his example and advice which most of these poets feel, are: Roque Esteban Scarpa, "The work of Vicente Aleixandre is now a diaphanous eternal truth in Spanish poetry . . . in truth young poets follow no other with as much enthusiasm"; Guillermo Díaz-Plaja, "one of the great masters of the young generations"; Ramón Castelltort, "He is today the master and guide of a Pleiad of poets and one of the most outstanding figures of contemporary Spanish poetry"; José Luis Cano, "one of the most extraordinary and suggestive figures of our contemporary literature . . . influence through the spirit and personal contact as much as through his works . . . without equal in the panorama of our current letters."[60]

Aleixandre's house in Madrid became a place of pilgrimage for almost all young poets, and he continues to play a large role in the poetry of the day. His greatest influence, perhaps, was that on the poets of the Generation of '36, Luis Rosales, Luis Felipe Vivanco, and Miguel Hernández, among others. José Luis

Cano feels that "it would be difficult to find in all the history of our poetry a similar situation. His book, *Destruction or Love,* came to be for not a few of those youths now since the days of the war, a kind of burning Bible with which to satiate their thirst for poetry in hours of hope or of anguish. And that influence became even more intense with the coming of peace and the publication in 1944 of his great book, *Shadow of Paradise.*"[61]

Aside from his undoubted influence on younger poets, Aleixandre is considered by many to be the master poet of Spain today. These analyses range from the "beloved and admired poet" generalization to be found in reviews like *ABC,*[62] to the perhaps equally exaggerated "one of the greatest and most significant Spanish poets of all time."[63] More tempered evaluations of his place and significance include: (a) "The value of his contribution to Spain's little Golden Age lay in his vigor and in the authentic harshness of his imagery"; (b) "Because his books of poetry have brought an essential liberty . . . to Spanish poetry; he now counts among those who both innovate and remain"; (c) "Aleixandre comes to enrich the expressive treasure of our poetry and the imaginative force of expression with a surprising extravagance"; (d) "the only important poet of the generation of '25 who has lived Spanish reality of our last twenty years . . . his importance consists not only in that he has been the master of new generations"; (e) "When at the end of a few years one studies the development of Spanish poetry during the first half century the work of Vicente Aleixandre will appear without doubt as an exigency and at the same time a reaction of unheard of vigor with respect to the period . . . it will be valued . . . not exclusively for what it is of itself, but perhaps in a more decisive way, heeding its character of an open breach toward a poetic world almost totally unexplored in our poetry."[64]

One must be careful in discussing the place of a living poet, especially a Spaniard, to take with a grain of salt the encomiums of fellow poets. Nevertheless, it may well be that one should accept the panegyrics of Gómez de la Serna that he is one of two poets who "head the whole contemporary Spanish movement"; acknowledge with Bousoño "that never has such a complex lyric poetry been produced in Spain from the point of view of the imaginative, discounting the baroque complications of the seventeenth century . . . it does not appear exaggerated to affirm that Vicente Aleixandre is, from the point of view of the imagination, one of the maximum creators of our lyric poetry"; and finally agree with Alfaya that he is "one of the greatest — if not the greatest — of living poets of the Spanish language."[65]

CHAPTER 3

Freud, Surrealism and the Sea

I Freudian Themes and the Sea

WHILE it is true that a psychoanalytic interpretation, where applied, may not be clinically valid without the cooperation and interpretation of the poet himself under expert analysis, and although in dealing with half-conscious remote associations, shifting illusions, and confusing images, the recurring themes may not give definitive answers, an examination of the sea symbolism in Aleixandre's poetry reveals the neurotic motivation behind and preoccupation with the equation that love equals death. As Freud points out, love and death instincts fuse and blend with one another and reveal themselves in an ambivalent attitude towards various objects: "for the opposition between the two classes of instincts we may put the polarity of love and hate. There is no difficulty in finding a representative of Eros; but we must be grateful that we can find a representative of the elusive death instinct in the instinct of destruction to which hate points the way. . . . In lower animals some die in the act of reproduction because after Eros has been eliminated through the process of satisfaction the death instinct has a free hand for accomplishing its purposes."[1] Melanie Klein has shown that in this tension "destructive and libidinal instincts are fused together; but its effect of causing anxiety is referable to the destructive."[2]

Whereas Jung's theory of the artistic insists on the separation of his personal life and his impersonal creative process,[3] Freud views the artist as one who compensates, through his creativity, for his inability to lead a satisfying personal life. Imagination, according to Freud, is a refuge which provides a substitute pleasure for narcissistic wishes which the artist had to abandon in real life. In a sense the poet resembles the neurotic who rejects reality for a world of fantasy which he disguises and distorts to avoid confrontation with strong repressions; he shares these fantasies with the audience as reflections, possibly of subconscious wishes possessed by all mankind. "An artist is originally a man who turns away from reality because he cannot come to terms without the renunciation of instinctual satisfaction which it at first demands and he allows his erotic and ambitious wishes full play in the life of phantasy. He finds the way back to reality, however, from this world of phantasy by making use of special gifts to mold his phantasies into truths of a new kind, which are valued by men as precious reflections of reality."[4]

Many psychoanalysts have interested themselves in the relationships between art and neurosis, symbols and illness. Freud himself analyzed *Gradiva*[5] by the Scandinavian writer W. Jensen and wrote a psychoanalytic biography of Leonardo da Vinci, shedding light on the relation of his sexuality to his creative work. Freud felt that such knowledge enhanced rather than detracted from the enjoyment of a work of art.[6] As Lawrence Kubie has shown, creativity and illness are not mutually dependent.[7] Nevertheless it is equally apparent that a man who suffers grave illness has time to daydream and think of death. Dr. Kubie admits: "Wherever unconscious influences play a dominant role the creative process in science or art becomes almost identical with the neurotic process — merely transmitting unconscious conflicts into some socially and artistically acceptable symbolic form."[8] Flanders Dunbar shows that "Freud . . . never lost sight of the essential unity of psyche and soma and he often dealt with somatic symptoms."[9]

In April of 1925 a serious illness caused Aleixandre to retire to the countryside for two years. This illness left an indelible impression on his poetry, which concentrated on an evasion of reality and a preoccupation, at least in part, with his own physical necessities. Juan José Domenchina phrases it thus: "The poet suffers from an illness which submerges him into an almost absolute withdrawal — it is a Biological poetry."[10] For Max Aub, "The sickly life of Vicente Aleixandre marks his poems indelibly, desperate songs of unsatisfied love . . . poetry of a bedridden man who sees pass through the heavens the phantasmagoria of his imagination."[11] Dámaso Alonso saw in him a poet whom God "touched as he touches that which he wishes to refine, with pain. Physical pain which left a deep imprint on his body and in his soul."[12] Luis Cernuda recalls

Aleixandre as "Sickly and alone, he lives there on the soil. That it were mine."[13] Aleixandre refers to his own illness and its effect on his career: "I shall detail that the initiation of a poetic consciousness — consciousness of a decided and possible vocation — flowered with the change which years later a long and grave illness impressed on the direction of my existence. . . . Countryside and Solitude. . . . This total change decided my life."[14]

In 1932 a new illness which proved to be almost fatal struck him, and he had to have a kidney removed and spend a long period of convalescence.[15] Sickly, alone, withdrawn, a man who fought death constantly and sought life instinctively,[16] Aleixandre wanted a refuge from a world indifferent to his pain and found it in a dream world of the unconscious where he might escape the reality of his impotence. In his poetry orgiastic Dionysian efforts to recreate a reality through imagery struggle with Apollonian tendencies to control his subconscious fantasy world. Aleixandre was never able nor willing to give an adequate explanation of his poetry, but he recognized it as a necessity based on subconscious desires. "I do not know what poetry is and I mistrust profoundly all judgment on the always unexplainable. . . . And I do nothing more than live as much as I can and what I can, writing poetry because it is my necessity still."[17] Sáinz de Robles, sensing Aleixandre's struggles and tensions, feels he writes as do very few poets "exclusively for themselves, without any other necessity than that of eliminating from himself a pressure which would end up by choking him, without any other interest than to 'see himself outside of himself,' as one who looks for a mirror only to 'discover himself' in the exterior."[18] The poet, then, is only one more object of nature which reflects in its total reality his personal problems and anguish, as Aleixandre seems to imply throughout his work.

Whatever the unconscious fantasies and their intensification through Aleixandre's illness, he consciously admitted the direct influence of Freud's works. "I know that without the impression of Freud, *Passion of the Earth* would not have taken the form which it took, although I then was not aware of it."[19] "I must confess the profound impression which the reading of a psychologist [Freud] of decisive influence, produced on me in 1928, and the basic change which was then produced in my modest work."[20]

In *Ambit* Aleixandre sets the stage for the sea as the battle-ground between Eros and Thanatos. "Mar y Aurora" ("Sea and Dawn")[21] shows us the sea as a living entity whose timid waves and passive foam awaken with the dawn. Gradually the sun's rays disperse the shadows, and the sea becomes more active as it renews its daily symbolic relationship with the sunlight. A primitive belief held that the sea had previously swallowed the old sun and like a woman gave birth the following day to a new one.[22]

"Mar y noche" ("Sea and Night"), the counterpart of the life force of the previous poem, reveals a dark and threatening sea viewed as a mouth, throat, and gullet waiting eagerly to devour the night:[23]

> Mouth—sea—all of it, asks for night;
> extensive night, quite black and large,
> for its horrid fauces, and shows
> all its white teeth of foam.
>
> *(Boca—mar—toda ella, pide noche;*
> *noche extensa, bien prieta y grande,*
> *para sus fauces hórridas, y enseña*
> *todos sus blancos dientes de espuma.)*

Seeking to swallow its enemy, the sea, chained to its black bed, vainly strains its muscles to free itself:

> The sea seems tied to the deep
> abyss, crucified, looking at
> the high heaven, to disengage itself,
> violent, roaring, nailed to its black bed. (pp. 101-2)
>
> *(Parece atado al hondo*
> *abismo el mar, en cruz, mirando*
> *al cielo alto, por desasirse,*
> *violento, rugiente, clavado al lecho negro.)*

"The moment before falling asleep (when the sense of being engulfed is strongest) . . . there is a pool or lake which will 'swallow her up,' or there is a yawning or gaping chasm or canyon. More elaborately the dreamer may be threatened by the jaws of death. . . ."[24] In these two poems Aleixandre produces a kind of primal relationship and reciprocal cannibalism as the day drinks the sea and the sea attempts to devour the night, again implying that the drive for life and the impulse to destruction are mutually independent factors.

More clearly in *Passion of the Earth* the poems emphasize a combination of death and sexuality. "Ser de esperanza y lluvia" ("Being of Hope and Rain") pictures a dying poet who does not know whether life can be found in the sea. In his hand he holds a breathing lung and "a broken head has given birth to two live serpents" (p. 159). Aleixandre here and in future sea imagery, in extrarational and compulsive symbolism, stresses his need for loving and being loved, and his impotence, and thus in a sense death state, at fulfilling that need. According to Ernest Jones, "Themes of death and castration . . . are extremely closely associated and . . . anxiety concerning indefinite survival of the personality constantly expresses the fear of a punitive impotence."[25]

"Ansiedad para el día" ("Anxiety for the Day") implies death, breast, and castration fantasies. Aleixandre misses a finger of his hand which he does not wish to recognize in the beak of a sea gull. The poet feels "lost in the ocean" against the background of a giant wave made up of handfuls of umbrellas, and wants to wet his tongue in the ecstatic blue of heaven. Both the pleasurable and the unhappy are conveyed in the screen memory which seems to be equated with a primitive wish to sleep and to join the mother. Being one with her at the breast and in sleep means also to lose one's individual consciousness or ego, and thus in a sense to die.

To merge or be lost in the ocean clearly reflects the loss of individuality, characteristic of going to sleep. The poet is both buoyed up and supported by the waves and yet he is threatened; this is a typical reaction of anxiety dreams.[26] But the earless monster will carry "in place of his word a short scissors, exactly right for cutting the open explanation." He is also threatened by the "throats of humid sirens." The defenseless poet delivers himself up to the powerful shears, and, indulging in a kind of autocannibalism, instead of tears cries his head off, which "rolls down his chest," while a dried-up girl demands whether he has enough skin left for two arms (p. 201). Sinking and smothering sensations, or the loss of consciousness, are found in fantasies of oral incorporation or being eaten. A baby treats the breast as it does its own fingers or other parts which it stuffs into its mouth, indulging in a kind of autocannibalism. This type of anxiety comes from childhood fantasies about the prenatal state, an aspect of which is the child's imagining it entered into the mother by being swallowed."[27]

"El amor padecido" ("Suffered Love"), the last poem in this collection, shows phallic and oedipal fantasies. "I prefer that muscular wing, made of firmness, which does not fear to wound with its extremity the jail of heaven. . . . Those limits of the horizon are not teeth . . . to love the perpendicular form of oneself. . . . I did not shout although they wounded me. . . . I felt the sun come from within my soul. Interiorly the points of the hedgehog, if they guess right, can come from within oneself and attract the vengeance, attract the lightning bolts . . . which penetrate and seek the mystery, the empty room where the mother did not live, although she moans, although the sea with jaws names her" (pp. 211-12). Karl Abraham shows that the sun may be a symbol of the father's phallus. He continues: "I might briefly mention that in many neurotics the father is not represented by the sun, but by lightning. . . . Lightning furthermore especially represents the punishing (killing) powers of the father."[28] The breast, the empty room associated with the mother, and the sea with jaws help support such a meaning. In Aleixandre's sea symbolism, what is commonly called a castration complex, in a sense psychological death, recurs constantly.[29]

Swords Like Lips continues the fantasies. "El más bello amôr" ("The Most Beautiful Love") rejects the false love of women. "False even to the simple manner with which the young girls/ nightly hang up their untouched breasts." Sexual passion and outlet can only be satisfied in a sexual fantasy of copulation, the wish to be devoured ("an imposing mouth like a bestial fruit/ . . . a bite that might embrace the entire water or the night") which smacks of the hallucinatory.[30]

> But I found myself a shark in the form of love;
> no, no; in the form of a beloved shark;
> clean dogfish, extensible heart, ardor or crime,
> delicious possession which consists of the sea
>
> .   .   .   .
> Thus, without ending mute that bloody coupling,
> breathing over all a thick ink,
> the kisses are the stains, the extensible stains
>
> .   .   .   .
> I penetrate you, silently, while I shout or rend,
> while my shrieks make music or dream,

because I kiss the walls which will never have eyes
and I kiss that easy yolk sensitive as a feather.

(pp. 243-44)

(Pero me encontré un tiburón en forma de cariño;
no, no: en forma tiburón amado;
escualo limpio, corazón extensible, ardor o crimen,
deliciosa posesión que consiste en el mar.

. . . .

Así, sin acabarse mudo ese acoplamiento sangriento,
respirando sobre todo una tinta espesa,
los besos son las manchas, las extensibles manchas

. . . .

Te penetro callando mientras grito o desgarro,
mientras mis alaridos hacen música o sueño,
porque beso murallas, las que nunca tendrán ojos,
y beso esa yema fácil sensible como la pluma.)

The poet's psyche appears to reject reality for a regression to
the past where his sexual instinct operated freely. The fish
inhabiting the life-giving seas represent a vital sexual force
of destructive capacity. One finds unacceptable, in this connection, the criticism of Bousoño and Dámaso Alonso. The
former insists that "nevertheless, the erotic pantheism which
has been pointed out so many times as characteristic of the
first Aleixandre has a moral root" (p. 21), and the latter that
Aleixandre's animals are primitive, uncorruptible beings who
love in intimate union with all the elemental forces of nature.[31]

In "Playa ignorante" ("Ignorant Beach"), pp. 279-80, the
poet comes from the exhausted world and desires to become
one with the sea. He is buoyed up, rocked by heat, pierced by
the water, as the sea with which he has fused strikes his
unmovable body, a sea which in "Formas sobre el mar" ("Forms
Upon the Sea"), pp. 291-93, represents death or sleep and
the unknown frontier to which life, "the world is the not
departed," leads one, "while now time passes like a nut,/ like
that which the impetuous sea has dislodged with kisses."
Aleixandre shows that through dying symbols of detumescence
a life may ensue. The creatures which inhabit his seas, then,
may be "deaf fish," "rotten fish," "fish which drown," "fish
which rot," "fish like stone," "dainty fish," "fish which nest,"
and "fish colored with the flush of living."[32]

The poems of *Destruction or Love* continue Aleixandre's sea
imagery. In "La selva y el mar" ("The Forest and the Sea"),

the human ego is overwhelmed by elemental forces of fantasy, represented by a variety of fierce animals who show their swords or teeth,

> open on the necks there where the artery beats,
> where one knows not if it is love or hate,
> which shines on the white tusks.
>
> . . . .
>
> The tiger, the hunting lion, the elephant who in his
> tusks carries some suave collar,
> the cobra who resembles the most ardent love,
> the eagle who caresses the rock like hard brains,
> the small scorpion who with his pincers only
> aspires
> to press life for an instant,
> the diminished presence of a body of man
> which
> will never be confused with a jungle,
>
> . . . .
>
> All sounds when the noise of the forest always virgin
> rises like two golden wings,
> shards, bronze or round snail,
> facing a sea which will never confuse its foams with
> the tender branches.
>
> (pp. 299-300)

> *(al descubierto en los cuellos allá donde la arteria golpea,*
> *donde no se sabe si es el amor o el odio*
> *lo que reluce en los blancos colmillos.*
>
> . . . .
>
> *El tigre, el león cazador, el elefante que en sus colmillos lleva*
> *algún suave collar,*
> *la cobra que se parece al amor más ardiente,*
> *el águila que acaricia a la roca como los sesos duros,*
> *el pequeño escorpión que con sus pinzas sólo aspira a oprimir*
> *un instante la vida,*
> *la menguada presencia de un cuerpo de hombre que jamás*
> *podrá ser confundido con una selva,*
>
> . . . .
>
> *Todo suena cuando el rumor del bosque siempre virgen*
> *se levanta como dos alas de oro,*
> *élitros, bronce o caracol rotundo,*
> *frente a un mar que jamás confundirá sus espumas con las*
> *ramillas tiernas.)*

Aleixandre views the instinctive attack of primitive animals as a form of love, but the implied sexual force may also

VICENTE ALEIXANDRE

represent a passive masochistic gratification or even a passive homosexual implication, for he both loves and fears these symbols of masculine virility, the lion, the cobra, and the eagle. To wish to be eaten by menacing animals often represents a death fantasy equivalent to a fear of castration,[33] or as Melanie Klein has shown, the neurotic dread of death is primarily related to the fear of being devoured.[34] The fear of death may also be an "anxious transmutation of the original pleasure of falling asleep. The idea of oral impregnation includes not only the active eating process, but the passive 'being eaten' as well."[35]

As Bousoño has shown, Aleixandre establishes an inverse hierarchy in which the non-living triumph over the living, the mineral over the vegetable, the vegetable over the animal, and the animal over man (pp. 21-22). Aleixandre welcomes life and love as a longed-for enemy which he fears but which will nevertheless relieve his own dammed up sexuality. Thus the forest is viewed as virginal and untouched by the impregnating sea, and the powerful claws of the animals, "the love which pierces," cannot fertilize,

> no matter how much the jet is prolonged,
> no matter how the breasts half opened in the earth
> project their pain or their avidity to the blue heavens.
> (p. 300)

> *(por más que el surtidor se prolongue,*
> *por más que los pechos entreabiertos en tierra*
> *proyecten su dolor o su avidez a los cielos azules.)*

His exploding sexuality, "the burning blood which spurts from the wound," is impotent against the rejecting virgin forest which must be punished, "love or punishment against the sterile trunks," as it faces the far-off withdrawing sea of life.

The fierce attacks of and identification with the long list of animals which the poet projects outward against the world may also serve as a father substitute onto which the fear of a father, a derivation of the Oedipus complex, has been displaced.[36] Otto Rank's idea is that a fusion through primitive life with animals may be "a rationalization . . . of the wish—through the desire to be eaten—to get back into the mother's animal womb."[37] Monroe Meyer points out "there does not exist in the mind of the little child the flattering if somewhat fictitious gulf that adult man places between himself and other species."[38]

"Después de la muerte" ("After Death"), pp. 303-4, equates the sea, filled with threatening tongues and furious foam, with both life and death; a sea which is "a thief who robs the breasts,/ the sea where my body was in life at the mercy of the waves." This death is both good and bad, for the sea may represent a kind of timeless afterlife which deletes the distinction between annihilation and immortality.

In "Mar en la tierra" ("Sea on the Earth") death may be a happiness, "the dark happiness of dying," which will triumph over life and a world which is merely a dissolving grain born for a divine water, "for that immense sea which lies on the dust." According to Freud, water or the sea symbolizes the original fountain of birth or the genesis of the individual either in association with the concept that the sea is the vital element from which all animal species came or in simple relation to the uterus of the mother, where the child originated in liquid. Fantasies and unconscious thoughts relating to life in the womb contain "the profoundest unconscious reason for the belief in a life after death, which represents only the projection into the future of this mysterious life before birth."[39] Aleixandre's pseudo-animistic theory holds that man returns in death to the place from which he came, to the sea which gave him birth, and thus a dark happiness.

The state of sleep bears a marked resemblance to the prenatal state, and it is easy to postulate an intrauterine regression, the dark joy of dying, of fusing with the sea, that is, returning to the womb. "La muerte" ("Death"), the last poem in the collection, stresses the poet's search for life against a powerfully threatening sea.[40] He wants "the color pink or life," but the sea offers him a love which must end in death, "a love which ends with death," for which the poet is prepared. "Ah, suddenly, suddenly, I want to die facing you, sea," but the sea, both love and death, withdraws, and the poet is drained and empty. In death he seeks surrender to his beloved nature, his final and greatest act of love; only thus can he achieve freedom.

> Death like a handful of sand,
> like water which remains solitary in
>   the grave,
> like the sea gull who in the middle of
>   the night

has a color of blood on a non-existent sea.
(p. 415)

(Muerte como el puñado de arena,
como el agua que en el hoyo queda
solitaria,
como la gaviota que en medio de la noche
tiene un color de sangre sobre el mar que
no existe.)

World Alone repeats Aleixandre's idea of an elemental world in which the sea plays a prominent part. "No existe el hombre" ("Man Does Not Exist"), pp. 423-24, stresses that "A sea is not a bed where the body of a man can stretch out alone/ A sea is not a winding sheet for a lucid death."[41] The sea is nevertheless a death, "a box always,/ which is a block without limits which nobody, nobody narrows." "Pájaros sin descenso" ("Birds Without Descent"), pp. 429-30, shows human life which lives and dreams at the edge of a non-human sea. "No, no, do not confuse the sea, the inert sea, with an agitated heart." Even though man may choose to ignore it, the sea is there, eternal and waiting. In "Al Amor" ("To Love"), pp. 441-42, the sea has many faces, promising or threatening, sweet and warm, or cold and burning. The sea is man's traditional enemy untroubled by man's weakness. It is "the harsh, the terse, the transparent, menacing sea which seeks shores . . . and which rolls by the feet of some human beings." This transitory, impetuous, furious, loving sea is nevertheless "Mortal enemy which hand in hand conquered me,/ to escape triumphantly to your ignored country," an image repeated in "Mundo inhumano" ("Inhuman World"), pp. 449-50, where there beats a sea where man does not exist. "Los cielos" ("The Heavens") repeats that love and life are to be found in the sea,

In the midst of the seas and in the high spheres,
under the deep basins of the powerful sea,
search for life perhaps as an unstable brilliance
profound darkness for a single breast.
(p. 459)

(En medio de los mares y en las altas esferas,
bajo los cauces hondos de la mar poderosa,
buscad la vida acaso como brillo inestable,
oscuridad profunda para un único pecho.)

But even though the sea offers itself and its love, man is incapable of reciprocating. Man may return to the primitive sea to be with nature and life, but his sterility and incapacity for loving cause his own destruction.

Shadow of Paradise contains some of Aleixandre's most provocative sea imagery. Aleixandre lived in Málaga between the ages of two and nine, and as Bousoño has pointed out: "The sea, blue and enormous, was perhaps what he loved most: sky, sand, foam."[42] Dámaso Alonso feels that Málaga represented for Aleixandre "the blue infancy of the poet himself elevated to an Andalusian paradise."[43]

Aleixandre himself stresses the importance of the temporal in contemporary Spanish poetry. "Thus the frequency with which there appear in their works the theme of 'lost time,' of human age, and with it of first order, as a representation of temporality, the theme of infancy transcended and mythified; now it is a question of a childhood which the poet evokes to symbolize through it the *fugit irreparibile tempus*."[44] Aleixandre views his childhood world as Eden in mythopoeic fashion, no longer the victim of an impassioned sexuality represented by the sea. Rather in the sea and in himself he sees a need for affection and identification with nature:

> A robust breast which reposes pierced by the sea,
> breathes like the immense celestial floodtide
> and opens its lying arms and touches, caresses,
> the extreme limits of the earth.
> > ("El poeta" ["The Poet"], p. 464)

> *(Un pecho robusto que reposa atravesado por el mar*
> *respira como la inmensa marea celeste*
> *y abre sus brazos yacentes y toca, acaricia*
> *los extremos límites de la tierra.)*

This is not to say that the psychological connotations so obvious in his earlier works are no longer germane. On the contrary, the poet's return to his youth gives ample opportunity for continuing interpretations. "Destino trágico" ("Tragic Destiny"), pp. 470-72, presents a silent sea which Aleixandre tries to define, not as foam, wind, a bird, a stone, or fleeting kiss. Under the ocean he sees a forest and birds as the waves, in this case, wind, move the branches, and the poet listens to the song of the birds. The sea still recalls an animal, but it is now tranquil and "his white visible teeth in the golden jaws,/ shone now in peace." But the peace is not what it appears, for he falls, "foaming into the breasts of the water," as the noise of his falling is covered by the "happy trills of the nightingales of the bottom." The poem may symbolize union with the mother, her triumph as she summons one back to the earlier, simpler prenatal life, in a sense, non-life or death, and thus "tragic destiny."

In other poems in this collection, Aleixandre represents the sea as the noise of life, a breast receiving the caresses of the sun, as the poet sees in the warmth a means of rekindling his old identification with nature. The sea was youth and joy of life, but those days are far away. Although still beautiful and kindly, the sea now has another face, for the passing of time stills life and love, just as night puts an end to the day. Through the sea's generative force, the poet kindles his memory and thus evokes an emotion previously felt. He enjoyed and suffered his youthful memories through the sea, and there he had the pleasure, youth, love, and things of far more value than the empty reality in which he now lives.

The sea in "Mar del paraíso" ("Sea of Paradise"), pp. 516-18, represents the most positive identification of the sea as life, and the realization that one can manage to live in spite of the worst that can happen to one; a person can convalesce from his impotence and manage life on new terms. The poet dreams of happiness and love, "a vast sea without weariness,/ ultimate expression of a love which does not end." In his youth, the first vision of life included the sea. In maturity the poet still faces the sea with the hope of regaining his lost desire, even though dimmed by adult experience.

> Therefore today, sea,
> with the dust of earth on my shoulders,
> impregnated still with the ephemeral slaked desire
> of man,
> here I am, eternal light,
> vast tireless sea,
> rose of the burning world.
> Here I am facing you, sea, still . . .

> *(Por eso hoy, mar,*
> *con el polvo de la tierra en mis hombros,*
> *impregnado todavía del efímero deseo apagado del hombre,*
> *heme aquí, luz eterna,*
> *vasto mar sin cansancio,*
> *rosa del mundo ardiente.*
> *Heme aquí frente a ti, mar, todavía . . .)*

In "Destino de la carne" ("Destiny of the Flesh"), Aleixandre shows that man is born for a moment to be a spark of light, consumed with love, and then he becomes one with nothingness.[45] The poet sees tired human bodies who retain at the shores of the sea the consciousness that life never really ends. Nevertheless the bodies continue to pile up in mountains of flesh, endlessly and apparently hopelessly, at the sea which is both the origin of life and also the end of life in an ever-recurring process.

> Human bodies, tired rocks, gray bundles
> who at the shore of the sea are conscious
> always that life does not end, . . .
> toward some mute, finite hands which imprison,
> where tired always, vital, we are still born.
>   (pp. 562-63)

> *(Cuerpos humanos, rocas cansadas, grises bultos*
> *que a la orilla del mar conciencia siempre*
> *tenéis de que la vida no acaba, no, . . .*
> *hacia unas manos mudas, finitas, que aprisionan,*
> *donde cansados siempre, vitales, aún nacemos.)*

The unconscious identification of the state after death with the state before birth is one of widespread occurrence, as is the conception that at death we pass away by the same road that we traveled when we entered into life at birth. Thus the sea may be especially identified with both birth and death.[46] Otto Rank stressed that the earliest place of abode, the "mother's body, where everything is given without even asking, is Paradise. To be born is to be cast out of the Garden of Eden. And the rest of life is taken up with efforts to replace this lost Paradise as best one can and by various means."[47]

In *Final Birth* the far-off sea reflects a continuing desire for love and life as well as death in poems such as "La estampa antigua" ("The Ancient Print"), p. 597, and "Eternamente" ("Eternally"), p. 598, where young girls wait for strong men "who impetuously end with them/ in the sea . . .," and "Junio del paraíso" ("June of Paradise") which considers the sea as an eternal life symbol which gives the world a constant rebirth.

> The sea . . . . It is not that the sea was born. Intact, eternal,
> the sea, only it was the sea. Each morning, there it was.
>   (p. 650)

(El mar . . . No es que naciese el mar. Intacto, eterno,
el mar sólo era el mar. Cada mañana, estaba.)

This sea brings passion with its "boiling splendor," as human beings love one another along the beaches. But the sea also promotes purity, as the graceful roe deer on whom no hand has yet set its love finds its fruition through the sea. For age does not destroy the contemplation of life and love, and through the sea one may find eternity and life, a death and love which are but fleeting moments in the eternal scheme of things, "and feel the ageless fire of what was never born,/ at whose shore life and death are a kiss, a foam."

In *History of the Heart* the poet seeks his real human existence, unable to rediscover the certain constants of the past in fusion with love or nature. Nevertheless, the sea appears still in its psychological and spiritual aspects, as it recalls memories of his infancy, youth, and maturity.

The idea that love equals death is the leitmotif of almost all Aleixandre's poetry and not exclusively an aspect of his sea imagery. However, since the sea meant so much more both consciously and unconsciously to Aleixandre, the man, and since the sea as the origin of life and a place of death have been universal constants in man's inheritance, it is through its symbolism that his ideas become clear. In addition to a repressed sexuality common to many poets, a neurotic and somewhat limited group of fantasies recur throughout. Aleixandre's youth in Málaga impressed the sea on his consciousness so that it became for him the symbol of that youth which he equated with innocence, happiness, and his mother. In psychoanalytic literature the sea and ocean in dreams often symbolize the mother. His desire to return and merge with that happiness and all it represents implies his death as an individual, as he is absorbed by a larger unit.[48] Intrauterine life, being pre-mortal, except to the Church, is easily equated with post-mortal life; so that life before birth equals, as a fantasy, life after death.[49]

The sea occupies a high place in Aleixandre's poetic scale of values. Of the 336 poems of his *Poesías completas* (1960), the sea appears 182 times and in addition is utilized as a central theme in sixteen poems. The sea, a recurring symbol or archetype which integrates all his poetry,[50] represents primitive, instinctive life, truer values lost by modern civilized man and maintained by simple sea creatures, a constant interplay between Thanatos and Eros, and a variety of sensual, erotic states involving repressed sexuality. Often Aleixandre juxtaposes the sea with the forest, the beach, teeth, tongue, birds, the sun, the moon, and the breast. The sea in Aleixandre's poetry is pathognomic in its psychological connotations, anxieties, and fantasies, rooted in the painful dynamic of Aleixandre's own life, although at times it evokes a happy, innocent childhood, much as the gypsy symbolized that of García Lorca. Aleixandre disguises the relationship between the symbol and its meaning at unconscious levels; he distorts and represses it so that the symbols may lend themselves to many interpretations which only psychoanalysis can fully bring out. However, in most instances unconscious influences play a dominant role in the creative process. The unconscious tries to divert stresses of reality into other channels, projecting the shape of actual dangers into symbols whose shape helps identify the fear and guilt. The subconscious defense mechanism, alert to the danger, seeks through complex patterns to avert the danger and shift the responsibility. As Frederick Prescott has pointed out, poetry may serve as a catharsis. "The catharsis is accomplished by a psychological 'analysis' to which Stekel likens poetry, except that in poetry the patient ministers to himself."[51] These unconscious forces account, for example, for the recurring breast motif associated with the sea, one of Aleixandre's most constant neurotic projections. Throughout his poems Aleixandre seems to use the sea as a surface on which to project his images, which causes the reader to think of the analogy to the "dream screen." According to the dream-screen theory, the original blankness of the dreaming infant is considered as its dreaming of the breast, and the later events and situations seem projected onto this original blankness (an image of the breast during the infant's sleep) as if it were a cinematic screen.[52]

In Aleixandre's poetry the sea takes on various hues, colors, and attributes. It can be "unstable sea" (p. 573), "imperious sea" (p. 664), or "contained sea" (p. 737), and it serves as the principal though not exclusive vehicle for the projection of neurotic fantasies where the poet employs symbols to convey meaning he might wish to suppress consciously. His sea imagery irrationally and yet imaginatively challenges his reader's established preconceptions, as the poet attempts deliberately or otherwise to recapture an unconscious knowledge and create a unity of perception.

II   Surrealism

Aleixandre's fondness for Freudianism enabled him easily to accept surrealistic imagery. Yet a continuing polemic exists over the impact of Surrealism on Aleixandre's poetry. André Breton defined Surrealism as a psychic automatism through which he proposed to express the real functioning of thought without control by reason and beyond all aesthetic or moral preoccupation, revealing the narrow relationship between the real and the imaginary. For him perception and representation, which to the ordinary adult seem to be opposites, are simply products of dissociation of a single original faculty which the eidetic image recognizes and which is to be found in the primitive and the child. For him automatism was the only thing which led to the ability to define the human condition. The distinction between the subjective and the objective lost its value, as the poet sought to engage in a kind of automatic writing. Breton found that through this *automatisme psychique pur,* one might express himself without the control of the conscious mind.

Vicente Aleixandre himself rejected automatic writing. "I have never believed in the strictly oneiric, in automatic writing, in the abolition of the creative conscious."[53] Charry Lara concludes that Vicente Aleixandre cannot be judged as an authentic poet of Surrealism, although he may be superficially catalogued with the French group, for he could never accept purely automatic writing.[54] The theme that Aleixandre was not a true Surrealist, that he owed nothing to the French school, and that his Surrealism soon gave way to other forces is a constantly reiterated theme of Dámaso Alonso and Carlos Bousoño. They imply that Aleixandre may have helped initiate Surrealism in Spain, but that it was never carried to extremes. "Vicente Aleixandre might write a surrealistic book of poems in prose . . . without any intention whatsoever of 'creating surrealism' and without knowing directly the French School."[55] "In this way if we refer to Aleixandre, the surrealistic ingredients visible in *Passion of the Earth* proceed . . . from the Spanish visionary tradition . . .[56] the initial surrealism of our poet, which in a certain way we can consider closed after *Destruction or Love,* has left, nevertheless, a profound mark on his total work, while intensifying enormously a vast imaginative phenomenon, the visionary, which was being elaborated painstakingly from the times of Bécquer."[57] Ricardo Gullón somewhat ambivalently agrees that Aleixandre's Surrealism is neither French nor complete, ". . . when one speaks of surrealism in Spanish poetry it will be necessary to understand it was a heterodox surrealism, never resigned to abdicating the artistic conscience, although, as occurs in these books of Aleixandre, the poet seems ready to allow himself to be overwhelmed, on special occasions, by impulses from the subconscious."[58] Jorge Guillén, a great poet in his own right, states that "In Spain, nobody was ever pleased with the surrealistic document."[59]

Other critics have no hesitancy about proclaiming Aleixandre's Surrealism. Alberto Monterde states: "Of the Spanish surrealistic poets the most fervent, the most definitely surrealistic is Vicente Aleixandre. . . . If one can include surrealistic poets within the pure poets . . . in the sense understood by Brémond, one could not select more obviously any poet but Aleixandre. . . . At the same time (with the publication of *La destruccion o el amor*) surrealistic poetry became established forever in Spanish letters, and its great poetic achievements definitely destroyed all skepticism."[60] Guillermo Díaz Plaja views Aleixandre's Surrealism as the standard literary version of the subconscious world unbound by rational norms. "Another great poet immersed in the oceanic world of surrealism is Vicente Aleixandre. . . . He dives through a diffuse, emerald aquarium light in which the forms navigate with the phantasmal inconsistency of the dreamed . . . Without any other logic but that which presides over the constant association of ideas, sentiments and sensations, originating from a Dionysian dynamism, Vicente Aleixandre spreads his irrepressible and vital song like the blood from a wound."[61] Luis Cernuda, himself a Surrealistic poet, insisted that Aleixandre was one of two poets, along with Emilio Prados, who knew and had read the French Surrealists. He further stated that "French surrealism obtains with Aleixandre in Spain what it did not achieve in its land of origin: a great poet. . . . Now, perhaps for Aleixandre this was not so much an aberration as a mask, a mask under which he could half say what in other terms he would not have had the courage to allude to in his work. Of all the poets of the group Aleixandre has been the one

who for the longest period of time remained faithful to surrealism as a form of expression for his own poetry."[62] Angel del
Río agrees, especially with reference to *Destruction or Love* that
it is "frank surrealistic poetry, of a surrealism much more specific
than that of any other of the contemporary Spanish poets."[63]

Aleixandre, thus, rejects the Surrealistic label. Dámaso
Alonso, Ricardo Gullón, Fernando Charry Lara, and Carlos Bousoño, who perhaps knows him best, concur to a great degree;
but a great many critics find in Aleixandre's subconscious world
and obsession with voluptuous themes a Surrealism which, if
not apocalyptic, is quite French and quite orthodox.[64]

CHAPTER 4

The Early Works

I *Ambito*

A MBITO (*Ambit*), Aleixandre's first volume of poetry, was composed between 1924 and 1927. It went to press in the summer of 1927, appearing the following year in *Litoral*, the poetry review of Emilio Prados and Manuel Altolaguirre in Málaga. *Ambit*, supposedly a marginal work in the author's production, is somewhat related to *Shadow of Paradise*, to be published years later. Composed of seven sections plus eight "Nights," including an initial and final "Night" and one "Sea," it contains classical and gongoristic forms, not unexpected at the time, since it was partly composed during the tercentenary of Góngora when baroque formalism ruled the day. One can find a minor delicate reminiscence of the poetry of Juan Ramón Jiménez. Nature is everywhere, but although there is a faint reflection of the cosmic force, the poet is largely descriptive and objective in a somewhat traditional way. He contemplates nature as in later works he will seek to possess her and be one with her. Written during his illness, the book sensually examines the fleeting aspects of time. Within his own boundary, the limits of his sickroom where he lived a solitary existence, he waxed both tender and uncontrollably passionate. Yet *Ambit*'s formal beauty, pleasure in the contemplation of nature, desire for perfection, and joy in life reflect both Juan Ramón Jiménez and Jorge Guillén more than the later Aleixandre. The poet himself claims: "*Ambit*, the first book, is born within a climate in a certain way traditional, although in its interior there strained, with expressiveness, the forces which later will reveal themselves."[1] Ricardo Gullón finds that it is "a complex of hidden nostalgias, an adolescent little book, clear in language and in sentiment, without anything revolutionary, nor even too daring."[2] Ventura Doreste feels the germ of all Aleixandre's later poetry is contained in these "delicious, moving, crystalline poems."[3] The poetry deals with the world of the senses, classic and cold at times, but also warm and romantic. The elusive imagery, the nature of shadows and clouds convey a meaning like the reverberations of a musical instrument. The poet employs traditional ballad form instead of the free verse he will later use almost exclusively, and his ten- and six-syllable lines and other experimentation reveal his great sense of rhythm.

"Cerrada" ("Closed"), a portion of the "Noche inicial" ("Initial Night"), is a descriptive humanization of night which he views as: "Oh flesh or light of flesh,"[4] as he makes us experience the loneliness of a cold, windy night in a naked field. "Idea," a somewhat baroque conception, apparently concerns the poetic process. Thoughts, like flocks of white birds, flutter in the waters of the forehead, while true thought emerges like a boat to project the threads of its sail left by the wind, outward to its farthest extremity, that is, to become words on the tongue which,

> knife which exempts it
> from its marine entrails
> and from the total landscape, profound and retarded,
> rends it.   (p. 56)

> *(cuchilla que la exime*
> *de su marina entraña,*
> *y del total paisaje, profundo y retrasado,*
> *la desgarra.)*

"El viento" ("The Wind") and "La fuente" ("The Fountain") convey placid, almost nostalgic nature symbols, but "Cinemática" ("Cinematic") shows a shadowy night again humanized:

> . . . Passion of night,
> lights up, lantern of the breast,
> the heart, and thou subduest
> thirst of blackness and silences.
>   (p. 62)

> *(. . . Pasión de noche*
> *enciende, farol del pecho,*
> *el corazón, y derribas*
> *sed de negror y silencios.)*

"Niñez" ("Childhood") recalls happiness on the beach; "Retrato" ("Portrait"), portraying Ramón Sijé, intimate friend of Miguel Hernández who died, his promise unfulfilled, pictures a lad who held the essence of things in his hands while painting the living landscape. "Forma" ("Form") reflects on temporality, for as he imprints his foot on the sand, the rising wind blows it away. "Riña" ("Quarrel") evokes a theme to recur throughout his poetry, that of the cruel moon which, as it struggles with the shadow, opens a bloody wound in gushes of light. The moon kills the night, but the poet hopes for dawn which will steal upon the moon by night and destroy it. "Adolescencia" ("Adolescence") laments the passing of youth. "Retrato" ("Portrait"), a common poetic title, here used in section three, is filled with tender emotion and vague sadness, as the poet watches a figure-skating friend who may dare both in life and in the rink. "Amante" ("Lover") enumerates the qualities of the loved one, the grace and hollow of her pillow, the warmth of her eyes, the light of her secret breast. Filled with subtle grace, the poem's imagery of light and hope are reminiscent of the lyrical ideal in Renaissance poetry. "Agosto" ("August") combines the standard elements of stars, wind, sea, and night, a limitless one which gives itself to open eyes.

The fourth section contains some of the themes which will preoccupy him in later works, the idea of limits, of time, of the need for light and joy, the naked body, as nature and youthful love link him to the security of childhood. In "Juventud" ("Youth"),

> One day there will fall,
> the limits. What a divine
> nakedness! Pilgrim
> light. Joy, Joy!
>
> (p. 87)

> (*Se le caerán un día*
> *límites. ¡Qué divina*
> *desnudez! Peregrina*
> *luz. ¡Alegría, alegría!*)

"Voces" ("Voices") conjectures that in the resounding valleys there still remain the voices of the day, refreshing themselves in the fresh lymph of the hours. The lyrical freshness and human and nature identification continue in "Cabeza, en el recuerdo" ("Head, in My Memory"), as in the play of light and shadows the poet identifies with light and growth.

> Sprouts grow from thy eyes, night
> rears tall its foliage, and thou sharest,
> pure sap, vegetable and human. (p. 91)

(Tallos te crecen de tus ojos, yergue
alta la noche su ramaje, y savia
pura compartes, vegetal y humana.)

As in many of his poems of this volume, it concerns an expanding *ámbito*, ambit, contour, limit, or boundary; "it broadens the boundary in my memory, and remains" (p. 91).

In a continuing "Night" section, "Pájaro de la noche" ("Bird of Night"), the bird is enslaved in the night, a mute block of ebony and a mold which keeps it motionless until it can be freed with the coming of dawn. The following section, "Mar" ("Sea"), contains "Mar y aurora" ("Sea and Dawn"), the first of many poems on the sea, which, as we have seen, has such symbolic value for Aleixandre. He evokes a pre-dawn sea with the faint sparks of day in the east. The still cold waters emerge from the night, running through the entire "ambit" as the streaks of light replace the sterile shadows of the night. The light disarms the dark skeleton of the air, exacting its daily worship as it drinks of the waves. "Mar y noche" ("Sea and Night") is the counterpart, the sea at night, seeking to swallow the heavens in a ravenous throat; the moon, round and pure, sinks and rises again from the waves, as the sea, crucified on its black bed, struggles towards heaven.

The fifth section continues the already familiar imagery, the interplay of day and night, the effect of light and its reflection on the earth, the birth of light in a new day. The "Night" section following, and Part VI, bring out the human element more strongly. In "Integra" ("Whole") the poet is alone at the hour of the setting sun as the harsh touch of night brushes him; in "Final," he sits in the cool breeze during the last twilight hour, after a walk. "En el alba" ("At Dawn") evokes the morning light "between the shores of night" (p. 119). Morning light continues to fascinate the poet, ecstatic in following poems over the beauty and light of day, the rays of the sun, and the yielding of night to the sweet hour of dawn. This interplay of light and darkness continues in his section "Reloj" ("Clock"), with its four hour poems, exemplifying in turn, warm light, afternoon shadows, and the power of night. Each landscape that inspires him reflects an emotion for him to experience, an ecstasy or exhilaration.

Section Seven, especially in "Alba" ("Dawn"), insists on the qualities of light which cleans the sleeping mountains, awakens colors and reflections, and finally consumes the shadows. The following poems, "Materia" ("Material") and "Memoria" ("Memory"), turn from feeling for the countryside to aspects of concrete and remembered, fulfilled and unsatisfied love.

The final poem in *Ambit*, "Posesión" ("Possession"), sums up Aleixandre's identification with nature. His love object is the night which he seeks to possess, a loving solidarity which converts the poet into an elemental fragment of nature, night itself, which with the moon, dew, dawn, and tactile senses, conveys allegorical symbols. The moon impatiently tries to build its bridges on the shadows as the poet, aware of the mature night on the spun snow, finds his mouth full of love and current fire.

> Drunk with lights, with night,
> of lustre, my body extends
> its members, treading stars?
> (p. 144)

> *(Ebrio de luces, de noche,*
> *de brillos, mi cuerpo extiende*
> *sus miembros, ¿pisando estrellas?)*

The poet then finally becomes the night, but on his tongue is "a taste of a growing dawn" (p. 144).

In this volume of youthful love, Aleixandre skillfully manipulates nature's elements and human love. He describes delicately, in gentle movements, his love affair with nature, a love of mental abstraction at times, whose equations resist completely logical interpretations.

II *Pasión de la tierra*

Aleixandre's second work, composed in 1928-1929 but not published until 1935 in Mexico, was originally announced under the title *La evasión hacia el fondo* (*Evasion toward the Deep*) and later as *Hombre de tierra* (*Man of Earth*), but the publishing company became bankrupt before it could publish the volume. Thus Aleixandre published *Swords Like Lips* first. Gerardo Diego, who arranged the appearance of the first edition of only 150 copies, originally called for twenty-one poems. Many of the poems beyond that number were eliminated.[5]

In the prologue to *Passion of the Earth*, Aleixandre claims that the poet is an "illuminator, the razor strop of light of a sesame which is, to a certain extent, the word of his destiny."

Seeking the authentic elemental life in these prose poems, with the minimum of elaboration, the poet considered them "poetry in a nascent state,"[6] written under the influence of Freud and Surrealism, poetry in which he could recognize himself. This passion for light and life must be seen as one of the keys to the work. The poems cannot be understood intellectually as individual entities without attributing to them arbitrary symbols. Ricardo Gullón says: "But—at least for me—certain fragments of *Pasión de la tierra* are so hermetic that their meaning has not yet been accessible to me."[7] In spite of the difficult dream symbols where tears become the head, the back, a celestial heaven, and the material of the visible world not distinguishable from an imagined one, the reader can sense the striving for emotional release and the search for identity for both the body and the soul. These prose poems possess a spiritual richness, interior flame, and the human aspects of pain and sorrow, which they convey in a rhythm all their own which has led critics to declare "the prose in its intention and result, pure, or impure, poetry."[8] Indeed, in Aleixandre's aesthetic word play combined with human passion, in his struggle to find himself as a creature of the earth and the world, there is already "implicit all his later poetry, while . . . the substantive poetry of the book consists, precisely in being implicit poetry."[9]

Ambit had a traditional coherence which *Passion of the Earth,* based on emotions and the subconscious drives of the poet, destroyed. It represents a fairly violent rupture with his first work, and according to the author, "with the crystallized world of a part of the poetry of the period."[10] Others have viewed this poetry in the same way. "But it is not *Ambit* but *Passion of the Earth* which is the beginning of a new poetry. . . . Here the whole purely real zone disappears, so that an interminable succession of enchained visions . . . form the nucleus of the work."[11]

"The poet is found on the eve of a profound human and aesthetic crisis. . . . But these poems in prose describe him, they discover the secrets of his passionate and fighting soul. Nothing more revealing than the contrast, the apparent contradiction between his sonnets . . . and these poems of *Passion of the Earth,* so overflowing, so without limits, so delivered voluntarily to the dark instincts."[12]

Passion of the Earth contains twenty-four poems, grouped in five sections, which have a vague connection with each other.

The title, of course, conveys the unifying force which is both "passion," in its human existential force, and "earth," the total reality for the poet and mankind. Whereas in following volumes the material of the universe is to predominate, in this early collection, the passion, spontaneous, instinctive, cries out. One sees Aleixandre's anguish in his relationship to the material universe which for him lacks order and, more important perhaps, which in its chaotic confusion offers no clear-cut destiny for man, a victim of the world and civilization, much as Aleixandre, sick and solitary, was a victim.

Ricardo Gullón called *Passion of the Earth* a "book of dazzling obscurity. . . . The poet has felt life like a stingy place, a sordid waiting room in which we wait for death to signal our turn. . . ."[13] Germán Bleiberg, himself a poet of considerable stature in the so-called Generation of 1936, finds it the "most anguished of the books of V. A.,"[14] a terribly sincere book, in sentiments and words, but one which the poet has not wanted understood in spite of his overwhelming uncontrollable compulsion to write it. It is therefore, says Bleiberg, " a long poem which ends in its very origin: in the poet."[15]

As stated above, these poems individually often appear illogical and senseless, but as a whole they form a meaningful pattern. In "Vida" ("Life") the poet is filled with a "shadow or masticated sadness which in passing, pains" (p. 149). He recalls a one-breasted mermaid, her breast like a mouth, who seeks to kiss him on the surface of the sea. As she floats face up in the purplish water, gasping for breath in what for her is airless air, her eyes, possessed by night, fail to stir life in him. The poet rejects his death, concomitant with that of the mermaid, rebounding to face life. "El amor no es relieve" ("Love Is Not a Relief") conjectures a loved one's charms which fail to arouse his love and passion as he faces approaching death in loneliness. "La muerte o antesala de consulta" ("Death or the Waiting Room") reveals the anguish of all mankind at the prospect of death. When death impassively issues her call, blind lovers can ignore her for a time, but they, too, must finally yield. He depicts shipwrecked people with the taste of dry earth on their tongues, the old with their fears, the young with their dreams of love, as their final hour approaches. "Fulguración del as" ("The Flashing of the Ace") outlines the frustration and empty promises of a future unfulfilled. Life evaporates much as a

game of cards is played, the individual cards serving as a kind
of horoscope which conveys a hypocritical hope, since one's "pal-
pitating heart does not know that high tide is a horizontal
dream under a moon of grass" (p. 157). That death awaits us
all continues to be the theme, and in "Ser de esperanza y
lluvia" ("Being of Hope and Rain") his illness and sterile
solitude prevail.

The second section starts with "Víspera de mí" ("Imminence
of Me"), concerning his fears of chaos and death, and his finding a kind of life through his words. He longs for life, its colors
and sounds, trying to be born again as an individual with a
name. This creative process or struggle, fixing limits on things
as the flux continues, converts hope into desire; sleep and night,
symbolized by drowned pianos, an extinguished note or sinking
harp, may give way to radiant dawn. The moon, with its cruel
yellow light, awakens his desire for love, one he cannot fulfill,
but he exclaims "Therefore I am here, now forming myself"
(p. 164). Gerardo Diego found this poem especially passionate
and lyrical.[16] "Rosa y serpiente" ("Rose and Serpent"), as well
as other titles in the section, continues the themes of love, anxiety, and pain. Love turns out to be an empty gesture in the face
of the threatening image of night. Death, the great serpent,
waits for us all, an illogical mystery we cannot solve. "La forma y
no el infinito" ("The Form and Not the Infinite") realizes that the
ultimate truth and reality is death, as the poet identifies with the
night, which, while it offers pain, also suggests joy, for love and
life are lies. The poet, indeed, becomes night: "I am Night"
(p. 169). "La ira cuando no existe" ("Ire When It Exists Not")
stresses his favorite themes of forgetting the limits of forms, the
play of light and darkness, the illogical moon, and his identification with the earth. "Thus I shall drag myself like a nard, like
a flower which grows in search of the entrails of the earth,
because it has forgotten that day is in the heights" (p. 172).

In Part Three, "Del color de la nada" ("Of the Color of
Nothingness") identifies love and night, in a meaningless and
hopeless place of scattered mannequins who uselessly offer their
nakedness to the surrounding air in a world where death is
inevitable; "Fuga a caballo" ("Flight on Horseback") notes the
poet's fear of nothingness as he enters the world of playing cards
in which one may identify with another world where the
capacity to love and live exists; but, in any event, when he dies

he will return to the earth, dissolve into it, "become pure vegetation" (p. 179). "El crimen o imposible" ("The Crime or Impossible") seeks the earth and death which will give him back the world as an innocent child. "El mar no es una hoja de papel" ("The Sea is Not a Sheet of Paper") opposes the sea life to the wormy earth. "Sobre tu pecho unas letras" ("On Thy Breast Some Letters") contrasts the sunlight of the day which for him is love and happiness, with the moonlight of the night.

Part Four views the moon in all its menace. "El solitario" ("Solitaire") is dedicated to a dangerous moon which seeks to hide its evil passions "while you seek the clear lymph, innocent, final, in which to bathe your ugly body" (pp. 18-19). The poet recalls his night of love and tries his fate at a game of solitaire, but the wind sweeps away his cards and only death remains. "Hacia el amor sin destino" ("Toward Love Without Destiny") warns his love of the new moon; "Fábula que no duele" ("Fable Which Pains Not") laments the destruction of the nightingale by the treacherous moon. "Del engaño y renuncia" ("Of Deceit and Renunciation") invokes in surrealistic imagery the inevitably menacing moon, as Aleixandre seeks to become one with various elements by breaking the limits of form. "Ansiedad para el día" ("Anxiety for the Day") fuses the poet with nature, the limits breaking. He rows, lost on the ocean of life, seeks to wet his tongue in the subheaven or ecstatic blue, becoming one with the shore and the ocean.

The final section stresses similar themes. "El mundo está bien hecho" ("The World Is Well Made") sings of his love for the forests, the cacti, the hills, all of which clamor for love. People, dragged by forces they cannot control, spend their lives within whitewashed walls which turn to boiling lava. They seek to escape their destiny, the great serpent which awaits them all. "El alma bajo el agua" ("The Soul Beneath the Water") opposes the beauties of nature to the creations of man. Aleixandre is sustained by an enormous sea, and his soul fuses with the light. He is saved by love as he becomes one with all nature. "Hacia el azul" ("Toward the Blue") paints the glory of the day, the sun on the water. The poet wants to fuse with the sun which will give flame to what is now ash. In the final poem, "El amor padecido" ("Love Suffered"), he longs for the world which he cannot fully possess, and feels at the mercy of the universe, because he can fuse with but portions of the mother earth.

The concept of mother earth in this collection combines with Aleixandre's Freudian preoccupations, discussed earlier, especially in his interest in breast symbolism. "Vida," as we have seen, contains a green, moon-colored mermaid who thrusts forth her "wounded breast, parted in two like a mouth" (p. 149). The idea of eating and being eaten by an object is also a way of becoming united with it, and as Otto Rank claims, "mermaids represent the primal mother."[17] In "Ansiedad para el día" Aleixandre views the potential threat of "the gullets of the humid sirens" (p. 201), as he fuses with the ocean and thus loses his identity to the larger whole. "A shore is my hand. Another my leg" (p. 201). As one psychoanalyst explains, "In anxiety dreams with this content (merging with a larger whole), the dreamer feels that he will . . . perish as an individual, absorbed by the larger unit."[18] The sea may represent then the devouring breast, and sinking and merging with it repeats the feeling of sinking, relaxing, and losing the sense of one's individuality, which is characteristic of going to sleep. "El alma bajo el agua" contains again the image of sinking and yet being supported by the immense sea. "If the waves ascend, if you soak in all the sad melancholies which flew by, managing to avoid grazing you with their hollow, fine woods, they will stop exactly in your throat, decapitating you with their light, leaving your head like the flower . . ." (p. 207).[19] The room in which the poet finds himself moves on the fearful waves, as he is borne up. "An enormous, extensive sea sustains me in the palm of its hand and demands respect of me" (p. 208). The symbols Aleixandre uses vacillate in significance to match the author's mood, often appearing incomprehensible to the reader whose sensibilities, nevertheless, quicken to empathize with the poet, inspired by the same life and challenged by the same sufferings and enigmas which belong to all mankind.

III *Espadas como labios*

Begun in the summer of 1929, *Espadas como labios* (*Swords Like Lips*) concerns the central themes of life, death, and love, which the poet, in his moment of inspiration and suffering, views in a new relationship. As Dámaso Alonso points out, ". . . it is useless to search through it for what it does not contain: history, anecdote and rational sequence. This poetry does not have—literally—common sense."[20] Clearly from the initial quotation from Lord Byron at the front of the volume, to the effect that the poet is "a babbler," no conventional "meaning" was intended. The work as originally presented was filled with poetic transpositions and capriciously arranged punctuation to help Aleixandre release what he considered his "interior fire." Many critics believe this work to be typically surrealistic, as Aleixandre confessed was his intention. "We find here this confession of the poet. It reveals that, in the years of greatest influence of that manner in modern French poetry, the Spanish poet participated in some form in its experience . . . tends to be, without achieving it completely, a typical surrealistic work."[21] As we saw in Chapter 3, Aleixandre's intention was not to induce a surrealistic trance, but to create a voluntary pattern of unusual images. Carlos Bousoño has shown that Aleixandre, in his somewhat illogically and incoherently developed poetic structures, does not know exactly what theme he will develop. The diffuse emotion he creates in this confused and disturbed work gives rise to apparent indecisions for the poet which transfer to the reader. ". . . will impose in his poetry, many times an idiomatic and mental illogicality which . . . will not entail . . . a detriment of lyrical value . . ."[22] Aside from syntactical tricks and an insistence on a great number of relatives and determiners, constantly repeated, the use of "where" with relative value, the constant use of the conjunction "or" in a comparative sense, and the like, Aleixandre in his oneiric representations utilizes visions, visionary images and symbols, as we have seen, characteristics of his highly rhythmical free verse.

His liberty of form and his use of varying lengths, greatly changed from *Ambit,* allow him to cover a variety of subjects in a dream atmosphere which hovers between sensation and thought. Dámaso Alonso finds two kinds of poems in this collection, short compositions of about twelve lines and longer poems, the first group in hendecasyllables and the second in free verse, the first restrained and elegant, the second less logical.[23]

Swords Like Lips, in its examination of reality, petrifies it, or, as one critic phrases it, indulges in the "immobilization of the moment."[24] Aleixandre's bitter-sweet perusal involves an imagery of dead roses, coals of silence (because they lack life-giving flame), and a series of other death representations.

In the world's changing reality he seeks to remove the charade of life which hides behind the mask of death, endeavoring constantly to establish an equivalence among various orders of reality. Leopoldo de Luis claims that *Swords Like Lips,* in its ironic and bitter projections, is "the rejection of a corrupt, outmoded society which must be ejected from its artificial and sycophantic shell . . . from its false and unjust principles."[25] Ricardo Gullón, admitting the bitterness and despair, finds in the poetry a principle of order and a spark of hope in Aleixandre's ascent toward the light.[26]

Almost all agree that this volume represents a break with *Ambit,* but critics express differing views as to its place in the development of twentieth-century Spanish poetry. Dámaso Alonso states it is part of the curious phenomenon between 1929 and 1932 of the so-called dehumanized poets to evolve towards a neo-romantic revival, and considers it a "bitter, disordered, harsh, suppurated, veined, livid, roseate, beatific, archangelic . . . mixture of pain and sarcasm, tenderness and delicacy."[27] Admitting to its passionate, tortured, stormy and grotesque aspects, he finds it "the most literarily revolutionary of all his works."[28] Eugenio de Nora sees *Swords Like Lips* as a rejection of pure poetry and "neo-juanramonianism" and says that it sweeps away with one blow "the affected world of exquisiteness in which poetry seemed to have been residing captive . . ."[29]

As one examines the individual poems, one encounters the poet's constant longing to be, combined with a fear of not being. "Mi voz" ("My Voice") relates his birth on a summer night; he senses in his beloved a possibility of hope and happiness; the sea like a warm medal gives promise of a possible light and life. But in "La palabra" ("The Word"), the poet cannot communicate and feels drained of life; in "Partida" ("Departure") his straining toward life gives way in the following poem, "Muerte" ("Death"), to "Under earth the unexpected kisses,/ that silence which is coal, not flame" (p. 223). In "Circuito" ("Circuit") Aleixandre seeks the love of virginal sirens beneath a harsh cruel moon; and in "Ya es tarde" ("Now It Is Late") he wants life, "ignoring that the rose has died forever" (p. 225). In following poems he continues to seek love and light as opposed to death and darkness until in his final poem of this first section, "Nacimiento último" ("Final Birth"), he fuses the two concepts and

sees death as joy and awakening. He becomes the sun, the happy
earth which welcomes the day, shifting in Spanish from masculine to feminine and thus implying a change from the concrete,
he visto el mar, la mar, los mares, los no-límites ("I have seen
the sea, the sea, the seas, the non-limits"), to the abstract. He
wants to break the limits which prevent things from returning
to earth:

> What clouds or what palms, what kisses or everlasting flowers
> seek that forehead, those eyes, that dream,
> that growth which will end like a newly born death?
>
> (pp. 230-31)

> *(¿Que nubes o qué palmas, qué besos o siemprevivas*
> *buscan esa frente, esos ojos, ese sueño,*
> *ese crecimiento que acabará como una muerte reciennacida?)*

The second section begins with the poem which has elicited
the most critical comment, "El Vals" ("The Waltz"). Dedicated
to García Lorca, who in turn dedicated a similarly titled
poem to him, the poem reflects Aleixandre's early awareness of humanity and society, to become so great a part of his
latest poetry. Aleixandre caricaturizes the end-of-the-century
salon as he describes a real or imagined social event in which
the poet recognizes himself as a participant. Sarcasm, sympathy,
tenderness, repugnance, death, and the macabre alternate. In an
elegant ballroom "the ladies await their moment seated on a
tear" (p. 235). The dancers swirl about the room. The imagery
grows more and more erotic, until at the height of the dance the
dresses change to birds, "the windows into shouts,/ the lights
into Help!" (p. 236) and the innocent kiss between two humans
into a thorn which death dispenses as it says: "I love you." For
Carlos Barral, who considers it Aleixandre's best poem, "The
rhythmic figure of the poem is like a perfect parody of the
narrated vertigo in which a most lively succession of images
assaults the imagination like a landscape seen from a pro-
gressively more rapid center, and toward which there converge,
as they approach, attitudes and things."[30]

In "En el fondo del pozo" ("At the Bottom of the Well") we
see death finally as a concrete reality. Subtitled "The Buried
One," the poem views the buried man (surely the poet) living
a death which is a prolongation of life. The cadaver feels sensations, for death is the only reality which can keep one in contact
with life. There where no wind blows nor sea threatens, perhaps

a voice or freed hand reaches toward the moon, recalling other times of warmth and light. Filled with temporal images, the poem stops and prolongs each moment of time, changing it into eternity.

> Thus the eternity was the minute
> Time only a tremendous hand
> on the long detained hair.
>   (p. 238)

> *(Así la eternidad era el minuto.*
> *El tiempo sólo una tremenda mano*
> *sobre el cabello large detenida.)*

Each moment, as it lasts, thus gives up all of the essence of its love to the poet.[31]

Other poems foreshadow future themes. "Toro" ("Bull") relates to cosmic fusion and self-eroticism; "Resaca" ("Undertow") involves an affirmative negation, "The flower in the water is not a moan" (p. 242). The poet thinks of the world in flux in which his hands become two mountains, his body an encompassing foam.

Love may take many forms; some of the Freudian ones we have already examined. The poet seeks truth and beauty in a hypocritical world where dreams are not fulfilled and where one must seek true sexual and erotic expression in the more primitive and even threatening natural forces. In "El más bello amor" ("The Most Beautiful Love"), his possessive anxiety for love is like the voracity of a shark. In other poems he identifies with those seeking love in America, and other world travelers in "Poema de amor" ("Poem of Love"); contrasts love and nature, adult passion and childhood purity in "Muñecas" ("Dolls"); becomes nature as he becomes a wasp, the breeze, a stone, in "Acaba" ("Complete"); and experiences the frustration of an incomplete love and identification with nature and life, "all is coal which hurts and sobs/ on the false vegetable which exists" (p. 252), in "Por último" ("Finally").

The third section, dedicated to the youngest member of his poetic generation, Manuel Altolaguirre (the first two sections were dedicated to Dámaso Alonso and García Lorca respectively), seeks truth in "Verdad siempre" ("Truth Always"); expresses his need for love from the forces of nature in "Siempre" ("Always"); stresses his identification with mother earth in "Madre, Madre" ("Mother, Mother"); acknowledges

the brevity of life in "Desierto" ("Desert"), and the inability of
his tongue to express the beauty of nature as expressed through
a naked girl in "Palabras" ("Words"). Other poems in this section reveal his love of nature, of different seasons and hours,
which he sees in human terms, of cold and heat, dreams and
light, temporality, and death.

> Thus death is floating on a memory not life,
> on that final blue made from overheard tears,
> from that labyrinth of threads which like dead hands
> place a lily as though girding a world.
> (p. 270, "Río" ["River"])

> *(Así la muerte es flotar sobre un recuerdo no vida,*
> *sobre ese azul postrero hecho de lágrimas oídas,*
> *de ese laberinto de hilos que como manos muertas*
> *ponen una azucena como un mundo ciñendo.)*

The final section, dedicated to Luis Cernuda, yet another
member of his poetic group, continues the already established
themes. "Salón" ("Salon") and its party of fainting ladies recalls
"El vals"; "Suicidio" ("Suicide") expresses the poet's wish to
live the eternity of love in singular form, but the world remains
deaf to his pleas and his desire for a fresh juxtaposition with
nature.

> Open the world to me, open to me;
> I want to illuminate only one kiss,
> lips which irritate,
> pitiless trees.
> (pp. 275-76)

> *(Abridme el mundo, abridme;*
> *quiero iluminar sólo un beso,*
> *unos labios que irritan*
> *árboles despiadados.)*

In this section the fusion with nature in flux, where a human
arm can weigh more than a star, takes on new dimensions.
Aleixandre searches for liberty to dissolve his limits in "Liber-
tad" ("Liberty") and wants to become a floodtide, appearing
on the beach as timid foam in "Playa ignorante" ("Ignorant
Beach"). The poet hears the music of distant planets and momentarily becomes the universe, but he is frustrated in his
desire to be the fish in the river. It serves him little to sink his
arm in the water, for fish are not hands, and thus the poet is

reminded of his tangible limits. These themes, occurring in "Con todo respeto" ("In All Respect"), "Blancura" ("Whiteness"), and "Mudo de noche" ("Mute at Night"), reach a peak in "Cada cosa, cada cosa" ("Each Thing, Each Thing"), included in the first edition of *Destruction or Love,* but later returned to *Swords Like Lips,* to which it really belongs. Aleixandre somewhat ironically investigates the limits and boundaries imposed upon him. In the remaining poems such as "Donde ni una gota de tristeza es pecado" ("Where Not Even a Drop of Sadness Is a Sin") and "Formas sobre el mar" ("Forms on the Sea"), he looks at form and matter while continuing to plumb the limits of a world where things are fixed in immobility, but where both love and time pass.

Swords Like Lips represents imaginative fragments grounded in the visionary. Its unity depends on the poetic sensibility and interest which permeate all of Aleixandre's poetry, but unlike his following masterpiece, *Destruction or Love,* its totality is not greater than the sum of its parts.

CHAPTER 5

La destrucción o el amor
and *Mundo a solas*

I *La destrucción o el amor*

MANUEL MACHADO, Gerardo Diego, and Dámaso Alonso were members of the jury which awarded the National Prize to *La destrucción o el amor* (*Destruction or Love*). In granting the award they found "the novelty is in the themes, in the landscape, in the image—many times, nevertheless, more reducible to reality than that of the previous book: a total renovation of the expressive means of language, which characterizes the entire work of the poet. . . ."[1]

One may view Aleixandre's poetry as both a reply to nature and a call to the original forces of life. The poet offers us a visionary transfiguration of the world in flux, a world of mystery and darkness at times, whose basic fabric is erotic love. Aleixandre proclaims here his romantic concept of love and the universe and sees the latter as a place of cosmic and human passion, of a frustrated and desperate clamor, and of unchained telluric forces which often prove fatal to man, absorbing him and destroying him. For Aleixandre men can obtain love only by destroying themselves and fusing with the cosmos, for human love is fleeting, and a final fusion with the earth will prove to be the most enduring love of all. Aleixandre excludes the life beyond and salvation, for his world matter, absorbed in the living unity of nature, evokes no religious connotations.

As part of the thematic structure of the collection, Aleixandre stresses the idea that the unity of the world includes man's works and his civilization, but they remain peripheral to the primary instinctive life. Perhaps love can save him from society's mask, for love fuses all things, animal, vegetable and mineral, into one substance. But to achieve fusion one must give up his limiting structures. Thus the title involves destruction or love,

81

that is, destruction identified as love. Concha Zardoya states it well when she says: "All is love nevertheless, and all is destroyed. A hunger of being in everything impels to that autodestruction: in order to be everything or something one stops being what one really is."[2]

The animal and the vegetable world constantly interact with the thoughts and feelings of the poet. In virgin forests ferocious beasts surround man who seeks to find himself fruitlessly, half glimpsing his salvation in an identification with nature in all its forms, and thus affirming rather than denying love for all creation. Animals, the forest, and the sea live in intimate union with elementary forces of nature, and tender small animals exist with large destructive ones, the beetle and the scorpion with the cobra, the eagle, lions and tigers. Bousoño has counted some thirty-one different animals mentioned, aside from the poems entirely dedicated to specific animals, all of whom in some way identify with the rest of the world. Thus, the tiger is an elastic fire of the forest, and the eagles resemble the ocean. These animals may be virginal and innocent or terrible and destructive, as may the other aspects of nature, such as the ocean, the moon, or the heavens. And in this vision of nature as a physical whole in which violence and love are but two parts of the total picture of the primary forces of life which include the wind, the sun, hills, and animals, a fusion of things by a creative paradoxical force which impels all to fulfill itself, to integrate, to fuse in the cosmic scheme of things for a final birth or death, everything attacks, destroys and loves everything, and in so doing, loves, attacks and destroys itself. Life is death. The limits between flora and fauna disappear in a new unity; the sea's fish appear to be birds; the foam is hair; a body becomes an ocean, a heart, a mountain; man may be metal or a lion. Throughout the scheme of things the eternal temporal verities of nature and the temporal brevity of love reveal themselves, but the erotic nature is exceptionally potent and its sexual symbols are singularly discernible.

Dámaso Alonso finds a mystic pantheism in Aleixandre's work. As the mystic poets of old, in order to fuse with God, had to die in order to find eternal life, Aleixandre offers a mystic fusion or death with the sea, the earth, the maternal earth which sustains him at her breast.[3] Others have commented on "the pantheistic vision of the world"[4] offered by Aleixandre. Pedro

Salinas sees a similar pantheism and the essential identity of love and death in the work corroborated "tragically at times . . . languidly . . . at others."⁵ Man's role varies; at times he hardly exists except as a sterile impotent being. Yet he suffers anguish, and albeit pessimistically, exhibits an existential feeling and longing to be. The pessimism may stem from the long illness suffered by Aleixandre in 1932. He began to write *Destruction or Love* at the end of the year, and with a rebirth of energy, finished it the following one in the little town of Miraflores de la Sierra, a mountain village. He composed it, he claims, "from the central thought of the amorous unity of the universe."⁶

This amorous unity, seen by most critics, impels some to insist that Aleixandre's work is neo-romantic. Pedro Salinas and Dámaso Alonso consider it passionate and romantic, and José Luis Cano states, "He does not believe it possible that any beating heart in life does not love, does not offer the gift of its blood to love . . . book of cosmic passion, fatal inexorable force of love . . . one only reaches the root of love by the self-destruction of the lover to be born—to live—in the blood of the loved being. And this human love is a simulacrum—the only possible—of total love which only in ultimate fusion with the earth—death—can be obtained. Therefore, in this book the poet identifies himself so many times with . . . the jungle, the light, the sea."⁷ Charry Lara finds Aleixandre's position a "spiritual one confronting the problem of love. An attitude entirely romantic; the only form possible of love is pain."⁸ Finally Juan Chabás, commenting on what he finds to be an instinctive and romantic exaltation stemming from Surrealism, sees in him the influence of Alberti, Neruda, and also Baudelaire and Nerval, especially in his thesis that love is no longer a fountain of life, but a destructive force of violent imprecations, a romantic world full of sobs, thorns, pain, death, dreams, tears, hearts, burning, pallor, sadness, sobbing, and suffering, all part of a romantic vocabulary where tigers are the size of hate, lions have hirsute hearts, and nature, earth, and the sea form one destructive poetic cosmos.⁹

Destruction or Love consists of fifty-four poems divided into six parts. Structurally, Pedro Salinas finds it difficult poetry, which rearranges normal values and confuses terms, stemming from "the new forms and lyric craving of a surrealistic type which . . . have encountered now . . . their perfection in this book of Aleixandre."¹⁰ Yet he finds in it an internal logic which subordinates the surrealistic elements, although he comments on the rather outward use of metaphors and the poetic transpositions. For him one of the principal values of Aleixandre's book is "having given to Spanish poetry an example of an instrument of lyric expression, of magnificent verbal altitude, moving, rich, of plastic force, accurate and of sufficient subtlety to reach the highest level of the poetic state."[11]

José Luis Cano, admitting the radical freedom of lyrical expression and richness and variety of lyrical elements, finds also an internal unity along with a powerful subjectivity, and a poetic world very much like that of Guillén, and "very rich in sensations of being, in life . . . resulting in a song full of insatiable impetus."[12] In this work one will find graceful lines of both peace and passion. Often Aleixandre's verbs will lead up to an explosive frenzy and then will give way to a lack of motion to convey peace and serenity. His adverbs and conjunctions possess unusual values.

Throughout, Aleixandre stresses a special use of the conjunction "or" as inclusive and equal rather than involving two mutually exclusive objects. Thus when he says kisses or birds, his kisses are like birds. He wants love or death, a fish or a dry moon, a body or a river, eliminating all but the one quality he wishes to emphasize. Aleixandre constantly uses negations with affirmative force: I am not the sea, I am not the sky, I'll never call the air, hands, nor the mountains, kisses." He repeats a word or words at the beginning of successive clauses: "that water like air, that fine dust, which is stirred up, which is pacified. . . ." Quite often Aleixandre will sum up in a final stanza or in a recapitulated last line the central theme of the composition. Although his metaphors often have objective reality where blond hair is gold and pearls death, his special imagery also allows him to reach the sun, the moon, or the stars. Writing his poems in free verse which "only occasionally descend into rhetoric,"[13] he shows little respect for traditional rhythms, ". . . the poet smashes to pieces the classic preceptive and breaks the syllabic harmony and logical sense of the phrases whenever in his judgment the integrity or purity of the expression demands it."[14]

Dámaso Alonso sees a bond between *Swords Like Lips* and *Destruction or Love*. Both are passionate, tortured, stormy books, but the latter is far superior in "efficacy and clarity."[15]

Eugenio Frutos feels that the poet achieved real authenticity only with *Destruction or Love.*[16] Del Río views it as a desperate desire to understand the enigma of things."[17] Dámaso Alonso finds it a "burning book, pierced by the darts . . . of a gale of a very dry summer,"[18] and also one of "the most genuine books, most faithful to the eternal heart of poetry, as well as one of the richest, and pierced by universal passion which Spanish literature in these last years has produced."[19]

"La selva y el mar" ("The Jungle and the Sea") exemplifies clearly the powerful destructive force of love, as well as a form-less world in flux where each being wishes somewhat existen-tially to be the other and through an erotic act partially discovers his real essence. Bousoño has shown, "in the act of killing which the beasts instinctively realize, Aleixandre sees the most simple form of amorous action."[20] Much as in Lorca's representation, the sword, the tusks, and the teeth are sharp instruments synonymous with death, but they and the threatening animals also represent a kind of overly energetic love which will result in the equation, previously discussed, that love equals death.

> The tiger, the hunting lion, the elephant who in his
>   tusks carries some soft collar,
> the cobra who resembles the most burning love,
> the eagle who caresses the rock like harsh brains,
> the small scorpion who with his claws only aspires to
>   oppress life for an instant,
> the diminished presence of a body of man which will never
>   be confused with a jungle . . .
>
> (p. 300)

> *(El tigre, el león cazador, el elefante que en sus comillos*
>   *lleva algún suave collar,*
> *la cobra que se parece al amor más ardiente,*
> *el áquila que acaricia a la roca como los sesos duros,*
> *el pequeño escorpión que con sus pinzas sólo aspira*
>   *a oprimir un instante la vida,*
> *la menguada presencia de un cuerpo de hombre que jamás*
>   *podrá ser confundido con una selva, . . .)*

The wild beasts kill not for hate but for love, and their power-ful claws, "the love which cleaves," seem to individualize the animals as poetic creatures as well as symbols of a desired fusion with all of creation, where "a hope ever green" is maintained. While tigers the "size of hate" and others "battle with the yellow hyena which takes the form of an insatiable setting sun,"

Aleixandre also contrasts the stars and meteors with the setting sun, fusing heavenly bodies with the animals. In relating to the latter, Aleixandre substitutes unreal for real images to convey to us what reality is for him. Thus, "The beasts show their swords or teeth like the beating of a heart" creates a vision of nature which may or may not be receptive to the blandishments of man.

Throughout this poem Aleixandre uses his creatures as representing the elemental force of nature where love and death are interchangeable. The animals, as forces of fantasy, represent a form of love, but the implied sexual force may also show a passive masochistic gratification previously referred to. To wish to be eaten by menacing animals may reflect a death fantasy, and Aleixandre's ambivalent attitude clearly conveys the fusion of the Eros-Thanatos instincts. As love and fear are mixed, so Aleixandre, while scorning man and deeming animals and the natural force they represent superior, longs for the very thing he fears. Thus, just as the forest remains virginal and untouched by the impregnating sea and its life, it cannot be fertilized either by the longed-for and yet feared powerful animal forces.

> The peaceful wait
> that ever green hope
> bird, paradise, pomp of untouched feathers,
> invents the highest branches
> where the tusks of music,
> where the powerful claws, the love which cleaves,
> the burning blood which gushes from the wound,
> will not reach, no matter how the fountain lasts,
> no matter how the half-opened breasts on earth
> project their pain or their eagerness to the blue heavens.
> (p. 300)

> (*La espera sosegada,*
> *esa esperanza siempre verde,*
> *pájaro, paraíso, fasto de plumas no tocadas,*
> *inventa los ramejes más altos,*
> *donde los colmillos de música,*
> *donde las garras poderosas, el amor que se clava,*
> *la sangre ardiente que brota de la herida,*
> *no alcanzará por más que el surtidor se prolongue*
> *por más que los pechos entreabiertos en tierra*
> *proyecten su dolor o su avidez a los cielos azules.)*

"No busques no" ("Search Not, No") shows a poet who has loved as never before. The woman he loves is seen as blue as the night, a place where all the beauty of life ends. Thus the living body of the woman evokes the same sensation as the night whose darkness ends the light of day. The poet strives to arouse love in "The living dryness of some withered eyes" (p. 301), but fails. As a poor man sleeps under the moon which scarcely grazes him, he vainly seeks heat, the minimum blood or tear. Aleixandre pities the poor human who, unable to fuse with the earth, cannot find love.

The following poem, "Después de la muerte" ("After Death"), seeks the reality which lives "in the depths of a sleeping kiss." Again a sea furiously but vainly crashes against the glass which encloses him as he lies peacefully in the earth, his reality. Since in the final analysis everything happens and changes, eventually the sea will triumph, "those thick waters which like black lips now erase the difference" (pp. 303-4). "Noche sinfónica" ("Symphonic Night") uses to good effect a stanza beginning with "Perhaps" which governs following stanzas and coordinates a series of different imagery. He achieves thus the same effect as with his equivalent "or," employed so effectively in much of the poetry of this volume. His head may fall on a sounding turf where the tongue may be a sweet savor of violins, the breasts have the form of a harp, and the lips form an arpeggio of water.

One of the frequently anthologized poems from this collection, "Unidad en ella" (Unity in It"), is one of the clearest statements of Aleixandre's position. From the first lines we see the mystic fusion and the human love of the poet for a loving creation.

> Happy body which flows between my hands,
> beloved face where I contemplate the world,
> where graceful birds fugitively copy one another
> flying to the region where nothing is forgotten.
>
> (p. 307)
>
> *(Cuerpo feliz que fluye entre mis manos,*
> *rostro amado donde contemplo el mundo,*
> *donde graciosos pájaros se copian fugitivos,*
> *volando a la región donde nada se olvida.)*

Throughout, the poet Aleixandre suggests that human love, his own love for nature, and the erotic force of nature are all fragments of the same unity, as the poet dissolves in living flesh against a cosmogonic background where nature is both destroyed and engendered. The creative force may also prove destructive in a constant interchange of cosmic human relationships. Thus, tinged with love, as he beholds his beloved, he will die and renounce life forever. While the loved one as a symbol takes a human form, these human aspects play a secondary role to cosmic infinity, and as the poet contemplates the beloved face, he seeks a special reality and passion. To love is to feel truly the limits of life and the nearness of death, and to die completely one must have passed through life, the hot blood of one lover burning that of the other. The poet exclaims:

> I want love or death, I want to die completely,
> I want to be you, your blood, that raging lava
> which enclosed, irrigating beautiful extremities,
> feels thus the beautiful limits of life.
>
> (p. 308)

> (Quiero amor o la muerte, quiero morir del todo,
> quiero ser tú, tu sangre, esa lava rugiente
> que regando encerrada bellos miembros extremos
> siente así los hermosos límites de la vida.)

The passionate call to the eternal communion of a final total love which only death can offer, reveals death transfigured into love itself. The romantic invocation continues, and in his final stanza, as is usually his custom, Aleixandre gives us the meaning and title of his work.

> This kiss in your lips like a slow thorn,
> like a sea which flew made a mirror,
> like the sine of a wing,
> is still some hands, a review of your crackling hair,
> a crackling of the vengeful light,
> light or mortal sword which threatens at my neck,
> but which never can destroy the unity of this world.
>
> (p. 308)

> (Este beso en tus labios como una lenta espina,
> como un mar que voló hecho un espejo,
> como el brillo de un ala,
> es todavía unas manos, un repasar de tu crujiente pelo,
> un crepitar de la luz vengadora,
> luz o espada mortal que sobre mi cuello amenaza,
> pero que nunca podrá destruir la unidad de este mundo.)

Thus Aleixandre in his poetic pantheism suffers a slow thorn, a carnal love, a mutual destruction and yet a fusion with the elementary aspect of the earth.

Similar themes occur and recur, emphasizing now the sea, now other natural elements, now the light, now the darkness, at times joy, at others anguish. "Sin luz" ("Without Light") imagines a swordfish in a marine cosmos where fatality and limits rule but where there exists a desire for freedom, light, and love. In "Mina" ("Mine"), claiming he is not the sea nor sky nor world, Aleixandre identifies with the sun and becomes the sun.

In "Ven siempre, ven" ("Come Always, Come"), the last poem of the first section, an obviously erotic poem, the poet is struck by the thought of shining kisses and the idea that if he drank at that shining fountain he would have the life of a star, a star without love. He feels, nevertheless, the temptation to fuse with the loved object which brings love and death. The usual pantheistic mysticism is visible, as orgiastic Dionysian efforts to recreate reality through imagery struggle with Apollonian tendencies to control the subconscious world of fantasy. The poet becomes almost desperate, longing for love or death, as he contemplates the solitary cold and loveless stars. The poet searches for the right word to convey his thought and emotion, repeating in almost frenzied fashion and with punishing intensity, "that brilliance which . . . that contagious brilliance . . . that luminous river . . ." (p. 316). Identifying man with cosmic force, Aleixandre invokes the loved one, again recapitulating the theme in the final stanza.

> Come, come, death, love; come soon, I destroy you;
> come, for I want to kill or love or die or give you all;
> come, for you roll like a light rock,
> confounded as a moon which asks for my lightnings!
>
> (p. 316)

> (¡Ven, ven, muerte, amor; ven pronto, te destruyo;
> ven, que quiero matar o amar o morir o darte todo;
> ven, que ruedas como liviana piedra,
> confundida como una luna que me pide mis rayos!)

The second section continues in the same vein, stressing especially temporal matters as in "Mañana no viviré" ("Tomorrow I Shall Not Live"). The poet searches for light and love against the background of the forest and the sea in "Ven, ven tú" ("Come, Come Thou"); feels repulsion and attraction at the thought of an unyielding and eternal nature, finding optimism in the illusion of youth which conveys warm happiness, watching the flowing of time and the ebb and flow of love, an eternal river which passes constantly, in "A ti, viva" ("To You, Alive"); and discovers solidarity and mystery as he looks for answers in nature in "Quiero saber" ("I Want to Know"). Aleixandre sees the universe as a development of mysterious unknown forces, but he keeps seeking for meaning. At first he denies the identity of that force but seeks to define it, asking whether the heart is rain or a margin, and what the limits are among flowers, doubt, thirst or sun, but he concludes that "the world all is one" (p. 335).

Section Three is labeled "Elegies and Elegiac Poems." "A la muerta" ("To the Dead Girl") declares man's great need to love. Indeed, the poem conveys the central message, if message there is, in *Destruction or Love.*

> To love, to love, who does not love if he is born?
> Who ignores that the heart has limits,
> has form, is tangible to the hands,
> to recondite kisses when one never cries?
>
> (p. 342)

> *(Amar, amar, ¿quién no ama si ha nacido?,*
> *¿quién ignora que el corazón tiene bordes,*
> *tiene forma es tangible a las manos,*
> *a los besos recónditos cuando nunca se llora?)*

In "La luz" ("The Light"), light is a loving, living form in an harmonious breast, the noise of celestial music. Aleixandre views it as a "celestial tunic which with the form of a luminous ray/ caresses a forehead which lives and suffers . . . " (p. 343). Light is a kind of messenger, and the poet conveys the idea of striving optimistically upward. Aleixandre uses an interesting imagery transposition, for the luminous ray is not clad in a celestial tunic, but rather it is the celestial tunic which has the form of a luminous ray. In "Humana voz" ("Human Voice") "the scar of light gives pain" (p. 345). The entire world suffers, day and night, and death is present in the room "where white doves like blood/ penetrate the skin without stopping at the lips" (pp. 345-46). "Canción a una muchacha muerta" ("Song to a Dead Girl") points out that if death is a continuation of life, then destruction or death is necessary for a complete love. The buried girl longs for life as she senses the sky and beloved feet which tread the soft turf above. "Plenitud" ("Plentitude") exclaims that all love is truth, that "All is blood or love or beat or existence,/ I am all for I feel how the world is stilled/ and how thus the sob or earth gives me pain" (p. 352). In other poems of the section he visualizes the cold moon, the setting sun, and an October day, but all are within the cosmic framework of love, light, and death.

Section Four comments on his happiness as he sings to the blue heavens, to love and to existence in "La dicha" ("Happiness"), and an unjust moon, the solitude of the world, and the glory of a fragrant naked body, a fairly constant image in his work, in "Triunfo del amor" ("Triumph of Love"). "El frío" ("The Cold'), the final poem of the section, sums up both its theme and its imagery, as Aleixandre once more stresses his pantheistic mysticism. As the wind pierces his bones and the sea his veins, in a burning freezing contrast, the poet evokes the wind as a living being, a fish within its own waters, a gigantic hand which oppresses the world, and creates other analogies. Man then becomes an absolute ocean, and his body is the sea shaken by the wind, under the light of the stars. But the same wind,

> Black secret wind which blows between the bones,
> blood of the sea I have in my closed veins
> absolute ocean that I am when, asleep,
> I irradiate green or cold a burning question. . . .

> *(Viento negro secreto que sopla entre los huesos,*
> *sangre del mar que tengo entre mis venas cerradas,*
> *océano absoluto que soy cuando, dormido,*
> *irradio verde o fría una ardiente pregunta.)*

which assumes the form of a fish or a human, is finally one with man, for it exclaims "I am your shadow, a road which carries me to that limit" (p. 370).

The fifth section begins with "Soy el destino" ("I Am Destiny"), an ardent poem of implacable passion which reveals his anxiety to fuse in amorous communion with the beings who populate the earth. He wants to live like the grass, or the snow, or the coal, for he is music, an innocent bird with bloody wings, the sea, a horse, a line, a tiger, a beetle—in short, the world. "Mar en la tierra" ("Sea on Land") is especially interesting because of its breast symbolism and suggestion of a dream screen occurrence. Throughout the poem Aleixandre seems to use the sea as a surface on which to project his images. According to the dream screen theory, the original blankness of the

dreaming infant is considered as its dreaming of the breast,
and the later events and situations seem projected onto this
original blankness (an image of the breast during the infant's
sleep) as if it were a cinematic screen.[21]

> The resounding sea converted to a lance
> lies on the dryness like a drowning fish
> clamoring for that water that can be the kiss,
> that can be a breast which is ripped and flooded.
>
> But the dry moon will not reply to the reflection of pale scales
>
> .   .   .   .
>
> Then the happiness, the dark happiness of dying,
> of understanding that the world is a grain which will dissolve,
> which was born for a divine water,
> for that immense sea which lies on the dust.
>
> Happiness will consist in dissolving into the minuscule,
> in transforming into the severe thorn,
> remains of an ocean which disappeared as the light,
> a drop of sand that was a gigantic breast
> which upon leaving through the throat lies here like a sob.
>   (pp. 379-80)

> *(El resonante mar convertido en una lanza*
> *yace en lo seco como un pez que se ahoga,*
> *clama por ese agua que puede ser el beso,*
> *que puede ser un pecho que se rasgue y anegue.*
>
> *Pero la seca luna no responde al reflejo de las escamas pálidas.*
>
> .   .   .   .
>
> *Entonces la dicha, la oscura dicha de morir,*
> *de comprender que el mundo es un grano que se deshará,*
> *el que nació para un agua divina,*
> *para ese mar immenso que yace sobre el polvo.*
>
> *La dicha consistirá en deshacerse como lo minúsculo,*
> *en transformarse en la severa espina,*
> *resto de un océano que como la luz se marchó,*
> *gota de arena que fue un pecho gigante*
> *y que salida por la garganta como un sollozo aquí yace.)*

Aleixandre's dark happiness stems from the sea which gave
him birth. The "gigantic breast" gives the theoretical genetic
origin of the screen, that is, the way it would look to a baby.
Aleixandre's fantasy, in contrast to the general run of adult

dreams in which the screen-ocean itself occupies part of the manifest content, is projected on the sea screen in many different forms at the same time. The gigantic breast which comes out of the poet's throat may be viewed as a withdrawal from the breast. The *dry* breast is a frustrating one and explains the "dry" ocean. A desert is, in a way, a dry ocean, and we speak of a camel as a ship of the desert. The dry moon, naturally, symbolizes the dry breast. "It is striking that the screen is frequently represented precisely as something inedible, tasteless or even disagreeable to the mouth such as a . . . desert, or other wastes and barren tracts."[22] Throughout the poem Aleixandre stresses the relationship of the sea and dryness. The dry moon fails to respond, and the immense sea lies on the dust. The dryness and sand represent thirst sensations, much as a gritty mouth would be projected onto the breast symbol.

The moon, love, and death continue as symbols in "La luna es una ausencia" ("The Moon Is an Absence"), "Quiero pisar" ("I Wish to Tread"), "Sólo morir de día" ("Only to Die by Day"), and "Cuerpo de piedra" ("Body of Stone"). Animals merit their own poems, in "Cobra" and "El escarabajo" ("The Beetle").

The sixth and final section of *Destruction or Love* includes a series of blander images in "Nube feliz" ("Happy Cloud"), such as the "breeze in search of dawn," and the beauty and innocence of a childhood love in "Hija de la mar" ("Daughter of the Sea"). Yet one of the most powerful projections of the love-death force is to be found in "Las águilas" ("The Eagles"). Bousoño states that "the visionary imagery, the quality which the sphere of fantasy emphasizes, will result more or less . . . indeterminate . . . determinable only in a generic and not specific way."[23] In this poem the powerful and destructive eagles, with their metal feathers, powerful claws and "that zeal for love or death" (p. 401), with their violent wings which destroy veins and section congealed blood, "break the wind into a thousand pieces,/ marble or impenetrable space" (p. 402). The wind is marble to show how impenetrable space is, thus setting off the violent intensity of the eagles who are so strong that they can even destroy the impenetrable. In "La noche" ("Night"), commenting on a heart or a breathing breast which may have limits, Aleixandre sees them converted into a star in the water. Animal, vegetable, and human limits disappear, and fusion occurs as human beings abdicate their responsibility to exterior force.

The final poems of the volume recapitulate previous themes in a rising crescendo. "Se querían" ("They Loved Each Other"), listing lips, faces, moonflowers, earth, and a series of other emphasized nouns, stresses love outside of time. Filled with a languid melancholy, the poet recognizes the harsh reality of the loving lips which involve an inevitable fatality in the closed system of night which is death, and yet he sees the possibility of communication with the rest of the universe, for everywhere and at all times, day, night, twilight and dawn, on sea or on land, love abounds. "Total amor" ("Total Love") also seems to involve an eternal love not limited by time, for the poet's body dissolves happily in the sea, finds the limits of the world like remote shores, becomes one with nature, and the sunlight on his skin, like the far-off noise of young teeth, devours its daily ration. The poet longs to live in the folds of the mountain or the sea. "Hay más" ("There Is More") claims a kiss is a dove which becomes a whiteness between his hands, the sun is a cloud and then a heart, a dove-like winged heart capable of flight. In an unusual use of synecdoche, where the part becomes the whole, it is also a flying world with the light of a live star like a body, or two souls or a final bird. "El desnudo" ("The Naked One") views death as the clothing, the accumulation of centuries on which a sobbing breast looks in vain for love or the naked body. "Cerrada puerta" ("Closed Door") continues the symbols of love and death,

> A hand the size of hate,
> a continent where veins circulate,
>
> .   .   .   .
> where love was the clashing of crashing rays
> on human bodies demolished on the earth.
> (p. 413)

> (Una mano del tamaño del odio,
> un continente donde circulan venas,
>
> .   .   .   .
> donde el amor era el chocar de los rayos crujientes
> sobre los cuerpos humanos derribados por tierra.)

The last poem of Destruction or Love, significantly titled "La muerte" ("Death"), sums up Aleixandre's views of death as the final surrender to the nature he loves, hence the final and greatest act of love. To become one with the world through death will insure his complete liberty. In a final struggle with the sea, where names and limits cease, the poet is finally overwhelmed.

> Death like a handful of sand,
> like the water which remains solitary in the grave,
> like the seagull who in the middle of the night
> has the color of blood on a non-existent sea.
>
> (p. 415)
>
> *(Muerte como el puñado de arena,*
> *como el agua que en el hoyo queda solitaria,*
> *como la gaviota que en medio de la noche*
> *tiene un color de sangre sobre el mar que no existe.)*

José Luis Cano viewed the poem as of radical liberty in lyrical expression, and his "amorous poetics, his conception of love, as a copy or essential form of death."[24]

II *Mundo a solas*

Mundo a solas (*World Alone*), begun in 1934 and finished in 1936, originally bore the title of *Destino del hombre* (*Destiny of Man*). The Civil War kept it from being published, and it did not appear until 1950 in a very limited edition. Aleixandre feels it is a transition work, "segregated—degraded—man—of his primordial elementality, distant and extinguished the dawn of the universe . . . is what is sung in this book, perhaps the most pessimistic . . . of the poet."[25] Possibly the least known of his works, it is still filled with furious birds, wounding metal, frenzy, violence, tormented love, a world in which man is a vague shadow, but it also contains a virginal world of light and purity, to be so much a theme in his next work. Man is unworthy of living in a beautiful world because he destroys nature and his fellow man. The world, lacking a perfected logical order, still forms part of the destructive impulse, but the poetry involves "a first and powerful approach of the poet to human life."[26]

Yet it appears to be an imperfect approach to humanity. The world the poet portrays is an anguished one where humans are incapable of reaching paradise, a shadow world which might have been, a world where the moon, queen of death, reigns. Man is not kind and rejects the consolation or salvation which nature may offer. Thus the world is a terrible place, for man has not taken advantage of his opportunities. As the editorial note which precedes it says, it is a "terrible world, the world alone, without containing in its breast a perfect man, but what might have been and was not, the remains which an outraged life has left."

The volume contains only seventeen poems, a number of them previously published in literary reviews, in three sections, headed by a quotation from Quevedo, the great Spanish satirist, "Life lies enveloped in a dark forgetfulness" (p. 419). In the first part of the collection, the poet seems to reject civilization and seek cosmic unity. Man's presence is a mistake in this almost frozen world. In the second part, a loveless moon skims through a loveless world, for nobody can recognize love when it approaches on silent stars or invisible roads—nobody, that is, but the poet. The poems interchange between those of beauty and light and love, and those where indifferent suns and cold moons rule a desolate humanless world.

Concha Zardoya sees *World Alone* as a world given us like "a growth of tall trees without underbrush, not of natural elements, but of men."[27] Ventura Doreste feels that the poet identifies human life with evil and cruelty, an "attitude which is only the result of an excessive love."[28] Bousoño comments on the stupor and astonishment at the appearance of *Shadow of Paradise* six years before *World Alone*, its originality, and its explosion of serene, sweet and placid clarity. He considers *World Alone* the connecting link between *Destruction or Love* and *Shadow of Paradise* in its combination of exclamatory sentences with those of great simplicity.[29] An ABC review of *World Alone*, stressing this latter aspect, found in it "a classical tradition which gives strict continuity to his poetry . . . the language, patently rich, precise, profound."[30]

"No existe el hombre" ("Man Does Not Exist"), the first poem, sets the mood. The poet contemplates the world around him and finds that only the ghost of man, residual man who might have been, exists. Only the moon suspects the truth of man's non-existence, and it sees that inevitable death impedes man's progress to paradise. The moon rises from a limited sea in pursuit of the bones, of what once were man's veins and blood, "But man does not exist,/ He has never existed" (p. 424).

"El árbol" ("The Tree") is one which never sleeps. Unable to cast shade on non-existent mortals, it becomes a thigh reared from the earth, ever green, satisfied to be a tree. "Bulto sin amor" ("Loveless Bundle") finds no love in the loved one's body. The poet exclaims:

> I loved you . . . I do not know, I do not know what is love.
> I suffered you gloriously like blood itself,
> like the painful hammer which makes one live and kills.
>
> (p. 427)

> (*Te amé . . . No sé. No sé qué es el amor.*
> *Te padecí gloriosamente como a la sangre misma,*
> *como el doloroso martillo que hace vivir y mata.*)

Feeling that life is death and love a daily dying, he finds the earth indifferent to his kisses. Unable to love his loved one, he clutches a stone as though it were a bird, but finds only the harsh mountain, for his beloved is a shadow sharing the common non-existence of man on earth. "Pájaro sin descenso" ("Bird Without Descent") shows us escaping birds almost desires or foam, leaves of a radiantly beautiful sky. But man ignores the sea, the beach, a bit of grass, and cannot recognize the birds and life. The poem exudes graceful vigor and tenderness, but reveals a man still inert. In "Bajo la tierra" ("Under the Earth") Aleixandre knows that heaven exists. One lives beneath the earth with the rock and dark skyless water, and deeper yet can undergo a purifying fire, one normally forbidden to man. In "Humano ardor" ("Human Ardor"), the final poem of this section, knowing that love is death, he still loves the form which may never become human.

In the second section, in "Ya no es posible" ("No Longer Is It Possible"), Aleixandre has a tragic moon which casts its shadow on a loveless world; in "El sol victorioso" ("The Victorious Sun"), he shows a powerful cosmos which crushes great mountains, a killing sun from which he seeks death; in "Al amor" ("To Love") he reveals love's naked presence without artifice or cosmetics; it arrives in many ways, not as a river, nor the terrible beauty of the forests, but rather as the simple quiet of mountains. Nobody knows this love which comes on silent steps and invisible roads, but the poet feels her: "But I felt you, I saw you, I guessed you" (p. 442). Along with the terror goes the happiness, warmth, and light, such a central part of *Shadow of Paradise*. "Filo del amor" ("Edge of Love") allows the loved one to assume its cosmic form in all sizes and shapes, as a mountain, a rose, a butterfly, a pile of nubile wheat; in spite of destroying light, living lovers kiss.

The third section approaches most clearly the themes of *Shadow of Paradise*. In "Mundo inhumano" ("Inhuman World") elemental creatures and the forces of nature predominate. Man's supposed civilizing influence damages nature, which rejects him. The poet must then seek his identity in a hostile world with joys which mortals cannot know, where there is no night and where death clamors against life in vain. Walled off from this happy world to which he cannot aspire, man withers and is destroyed. "Tormento del amor" ("Torment of Love") shows the poet's love for a beautiful woman, but being human and mortal, by definition she is evil. Anguished at not knowing who he is in the blood-stained world, where he cannot hear his voice in the thunder "nor the bloody rain which tints the grass which has grown/ between my feet bitten by a river of teeth?", the poet wants to know who he is and whom he loves.

The poet realizes the limits of his love, its cruelty, and his own frustration and impotence. "Guitarra o luna" ("Guitar or Moon") portrays a moon fatal to the poet, for its mere cold touch spells danger. As the moon sings her song of death, animals bathe in her changing light where man does not exist. The moon moans disconsolately as she fruitlessly seeks a life not yet on earth, sadly becoming a tragic guitar. "Amor iracundo" ("Irate Love") pictures a beautiful woman, loved like the noonday sun, like a shadow, a lightning flash, like the sea and the beach; she is both light and blood, cruelty and lies, and life. "Nadie" ("Nobody") projects man into the solitary world where he partakes of the elemental cosmos. The poet, crossing rivers like panthers sleeping in the shade, hearing the unhearable howl of night, crossing the forests, breaking branches with his forehead, contemplates the heavens, but he can communicate with nobody in an empty world. In the final poem, "Los cielos" ("The Heavens"), he advises one to search for life beneath the sea, which sustains the heavens, a breast of love, on its arms. But the heavens, the luminous unmoving heavens, do not smile, nor fly; they are for eyes and ears where "the moon moans enclosed in air, in pure air" (p. 460), and man, sadly, is dead. Concha Zardoya feels that this collection "closes the door of chaos and opens the door of Paradise, or perhaps, just the opposite, if we want to find in it a more exact meaning within the Aleixandrine cosmic conception."[31]

CHAPTER 6

The Search for Paradise

I Sombra del paraíso

A LEIXANDRE spent the formative years of his life in Málaga, and "in that unforgettable age, Málaga, its coasts, heavens, sea foam and profound indefinable aura, were . . . the very core of his existence, and nobody knew it as well as he when many years later, he subjectively discovered, under a familiar light, all the buried landscape of Paradise."[1] That the point of departure for his poetic recreation of Paradise is Málaga seems fairly obvious without the poet's own admission in a prologue to an anthology of his own selections from *Sombra del paraíso* (*Shadow of Paradise*). "Without that city, without that Andalusian shore where all my childhood was spent and whose light was to remain indelibly in my pupils, that book, for which so many reasons can well be called Mediterranean, would not have existed."[2] His "sea of Paradise" is that Mediterranean, his "river," the Guadalhorce, his "city," Málaga.

Shadow of Paradise, begun in 1939 and finished in November, 1943, even before its publication created a sensation among young poets; when it finally appeared in 1944, "it inspired a movement of enthusiasm and fervor in the readers, principally in the poetic youth of the moment."[3] Aleixandre deviates somewhat from the tumultuous and disparate ambivalence of *Destruction or Love,* but in the old familiar distinctions between man and nature, he continues to denigrate the former. The old fire remains in sublimated form, although from time to time the frenzy and naked passion of *Destruction or Love* shine through, and the poet employs new dimensions of supplementary imagery. He returns to his innocent world of infancy, to a Paradise beyond original sin and knowledge, to be one with the heavens and the creatures of the dawn.

Aleixandre's Paradise, superficially, appears to be a de-

energized world, but the poetry of opposite equivalencies
remains, mediated but not resolved. He evokes a Garden of
Eden where he may find lost happiness to escape the evil
world of man, in its folly and malignity. The poet rejects them
or relegates them to a peripheral role somewhat egotistically,
and narcissistically reinvents his own reality, remembers it,
or perhaps imaginatively recreates a dimension before the
time of the child's horrifying and inevitable loss of innocence.
But, in his universe of serenity, order, and beauty, Aleixandre
implies an awareness of the world's true appearance and structure in which man must play his role, to be an increasing
concern of the poet through the years, the revelation of *Shadow
of Paradise* later ceding to the cognition of *Historia del corazón
(History of the Heart)*. The former vision of a glorious cosmos
before man's full appearance, with the concomitant limits and
pain, reveals him still as a transitory being preoccupied with
his destiny, anticipating in this way the human heart of the
second collection.

The poet himself claims that in *Shadow of Paradise* he sings
of the dawn of the world as viewed by current man, a kind of
song of light from the consciousness of the darkness, "a counter-
point which gives this work its pathetic depths."[4] Upon viewing
Aleixandre's Paradise, perforce a pre-human world and yet one
against whose purity of nature man committed original sin,
one must question man's basic evil, since he can nostalgically
recall a primitive world of clarity, a pure virginal world of
light and dawn and innocent children. Aleixandre's calm and
well-ordered world is one in which all beings share a brotherhood uncorroded by the corruption of the current world, but
the poet, as a human being of the present, in his briefly happy
recreation, based on the human emotion of love, is limited, not
only by recall and inspiration, but by the obviously human
limit of death. Anguished man longs for the radiant light of
Paradise, whose beautiful nature the poet recreates.

While some may find only a tenuous thread of topical rele-
vance connecting the poems of this collection, the arrangement
is neither shapeless nor random in its rejection of the destruction and decomposition and search for sublimation and rebirth.
The poet achieved a momentary glimpse of Paradise, but having
lost its substance, finds only a shadow; hence the title. But
the shadow world is clothed in living and beautiful flesh,

with seas and moons, cities and birds, realities, or at least invitations to reality. Illusion must imply disillusion as purity inevitably implies the existence of a less innocent reality, and the unreal fantasy of flying cities, humans of cosmic size, and fires which cannot burn, involves objects, however symbolically used, which are recognizable realities of the everyday world. The poetic leitmotif again is cosmic love. Although the city man, unaware of nature's beauty, cannot live that life, the poet's love for the world from which he came leads him to identify with the moon, the stars, the animals, of which there continue to be a great variety, and all creation. Love destroys all distinguishing boundaries among creatures, and death (the world before birth is a kind of death) continues to be the most perfect love in its prospective fusion with the material of the world.

Aleixandre's "creatures of the dawn" are part of his personal Paradise lost, but he includes "a love of the world which to me, a man in repose, makes me suffer or exalts me. I have a unitary vision of life . . . drinking a glass of golden wine I salute the luminous air, the powerfully maternal sea, the blue space, the miniscule blade of grass. . . . And on drinking the wine, lighted by the sun, I feel a communion with life."[5] Seeing the civilized world as a deformation of a previous one, the poet submerges himself in the womb and again becomes part of mother earth. In seeking an escape to Eden, he achingly evokes the romantic emotion of his lost youth. Exiled from Paradise, he exudes melancholy and nostalgia, recalling the hidden beauty at the fount of life, where naked creatures of a newly-created world listen to musical rivers and harmonious forests and seas. Pulsating purity, replacing tremendous telluric outbursts of destruction, demands a luminous nature, radiantly resplendent with a light which reflects an eternal celestial glow.

Aleixandre uses expressions such as instantaneous moon, rock, and kiss, or a sudden glance "to give us an idea of an eternity enjoyed with that freshness and the haste of the passing moment. He discovers the eternity of the moment, as he might discover a vast and noisy bloody flow in a single pulse beat."[6] His virginal beauty is as fleeting as the foam of the sea or the winged flight of a bird, an ephemeral and transient quality which would normally imply unhappiness. But as the poet identifies his loved one with heaven and earth, death and transformation, in addition to the cosmic themes and Platonic ideal, he seeks relief from the human condition through a love which is after all a familiar human emotion, communicating thus a poetic double vision, the instinctive one of innocence and the experienced one of adult knowledge.

Shadow of Paradise is divided into six parts. Of its fifty-two poems, forty are in free verse. Only a dozen have a definite metrical form, but through them all there exists free association among rhythms of different kinds. The free verse is of varying length, hendecasyllables, pentasyllables, hexameters, exciting combinations of anapestic lines, and irregular meters. Avoiding, through this prodigality of expression, monotony in his rhythmical movements, Aleixandre uses exclamations, interrogatives, and an almost musical progression of scales to form a polyphonic richness. As one critic states it: ". . . we have found the fundamental law which governs it: his formidable capacity to unify rhythms of different kinds."[7] But these rhythms depend on a fairly simple vocabulary. "The poet moves within a framework of current words, elegant, as he habitually is, but not recherché or vulgar. . . . His poetry is sufficient to maintain at the highest poetic tone, the most elevated lyrical temperature in any kind of language use."[8] His fetish for simplicity extends to his use of adjectives, which he occasionally employs adverbially, and rarely in double or triple combination. Many times his naked nouns convey his precise tone or mood; on other occasions, for special effects, he ends his poetic lines with a verb; infrequently he employs gerundives experimentally.

Aleixandre's metaphorical experimentation is less important than his complication of imagery achieved through the inversion of normal placement and relationships with reality and fantasy, a process in which he offers the reader contrasts between colors, between light and darkness, day and night, pain and happiness. Bousoño shows how eleven of the fifty-two poems contain one "continued image" extended from beginning to end, twenty-two have a single principal "vision" and some secondary ones, and nineteen have greatly varied imagery. The "vision," Aleixandre's basic material, gives attributes to a real object which it cannot have. Thus, "When Aleixandre attributes cosmic size to a human being, what he does is to emphasize the spiritual power that that human possesses."[9] José Luis Cano depicts Aleixandre's bubbling waterfall of words and passionate invocation as an "interior frenzy . . . in a form of classic beauty,"[10] but Dámaso Alonso find it has "nothing to do with classic form, but with a vital, individual and individualizing form, necessary to project superficially the profound unity of the poem."[11] Aleixandre himself sees his work as a fusion of romantic and classic tendencies, "this synthesis of romantic background and new expressive classicism . . . which is *Shadow of Paradise*."[12]

Shadow of Paradise has achieved almost universal acclaim. Carlos Bousoño, for whom it is a kind of "symphonic vision," feels it is the greatest work of Aleixandre's first period.[13] Concha Zardoya sees it as a peak of Spanish poetry. "Aleixandre writes . . . with the fire of fever, but since he possesses gracefulness, he does it with ecstasy, with . . . torment, melancholy, sadness, in an eternal spasm and voluptuousness of pain, love and joy. . . . In no Spanish poet is there received with as much force as in Vicente Aleixandre that beauty . . . does not hide exactly beneath the probable."[14] She states that his work is a basically optimistic book, written by a visionary. "With daimantine grace he surprises the mysterious origin of the phenomena, of time, of love. He is in part a man who dreams and in part illuminated by grace and natural knowledge. His poetic light has pierced the bark of life, to absorb from it the fluidity of its sap. . . . *Shadow of Paradise* represents—within the complete work of its author—a marvelous equilibrium in the conversion of the subjective to the objective, without thereby abandoning passion, fire or ascensional impetus."[15]

Ildefonso M. Gil considers it "the great book which announces the splendid maturity of a great poet."[16] Dámaso Alonso finds its keynote to be a kind of dazzling stone, both burning and cold, sculptured by a god, "this *Sombra del paraíso* in which Vicente Aleixandre, one sad afternoon of the world definitively encountered Beauty."[17] Luis Felipe Vivanco discovers in this poetry the flesh and sensuality which allows us to approach the residues of a natural paradise. Aleixandre, through this sensual expression, discovers the truth of nature as a feminine body, and " . . . with recent words, miraculously recovered, the unstable transparency of a world also recent: it is, I believe, what Aleixandre proposes and realizes in *Shadow of Paradise*."[18]

Max Aub concurs that it is Aleixandre's best book, and states that it might have reflected a former Spain of happiness which the poet lost because of the political adaptation he had to make. But in Aub's opinion, in spite of the constant purification of the poet he "has not been able to free himself from rhetoric and oratorical reiteration."[19] Finally, Rafael Benítez Claros insists that "Aleixandre's book is to be read in intimacy, slowly, many times. Without thinking of any other poetry or any other poetic world but his."[20]

In his first poem, "El poeta" ("The Poet"), Aleixandre states that the poem is not enough, that he must identify with the entire universe, that his vital passion is still a prolongation of amorous passion, and an invitation to a natural life.

> Yes, poet; cast off this book which pretends to enclose
>   in its pages a sparkle of sun,
> and look at the light face to face, your head supported
>   on the rock,
> while your very remote feet feel the final kiss of the
>   setting sun
> and your lifted hands sweetly touch the moon,
> and your hanging hair leaves a wake among the stars.
> (p. 464)

> (Sí, poeta; arroja este libro que pretende encerrar en
>   sus páginas un destello del sol,
> y mira a la luz cara a cara, apoyada la cabeza en la roca,
> mientras tus pies remotísimos sienten el beso postrero
>   del poniente
> y tus manos alzadas tocan dulce la luna,
> y tu cabellera colgante deja estela en los astros.)

Having established that love and sorrow belong in his kingdom, the poet in his next poem, "Criaturas en la aurora" ("Creatures in the Dawn"), seeks the original innocence of the universe which they know. Nakedly, pure and inviolate, they "say goodbye to men . . ." (p. 467). This sweet world of his infancy and tropical nature, the music of its rivers, the magic breath of its light, was the one in which the poet lived. "There you lived. There each day you saw the earth,/ the light, the heat . . ." (p. 468). These creatures of the virginal dawn are seen as the prime movers.

> There were born each morning the birds,
> surprising, all new, living, celestial.
> The tongues of innocence
> said no words:
>
> .   .   .   .
>
> Birds of initial happiness, who kept opening,

trying out their wings, without losing the virginal
    drop of dew.   (p. 468)

(Allí nacían cada mañana los pájaros,
sorprendentes, novísmos, vividores, celestes.
Las lenguas de la inocencia
no decían palabras:

. . . .

¡Pájaros de la dicha inicial, que se abrían
estrenando sus alas, sin perder la gota virginal
del rocío!)

The poet loves these innocent, amorous, mortal beings of a
virginal world, renewed daily. The language itself, involving a
number of "r"s in postvocalic position and other special combinations of sounds such as "s-rb" groups, not translatable or
reproducible in English, gives effects of implied sensuality.

In the next poem, "Destino trágico" ("Tragic Destiny"),
the dawn creatures become or are becoming human creatures
for whom fate and time exist. The claws of powerful eagles
detain the sun and oppress the night, but the white teeth of
tigers now shine in peace. Under the ocean in an unreal forest,
nightingales sing in the dark night without a moon, although
the latter suggests the idea of light or at least luminosity.

nightingale of the seas, tenuous moonless night,
shine beneath the waves where wounded breasts
sing warmly on perfumed coral branches.
                                         (p. 471)

(ruiseñor de los mares, noche tenue sin luna,
fulgor bajo las ondas donde pechos heridos
cantan tibios en ramos de coral con perfume.)

Thirsty with the confusion of the absolute, the elected human,
losing his individualism, throws himself into that sea, as the
nightingales joyfully sing and nature triumphs. This poem has
an overwhelming number of the "almost affirmative negations"
of which Bousoño speaks.[21] The sea is neither wind, nor its
image, nor the brilliance of a passing kiss, nor the moan of
brilliant wings. The poet tells us for six lines that the sea is not
an eagle, for five that it is not a stone, takes ten to inform us
that it is a forest, and then tells us for seven that it is a tiger.
The negations become almost affirmative alternates.

In "Sierpe de amor" ("Serpent of Love"), the poet, a serpent in Eden, longs to possess the naked, indifferent, beautiful

goddess, but the menace of light from her brow impedes his
sliding like a tongue between her living breasts. Yet he penetrates her, bathing in her blood, a celestial, destroying fire
which will consume him. In spite of the presentiment of death,
he kisses her and dies. As we can see, love can still destroy,
but in most of the poems it is a light, joyful, frothy evocation.

In remaining poems of the first section, the poet evokes
love in sadness, for its beauty is fleeting and perishable. The
more deeply he feels, the more keenly aware he becomes of the
fleeting quality. In "El río" ("The River"), he longs for that
of his childhood, which crossed his innocent city, a beautiful
river where one might disrobe and be close to a nature whose
songs man has forgotten. The note of melancholy increases in
"Nacimiento del amor" ("Birth of Love"). The poet, in the
golden autumn of his love, sees his loved one emanate light
even in its absence. This light of love envelopes him, and he
recognizes his mortality, "penultimate birth perhaps toward
death" (p. 478), but it also recalls the beauty of dawn and
birds. He hopes to enjoy love, almost drunk with the light of
day, for with twilight comes the night, "naked angel of
dead light, by master" of "Arcángel de las tinieblas"
("Archangel of Twilight"), and finally (p. 483) death, "Another dead beautiful sea,/ below has just smothered . . ." in
"Poderío de la noche" ("Power of the Night"). One enjoys love
until it dies, without imposed limits. Joyfully he welcomes his
golden love, the center of his cosmos, the absorbing light of
day, even knowing that nothing can last, as dawn becomes day,
twilight, and finally night and death, aesthetically and emotion-
ally the only possible final perfection.

In the second part, we meet the seductive "Diosa" ("Goddess"), unknowable for humans. A tiger guards her and her
intangible breast from man, for she is Paradise, warm with
light, which would swallow man by the infinity of her love if
he could know her. The following poem, "La verdad"
("Truth"), depicts not birds but only their memory, ashes and
not love. Love consummated is like the ash of a flame and
death. All which surrounds man is a copy, a false echo only.
His body takes on the aspects of a flowing stream, and he
awaits a death which is but the ember of the day.

In "No estrella" ("Not a Star") the poet invokes the star to
descend to be a woman on the grass, so that the poet and the

waiting earth may have her, for they both need her light to satisfy their love. "El desnudo" ("The Naked One") views primitive man as an elemental part of nature. Naked women occur as frequent themes in Aleixandre's poetry, for nakedness gives a kind of magic quality to the countryside. The poet possesses nature through this naked girl, a veritable daisy basket of delights. He invites her to rest on the turf at the edge of the river, and regards her neck which sustains the concentration of light over which virginal birds play. He wants to sink his lips where his loved one's feet have trod, to merge with her completely. She rises from the water, a song bird at her breast, and as the bird raises its ecstatic song to light and love, the poet, under the enchantment of her body, would also sing the glories of the world. Her body, dripping still with the light of day, fuses with the night and death to whose power the poet must surrender her.

Man becomes more of a factor in "Las manos" ("The Hands"), as the hands of dead lovers fly through space to search for the loved one. The hands, a visionary force of love, filled with transparency, move in the night. One hand, coursing with light, moves through the high vault of heaven, groping blindly in the noiseless sky for the other newly born hand with which it unites; then the hands of dead lovers fuse with immediate light which they shed on all mankind. "Los besos" ("The Kisses") symbolize the sweet passion that may triumph over death, which the poet, for the moment, forgets; but with the setting sun the kisses of life become also those of death.

The third section begins with "Primavera en la tierra" ("Spring on the Earth"). The poet recalls his love for a happy Spring when all creation resounded with yellow light, multicolored birds, flowers, rocks, and living waters. The naked youth runs through Spring, finding the primitive voice of love and fountain of truth, slipping through the sea like a dolphin, but he must return to the present of snow and heavy lead. He sees the obverse of nature in the horrors of civilization and the eternal conflict of those who suffer and die.

> and I descry the irons of the towers elevated by men
> like specters of all ephemeral desires.

> And I look at the vague clothes which men offer,
> masks which do not weep over tired cities,

while I hear in the distance the music of dreams
in which the flutes of Spring escape extinguishing themselves.

(p. 503)

(y diviso los hierros de las torres que elevaron los hombres
como espectros de todos los deseos efímeros.

Y miro las vagas telas que los hombres ofrecen,
máscaras que no lloran sobre las ciudades cansadas,
mientras siento lejana la música de los sueños
en que escapan las flautas de la Primavera apagándose.)

"Casi me amabas" ("You Almost Loved Me") quotes a line
from the famous Spanish Romantic poet, Espronceda, "Celestial
soul born for love," which gives us the theme. The poet sees
the play of light on the golden hair of his loved one. He is an
earth creature, "I arrived from there, from beyond, from that
dark consciousness/ of land . . . " (p. 504), and she is of the
sea. Moonlike, her coldness chills the light of day, and her
hair deafens the poet. She evokes the loved one of his youth who
gave him her warm body on the ocean waves, but she floats
freely in the heavens and reveals the world to him. "Los
poetas" ("The Poets") envisions vast painful wings of exiled
angels sleeping on the earth. Aleixandre recalls the naked shoulders of his love, and ". . . girls, happy rivers, their hands
foam, tie around his neck the flowers of a sighing light" (p. 507).

Among the poems of this section, three specifically devote
themselves to Paradise: "Luna del paraíso" ("Moon of Paradise"), "Mar del paraíso" ("Sea of Paradise"), and "Muerte en
el paraíso" ("Death in Paradise"). The first evokes his formerly loved moon as a beautiful nude girl, full of light on the
soft turf. Aleixandre relives the days of his youth, recalling
the nightingale's song of love. He recalls other nights of love,
light and happiness, when his lips drank the pure light at her
throat and fused with her hair, "and I felt that my blood, converted to thy light,/ ran through my veins sparkling in the
night" (p. 511). In the second poem he faces the sea with
the dust of earth on his shoulders, and in the final poem he
remembers the almost human voice of the jungle, evoking the
lips which are losing their words of happiness much as the
light gradually disappears in the twilight sky. The poet is
dazzled by the setting sun of blood, light, love, solitude and
fire, but night falls and he finds only a dream of life in his
beloved, as he kisses "her dead blue . . . love."

"Como serpiente" ("As a Serpent") offers a good illustration of what Bousoño calls "continued visions" which bear only an exterior resemblance to symbols. "The plane of reality in which they are based is not spiritual nor intangible, but an object with a material existence: a river, a woman, a tiger, a tree. . . . Its limits thus will not be diffuse but absolutely clear with massive, evident design."[22] Aleixandre, beneath the figure of a serpent, sees the figure of a woman, and the former's qualities supplant the concrete reality of the woman. The imaginary serpent, with its black magic head, which in turn becomes sharp steel, and the fatal cold light of its deep pupils, brings a frozen lightless abyss of night.

"Plenitud del amor" ("Fullness of Love") calls up a cloudless autumn afternoon. A charming blonde appears, to shatter the melancholy of a lost illusion. The countryside, a tree, the breeze, a sea, become a living reality between his arms. Realizing that it is not a vague illusion, the poet loves the human body, whose thighs of earth become boats rowed over a sea of tarnished love. But love is brief, and one must enjoy it to the full. Her body becomes the nocturnally beautiful sparkling arch of heaven, as night wets the poet with its foamy stars. He reflects on the beautiful day, the chirping morning birds, and future stars, and "I view myself in your body, in soft form, sweetly extinguished,/ as one contemplates the afternoon which ends fulfilled" (p. 521). Here the brevity of love ends not in death but in further contemplation of nature. The ending is but a prelude to a possible future. To have possesed the loved one for a moment is to have possessed a light which makes the poet forget the misery of being a mortal man, condemned to a fleeting existence. Now, at least, man is admitted to this Paradise, enjoying eternity as a moment in the eternal sea of time.

Finally, in "Los dormidos" ("The Sleepers"), night must not be a time of sadness. After the song of birds and lights, after the orchestra of the day, silence loses its opacity and acquires vibrations to fill the mute spaces. The light of stars changes to celestial wine, drunk by the poet, the night becomes his very body to illuminate the dreams of sleeping men. The planet now is "a bacchante, in the spaces, who shows a beautiful breast" (p. 522). This naked bacchante becomes a clothed victory. In a Dionysian fruition, the naked earth, recalling Greek

statues, cries out to the dead and sleeping. Aleixandre's thought
continues in "Mensaje" ("Message"), an affirmation of pagan
joy in which he tells his friends to live and exist joyfully without question, accepting the beauties of the clouds, the sea, the
sun, the beach and the light, while the universe consumes
itself.

Section Four, titled "Los inmortales" ("The Immortals"),
contains seven short poems on rain, sun, land, fire, air and
the sea. The first, "La lluvia" ("The Rain"), is typical of those
in this section.

> The waist is not a rose.
> It is not a bird. They are not feathers.
> The waist is the rain,
> fragility, moan
> which surrenders itself to you . . .
>
> (p. 533)

> (*La cintura no es rosa.*
> *No es ave. No son plumas.*
> *La cintura es la lluvia,*
> *fragilidad, gemido*
> *que a ti se entrega . . .*)

Again he uses negatives with partial affirmative qualities.
The rain, almost a rose or a feathered bird, is certainly a waist
which the mortal should embrace with his arms.

Section Five starts with "A una muchacha desnuda" ("To a
Naked Girl"), a continuing theme in the poet's work. The
delicate dark-eyed girl at the river's edge, her naked body
resting on a virgin turf, is morning love. The poet sees her
as a musical instrument against the green background of Spring,
but much water separates them, and so he must continue incomplete in his eternal but unattainable desire. "Desterrado
de tu cuerpo" ("Exiled from Your Body") shows us a poet
who feels lost without his love or the earth or a Republican
Spain which he is partially responsible for having lost.

> My name is mutilation. I have no name; only
> memory am I, torn from thee myself. Oh my country,
> oh body from which I live exiled,
> oh my land,
> reclaim me.
>
> (p. 544)

> (*Mutilación me llamo. No tengo nombre; sólo*
> *memoria soy quebrada de ti misma. Oh mi patria,*

> oh cuerpo de donde vivo desterrado,
> oh tierra mía,
> reclámame.)

"Noche cerrada" ("Closed Night") pictures night as op-
pressing mankind, above whom freed lights burn. The shadow,
an invincible black wave, suggests the idea of height and thus
becomes a columned night in whose heavens the stars shine.
In "Cuerpo de amor" ("Body of Love") Aleixandre's beloved is
a current, a cloud, the sky, a mirror. He kisses her lonely
breast, the dying day on his cheek, and the breast of love in his
mouth, a rotund morbidity of the afternoon. As the afternoon
dies, her abdomen becomes a pale light shining in the night,
into which with his words he wishes to convert her so that he
alone may possess her in a frenzy of love, as she and the light
become one. The kiss which unites them also joins them to
the universe and to a love for all creation.

The final section starts with a poem containing a rare religiosity, "Padre mío" ("My Father"). In a kind of biblical echo
of Genesis, he views the created world and finds it good. His
father assumes the role of God, much as Málaga becomes
Paradise, as the poet becomes increasingly aware of the lim-
itations of human love. God again acquires an anthropomorphic
shape in "Destino de la carne" ("Destiny of the Flesh"). Man,
a disturbing influence, has been expelled from Paradise because
he established the barrier between himself and nature; thus he
will remain a body without light, dying for his crime of breaking with the cosmos. The poet longs for the country of his
pure immortal beings, but eternally alive in the world, he
must agonizingly repeat himself, a reiteration the poet emphasizes with a series of repeated negatives, adverbial repetitions,
an unusual accumulation of adjectives, and a series of repeated
nouns. The poet starts in a slow tempo but accelerates the
movement through the image of the ocean which sends wave
after wave to the other shore.

> Always flesh of man, without light! Always rolling
> from there, from an ocean without origin which sends
> waves, waves, foams, tired bodies, edges
> of a sea which never ends and which always pants on its shores.
>
> (p. 563)

> (¡Siempre carne del hombre, sin luz! Siempre rodados
> desde allá de un océano sin origen que envía

ondas, ondas, espumas, cuerpos cansados, bordes
de un mar que no se acaba y que siempre jadea en sus orillas.)

In "Ciudad del paraíso" ("City of Paradise") Aleixandre
creates a suspension of time, of a sudden sun, a fleeting but
eternal moon, a scarcely felt divine breath which he eternally
evokes through his memory. "Men lived through a dream, they
lived no,/ eternally shining like a divine breath" (p. 565). That
which is valuable in man is close to nature, and youth being
nearer implies an immortality for which he longs together with
his beloved perfumed city of Málaga.

José Luis Cano called "Ultimo amor" ("Ultimate Love")
"perhaps the most beautiful, the most moving declaration of
love that has ever been written in Castilian verse."[23] The poet
seeks to discover love's essence, finding in her eyes "a nocturnal
sword," a familiar image he uses in the following poem of
the section, "Al cielo" ("To Heaven"), where "a long sword,
extended like blood, runs through my veins." Here Aleixandre
dislocates words, for he means "blood, extended like a long
sword, runs through my veins." He knows the perils of love,
that he may destroy himself in her glorious flame, and that to
possess her is to die.

> Is thy glance only death? Is it an angel?
> Or is it a long sword which cleaves me
> against the heavens, while I shine bloods
> and end in light, in quivering star.
>
> (p. 569)

> *(¿Es sólo muerte tu mirada? ¿Es ángel?*
> *O es una espada larga que me clava*
> *contra los cielos, mientras fuljo sangres*
> *y acabo en luz, en titilante estrella?)*

Love is both torment and happiness, bitter and sweet, and
the poet does not know whether he is experiencing love,
crime or death, as his lips, tarnished by the world's experience,
touch hers, warmed by young suns and dawn's recent light. Her
black hair presages in its mourning the poet's approaching
solitude. But, even knowing the fatality which will be his,
he exclaims:

> But it matters not! Let the world turn and give me,
> give me your love, and may I die in a futile
> science, while kissing you we roll
> through space and a star rises.   (p. 570)

(¡Pero no importa! Gire el mundo y dame,
dame tu amor y muera yo en la ciencia
fútil, mientras besándote rodamos
por el espacio y una estrella se alza.)

The final poem of the volume, "No basta" ("It Is Not Enough"), in its amorous pessimism, both sums up the metaphysical content of his trip to Paradise and previews his approach to humanity. The poet finds that the freedom he sought in Paradise, the sun, the rain, the sea, the dark mystery of a glance, although important still, are not related to his human existence. Returning from Paradise, even though nothing suffices, not even the world, he seeks a final embrace in his mother earth.

Oh mother, mother, only in thy arms do I feel
my misery! Only in thy breast martyred through my tears
do I surrender my bulk, only in thee do I dissolve.

(p. 578)

(¡Oh, madre, madre, sólo en tus brazos siento
mi miseria! Sólo en tu seno martirizado por mi llanto
rindo mi bulto, sólo en ti me deshago.)

He longs for his mother's beautiful breast and the support she once gave him and still gives him. Again we see the dream screen in operation. The sea appears as waves intangible to his hands. A weighty cloud stops above the water and then withdraws to a vanishing point on the horizon. The poet associates the withdrawal with a lost happiness which he specifically connects with his mother and his mother's empty breast,

mother mine of warm dusk,
single breast where emptiness reigns,
my love, my love, become thou, become thou alone.

(pp. 578-79)

(madre mía de tinieblas calientes,
seno sólo donde el vacío reina,
mi amor, mi amor, hecho ya tú, hecho tú sólo.)

The mother, while a symbolic earth, may also be the human reality. The poet wants to return to his mother's lap, or womb, to experience her warmth, the promise of God, and to be "rocked on the sea." The horizon and the clouds floating away in a perspective leading to a vanishing point may well be a

renunciation of the breast or the withdrawn breast. The poet
relates his ensuing emptiness to a lack of God, "An emptiness
of God I felt upon my flesh." As Lewin points out:

The optical impressions produced by the nursing situation attain some
permanence in the form of the dream screen, and later in development
become associated with and attached to the representatives of concrete ideas. We are then naturally curious to know whether the
nebulous and the intense but ill-defined perceptions enter into such
union too. . . . The invisible and formless elements become related
to invisible and formless things, which are then perceived in the
same direct immanent fashion. The invisible in the breast situation
may be brought into juncture with God, the invisible, so that He
may be perceived in this same way, directly.[24]

Aleixandre suffers a loss of identity or Ego in the absence of
God and the breast, "what an absence of God on my demolished
head/ watched my convulsed body without limits?" He tells
his mother that only in her bosom can he surrender his bulk.
The poet's use in Spanish of *deshacer,* to vanish or be consumed,
in connection with his mother's breast, may be a revived feeling or memory of the pleasurable as well as the unhappy which
would seem to relate to the primitive wish to sleep and to
join the mother—to be one with her at the breast and in sleep.
But whether she is the earth or mother or both, she is the
only consolation and support available to the unfulfilled poet.

II   *Nacimiento último*

Originally announced as *Desamor* (*Lack of Love*) in 1941,
this collection appeared in 1953 under its new title, somewhat
changed and with a number of new poems, in a small luxury
edition illustrated by Aleixandre's friend, Gregorio Prieto. The
poet abandons his previously established position on the flow
of causality and philosophically brings to completion his negative affirmations. Each object has its negative counterpart,
except life and death, which are not opposites, but the same.
Final Birth marks a moment of transition between *Shadow of
Paradise* and *History of the Heart*. In simple, sober, almost sad
poetry, Aleixandre broadens and humanizes his perspectives on
life and death, a process which will reach its fruition in *History
of the Heart,* which, without abandoning the quest for light
and love, will search for it in human existence and the brotherhood of man.

The title itself means a birth into death, for death and birth, confused in the mind of the poet who views death as a final birth, recall the religious "ashes to ashes and dust to dust." When man dies he finds his destiny. Cano claims that "The pantheism of the loving concept of Aleixandre's poetry is shown here in its deepest and most pathetic sense."[25] Although the volume marks a natural close to Aleixandre's cosmic cycle, for the only complete love lies in the final act of death, the poet is not resigned to the complete disappearance of the loved body which viewed the light and walked the fields. For him the dead do not die completely, as they live on in the earth or in the form of a tree which may grow from the departed's breast.

The volume, in reality, is three collections of poetry in one. The first section extols the emotion of death. A second section involves portraits of and dedications to other poets and friends, and other isolated poems, and a final section once more views Paradise. Aleixandre himself felt that the first part "closes the representation of the cosmos initiated with *Passion of the Earth*."[26] Gullón compares the poetry to that of Baudelaire and Rilke, for like theirs it exudes a "sensation of secret melancholy."[27] Far from being a minor work, says José Luis Cano, *Final Birth* must occupy an important position among the author's books, as it ". . . seduces us, rich and unique, through the supreme unity of the poet, and the variety of his power."[28]

The poet in "El moribundo" ("The Dying One") examines the words of life like "hope" and "love" to disappear with the warmth of his body. Silence prompts him to exclaim: "Love. Yes, I loved. I have loved. I loved, I loved a great deal, but nobody hears." Max Aub views this poem as an attempt to "free himself from the weight of unreason, but without treading still on firm ground,"[29] as the poet desperately sings songs of unsatisfied love. In "El enterrado" ("The Buried One") earth and man, confusedly, find the same destiny.

> Man who, dead or alive, may find life
> breathing the earth. Alone, pure,
> your limits broken, you burst,
> you resuscitate. Now land, beautiful land!
> Man: perennial land, glory, life.   (p. 593)

> *(Hombre que, muerto o vivo, vida hallares*
> *respirando la tierra. Solo, puro,*

quebrantados tus límites, estallas,
resucitas. ¡Ya tierra, tierra hermosa!
Hombre: tierra perenne, gloria, vida.)

Alfonso Alvarez Villar calls "El enterrado" "a manifest apology for death . . . one of the most beautiful, perhaps, that has been written and which will be written while there are men on the earth."[30] Other poems in the section continue to think of a former youth as a loving foam, of life like a spring afternoon, of buried lovers, of the far-off sea of love, of plains without poplars, natively round and warmly naked, of love as an instantaneous dagger which drained his blood, of the end of love, of peace and continuation beneath the earth, and similar themes. The very titles convey the tone: "Los amantes enterrados" ("The Buried Lovers"), "Eternamente" ("Eternally"), "Acaba" ("Finish"), "Acabó el amor" ("Love Ended"), "Sin amor" ("Without Love"), "El muerto" ("The Dead One"), and the final poem, "Epitafio" ("Epitaph"), which in a grave, almost pathetic tone views the earth as a liberation and not a tomb. Aleixandre continues the same techniques in these poems previously found, for example, hyperbaton in "Amor del cielo" ("Love of Heaven"), "For that which I guess song between some lips."

The first poem of the second section, "A Fray Luis de León" ("To Fray Luis de León"), written around 1927, was the poem which first convinced Gerardo Diego that Aleixandre was a great poet.[31] Others in the series are dedicated to Luis de Góngora, to Emilio Prados, to Julio Herrera y Reissig, a famous Modernist poet of Uruguay, to Gabriela Mistral, the Nobel Prize winner from Chile, and to Pedro Salinas. In his poem "La cogida" ("The Horn Thrust"), Aleixandre views it as a secret, blind, mortal kiss. "Elegía" ("Elegy") is a true funeral hymn to the manless world, an earth which flees from lost men and sails through the universe sustaining eternally its light without human beings. "Al sueño" ("To the Dream") is a song of life and its triumph over death.

The final section recalls *Shadow of Paradise.* "Junio del paraíso" ("June of Paradise") pictures the same innocent vision of "Criaturas en la aurora." "Bajo la luz primera" ("Beneath the First Light") repeats a variety of the themes from *Shadow of Paradise* (of one born in the dawn, caressing softly the tiger skin, of free eagles), as does the musical "Los besos" ("The

Kisses"), which the poet views as winged celestial birds who touch the sweet half-opened mouth of a girl with their golden light. "Cántico amante para después de mi muerte" ("Loving Canticle for After My Death") recalls his goddess of the naked body. The final selection, "El poeta niño" ("The Boy Poet"), is in prose. The boy is born and grows up in a city. Gradually he extends his vision and knowledge of life to the outskirts, to the noise of rivers, indeed, to the first creation of the world, as he spends his passing moment among sad men. Knowing that he cannot escape the world, the mature poet hopes the youthful one he was will eternally be reborn, with the age of centuries. In this way he may possess the cosmos in its primitive stage, infusing its shapeless mass with order through the love which illuminates his soul.

CHAPTER 7

The Human Equation

I *Historia del corazón*

WRITTEN between 1945 and 1953, *Historia del corazón*
(*History of the Heart*), dedicated to Dámaso Alonso,
"friend at all times, certain in all vicissitudes, from remote
adolescence . . . a third of a century of fraternal accord"
(p. 667), looks at human life in a somewhat new key. Aleixandre
says he started the work as another on love but broadened
it to include temporal considerations.[1] Man lives in a temporal
universe from childhood through adolescence to old age, but
"this suffering man, so far from Paradise, is not the 'dry'
figure against the wall; he lives, enjoys, suffers, he dies—
above all he dies . . . and waits and despairs . . . metaphysical
poetry this of Aleixandre. . . . No: poetry . . . is not metaphysical
mystification: it is only poetry. Therefore, through it, we come
to recognize and communicate along the deepest paths which go
from man to man, . . . which his revelation illuminates."[2]

Unlike previous poetry where nature was all-important,
it now serves only as the background against which human
history passes. Nevertheless, many find that the work of Aleixandre "represents a perfectly sustained continuity, since from
different angles . . . his glance . . . is identical. . . . The poet
was never a solitary being on purpose nor a narcissistic weaver
of dreams. And perhaps for many the appearance of the last
book (*History of the Heart*) has been revealing . . . one may
have a clearer comprehension of this social aspect in all his
work."[3] José María Souvirón agrees that, "the rediscovery of
that which is human, which had never disappeared from his
work . . . but which at times seemed to escape toward dangerous
impalpable and ethereal zones, toward regions anterior to
original sin . . . here the heart pumps blood through . . . life . . .
with a moving passion."[4] In a sense, then, the new volume is a
variation of an old theme, as it tells, not of cosmic fusion, but
of the unification of all mankind.

118

Many underlying crosscurrents of thoughts and emotions can be found in *History of the Heart,* but the central theme concerns human solidarity and compassion for the victims of injustice, the masterful epitome of the book as a whole. Although he reserves his deepest and subtlest meanings for the description of historical and existential man, the poet also portrays his own life and personal past. No longer the creature of telluric forces, man represents the difficult and dolorous of daily experience, "the life of man seen as an effort and disclosed via the meditated life of his finality and of his recognition in others. It is now the reverse of human solitude. No, man is not alone."[5] The poet, a man, becomes all men, destined like him to live and die, without the assurance of Paradise or eternal life, in a world where death is always with us. Nevertheless, it is not necessary to live desperate solitary lives, the poet exclaims with tenderness and optimism, as he sings for all mankind of fleeting time, social love, and human solidarity. Infants and oldsters mark the boundaries between being and not being, life and death. The poet recognizes that he is aging, but without despair, empathizes with his neighbor who must also stoically face the end.

Man's reality, then, both good and bad, involves daily living. Aleixandre, sensitive to the tactile aspects and wonders of the human body, may give us the characteristics of a human hand along with descriptions of daily events and quotidian tasks. He manages to project universal implications from the common object which has momentarily attracted him, in the full realization that the part belongs to the whole. As a poet he is keenly aware of spiritual distances between lovers, but he views the body and soul as one. Life is difficult, but its absence is worse, so it becomes the reason for life itself in the city, the streets, or the parks. The poet examines the anatomy and psychology of his loved ones, and now without cosmic illusions, finds comfort in the sensual (*History of the Heart* has twenty-six love poems) in an everyday world where love is not eternal and where life is brief, meaningless, and cruel.

The title is what it says, a history of mankind in general and of the poet specifically, their cycle of existence and circumstances, their rebellion or resignation, and the joys and sorrows of the heart. Most critics concur in this evaluation, summed up succinctly by Concha Zardoya's "The theme of

History of the Heart—as its title indicates—is the life of the poet and, through his, the life of man."[6]

We can see that man has a changeable nature, that existentially he helps create his own life. As time passes, he evolves new states of consciousness, an awareness which leads to a social conscience and attempts to identify with the community of man. But this new awareness that he is a part of the heart of humanity brings with it the knowledge of fleeting time and transitory life. Aleixandre, both a poet and a man, accepts his new existence with optimism, knowing that he must live the only life he has with joy. He reacts calmly to his temporal transiency, realistically interested in the ethical and social consideration of the survival of mankind. "But, at heart, there will continue beating in man, if not a belief, at least a necessity of permanence . . . a kind of faith or transcendental demand. Otherwise, there would be no poetry, for this is really nothing but a final and desperate effort of man to put some order and clarity into this dark chaos . . . of his existence."[7] In a sense Aleixandre's man triumphs over the existential boundary situations discussed by Karl Jaspers and symbolically, even over the final one of death.

History of the Heart is divided into five sections, "Como el vilano," "La mirada extendida," "La realidad," "La mirada infantil," and "Los términos." Concho Zardoya views the book as an organic whole within which each poem maintains its own unity while acting in coordinated and perfect symmetry. Although the symmetrical structure is an equilibrium with a substructure, Concha Zardoya sees *History of the Heart* in its use of long and short lines, as "spontaneous but rhythmical ametrics."[8] Others have seen the intricately cadenced free verse as "moved by shapes and textures, physical sensations, warmth, color and brightness . . . essentially buoyant. Their weakness lies in the ease with which they can descend into rhetoric and the recording of sensations disguises itself as emotion."[9]

The imagery is plainer and more pedestrian, as the author attempts to suit both his language and style, in a continuous simplification, to the need for communication with ordinary people. He uses simple sentences or a truncated style of short outbursts. One can more easily see the narrative framework which supports the lyrical emotion of the heart's history from birth to death because of the simplified and clearer ideas, and because each new poem seeks to indicate its link with the previous one.

Many opinions have been expressed about *History of the Heart*. Ricardo Gullón considers it a book of elemental movements like his others with "vision replaced by remembrance; imagination gave way to memory, although the remembering is imaginative and tends to live from his own fire."[10] Bousoño finds it "a consoling and hope-giving book."[11] One critic feels that the poet abdicates his own pain to sing of the pain of others. The voice issuing from his throat "must come from the depths of all the hearts which he interprets and for whom he sings. It is a voice like a path along which all travel. Collective and raised voice. The responsibility of the poet who must interpret his people could have no more beautiful image: a path along which the rest tread."[12]

Elsewhere, while agreeing that the fundamental principle is human solidarity and man's need for love, "The poet recognizes himself, that is: he discovers himself, he takes possession of himself, on seeing himself in the rest."[13] The poet does not lose his liberty but obtains a kind of communion. Sáinz de Robles rejects the above criticism. He feels the work should have been called "History of My Heart" for it is an enormously egotistical work revolving around the poet's own head and world. "It must be terrible for this great poet to understand that neither his body nor his world accompany him, most of the time, where his spirit and his sensibility culminate in a resolution of poetic fulfillment seldom obtained by any poet . . . work of shades, . . . of suggestions, of morbid pathos."[14] Finally José Luis Cano finds the work redolent with life which has been lived and therefore so full of human solidarity. "But the author has contributed also his enormous talent as a poet, and has given us perhaps his best book, the most transfixed with human emotion and the richest in naked and deep beauty."[15]

The first poem, "Como el vilano" ("Like the Thistledown"), in the first section, is filled with tenderness and a sad truth that reality thwarts the impossible flame of love. The poet realizes that life passes in a series of momentary states. He strives to find a permanent existence in an objective world of men of flesh and blood. He clutches for love but finds it too

ephemeral and only a shadow of reality, an illusion which he
may briefly and sadly accept.

> the lover knows that it passes,
> that love itself passes
> and that this generous fire which in him passes not
> witnesses pure the sweet passage of that which
>   eternally passes.   (p. 672)

> *(el amante sabe que pasa,*
> *que el amor mismo pasa,*
> *y que este fuego generoso que en él no pasa,*
> *presencia puro el tránsito dulcísimo de lo que eterna-*
>   *mente pasa.)*

Temporality conspires against his love and he, no longer able
to fuse with nature, knows that love will be his but for an
instant, because " . . . it passes and remains. And rises up, and
returns./ Always light, always here, always there; always./
Like the thistledown" (p. 673).

"Mano entregada" ("Delivered Hand"), the second poem,
uses the verb "to touch" in the first stanza, a verb to which
the others in other stanzas are subordinated. The poet caresses
the hand of his beloved, lingering over its form and structure,
feeling its soft sweet flesh and the hard bones of its reality
which his love can never penetrate. The lover feels transformed
into his loved one and runs through her veins, as his life slowly
penetrates her beloved body. The skeletal resistance makes
his love less than complete, but he obtains complete possession
of her flesh, "until your deepest total veins where I row,/
where I populate you and sing complete within your flesh"
(p. 675). "La frontera" ("The Frontier") again details parts of
the body as a fragment of the whole. Aleixandre gives his
exterior love to her skin, but she remains inviolate beneath,
"drunk with your remote, unattainable aromas" (p. 677), and
he recognizes the limits of his love.

He then becomes aware, in "Otra no amo" ("Another I Do
Not Love"), that while his loved one rejects him, another whom
he refuses loves him. He knows that love is unjust, but he kisses
the cheek of the pale girl who loves him and then her almost
naked body, forgetting her, even as he makes love, and thinking
of the other. In "Después del amor" ("After Love"), he feels
the musical, silent truth of her body, at rest after their love-
making. Knowing that love may be a menacing combustion, "a

fearful key of the enclosure of fire," he recognizes it as life. "Nombre" ("Name") concerns the secret name of his love which shakes within his soul, but which he will not pronounce, as he faces fleeting time with tranquillity. In "Coronación del amor" ("Coronation of Love"), filled with color, the golden lovers, crowned by the sustaining light, find that love does not destroy. The second part of the first section concerns hate, hopeless, abandoned love, and final despair. In the last poem, "Sombra final" ("Final Shadow"), the poet exclaims:

> Oh dark night. Now I expect nothing.
> Solitude lies not to my senses.
> The pure, calm shadow reigns.
>
> (p. 697)
>
> *(Oh noche oscura. Ya no espero nada.*
> *La soledad no miente a mi sentido.*
> *Reina la pura sombra sosegada.)*

The second part of the book, "Mirada extendida" ("Extended Glance"), involves the poet's attempt to alleviate his solitude through identification with the life of the world. Through the eyes of others he recognizes himself, and he can now identify with the misery and pain of old men who walk in the sun, a working family, or a mother and child, and he experiences a great feeling of tenderness. In "Ten esperanza" ("Have Hope"), he seeks understanding in himself and in the world. As an adult he still feels youthful force and he searches for new light, new life, and new hope. "En la plaza" ("In the Square") sings for all humanity. The poet feels it is not good "to remain on the shore" but one must find oneself ". . . in the movement with which the great heart of man beats . . . " (p. 703). The poet, in his search for light and love, with hope, with resolution, with faith, with fearful daring, is comforted at finding himself among men and knowing that he too is a man. He realizes that one exists only as part of humanity, "There where one can see himself and can be joyful and recognize himself" (p. 704).

This recognition of himself in others, as he joins his small heart to that of humanity, will insure the poet's salvation through his new identification. "A la salida del pueblo" ("At the Exit of the Town") sings of old men from whom one could learn of sadness, patience and truth, who take the sun, patiently wait for death and dream of a life of which they are almost no longer a part. In "El poeta canta por todos" ("The Poet Sings for All"), he conceives of the poetic mission as allowing humanity to express itself through him, while at the same time he recognizes himself in others, "And it is thy voice which expresses them. Thy voice, collective and raised" (p. 708). The solitary poet joins the wave of mankind, feels their common flow of blood, and finds new hope and love, and joyfully a part of the collective voice, he sings " . . . with majesty the entire echo of man" (p. 708). In "Vagabundo continuo" ("Continuous Vagabond") the poet recalls the remote origins of man's journey through life, his arrival at the settlement of humanity, white and black, men and women, old and young. Humanity, ". . . a vast only creature, forgotten, naked," a "continuous vagabond," still hopes. Pain and death take their toll, "But it continues . . ." (p. 710).

In the other poems of this section the poet continues to travel, seeking the motive of existence. He meets a child who dies in "El niño murió" ("The Child Died") and shares the suffering of the mother and mankind. Continuing, as "El visitante" ("The Visitor"), he comes to a poor house at whose door a workman labors while inside a woman sews and children play; discovers that he carries his mother with him, and is comforted on his travels by the realization that he is a man, her son, and a poet. The journey is long, but fate moves him on. He meets an old man, in "El viejo y el sol" ("The Old Man and the Sun"), bathed by the sun which fuses him with its essence so that he becomes the very light of the sun itself. Perhaps the poet's song will also purify old age, as he eternalizes it therein. He now knows, in "La oscuridad" ("The Darkness"), that all things wish to fuse with the material of which they are a part, and so man wants to unite with his brothers, "Because they are all one, one alone: he; like him is everyone./ A single living, suffering creature, with which each one, without knowing it, is totally solidified" (p. 718). The poet can find no real solution to life, but his search through the darkness ends in his acceptance. Finally, in the last poem of the section, "El niño y el hombre" ("The Child and the Man"), he realizes the temporal equality of life, that past and the future are really one, that all men were once children, and that if one searches the eyes of the child one can see the tragic adult. Thus a child who dies has within his soul the man who has died and never been born.

The third section, "La realidad" ("Reality"), restates that love is humanity's only reality, that one may seek perfection in human love, and that the body of the loved one is a soul which has taken bodily form in tangible material. Trying to imagine what life would be like without love or another reality, the poet half glimpses that his totality and existence may well be incomplete. Examining further, he sees love as a pure and innocent child, recalls a holiday once spent with his loved one, and describes the details of her body. Love is human and pure, but it changes as the human heart changes. The poet's awakening conscience views love as a dream in "El sueño" ("The Dream"). Surrounded by shades and shadows, and perhaps by the dream of one who sleeps among them, he concludes that lack of love may also be a dream. Viewing the outside world in all its sadness, he sits in a silence broken only by the respiration of the beautiful sleeping woman in whose dream the poet discovers the confirmation of his thought. In other poems of the section Aleixandre contemplates the flowers and light in a garden, content to fix the reality of his love in the present, and finally, in the last poem, "La certeza" ("Certainty"), he decides that love is a proved although limited reality.

Section Four, "La mirada infantil" ("The Infantile Glance"), returns to the poet's childhood. On a bicycle he passes by horse-drawn carriages, and innocently looks at baby-sitting mothers and working fathers. On the threshold of school in the first poem, in the second, like a little bird, he attends the class of a teacher who neither speaks nor listens. Reliving his childhood in following poems, the poet next recalls a little girl, sees her floating on the ocean, remembers a strange little boy who in his fantasy represented a variety of evil images and died, views the indecency of life with the innocence of childhood, longs to play with other children and, unable to do so because he is the smallest of them all, dreams that he will be a poet, and thinks of an older girl of sweet large eyes with whom he sometimes played who disappeared. The poet-child continues to ride his remembered bicycle, finds a lake, enters a boat, and finally, in the last poem of the section, "Una niña cruzaba" ("A Girl Was Crossing"), evokes his first encounter with childish love, a girl he views with dazed delight but whose name he never asked.

The nine poems of the fifth section, "Los términos" ("The Limits"), concentrate on the problem of human temporality, the existential aspects of life on earth. Life is a constant search for enrichment and knowledge with the certain conclusion that death, which may be a final illumination or salvation, awaits us all. Death may be, not a negation of life, but its final achievement, and only in the knowledge that death exists can man achieve an authentic existence in this life. In "La explosión" ("The Explosion") love appears as a torrent of light, growing until it is ready to burst its bounds. Through love the poet may achieve authenticity. He contemplates the life he has lived and now lives, and love limited by the experience of one unique afternoon of infinite duration. As the afternoon dies, it is as though life itself is ending.

> and in one afternoon they are and all the light gives itself
>   and bursts and becomes,
> and has been one single afternoon of love, infinite,
> and then in the darkness they are lost, and never more will
>   they see one another, because they would never recognize
>   each other . . .
>
> > > > > (p. 764)

> *(y en una tarde son y toda la luz se da y estalla, y se hace,*
> *y ha sido una tarde sola del amor, infinita,*
> *y luego en la oscuridad se pierden, y nunca ya se verán,*
> *porque nunca se reconocerían . . .)*

Life is brief, time is deceiving, and so one must make every moment count. Thus in the "whole afternoon of life I have loved thee," equates the poet's life with the one afternoon of an explosion of light and love. "No queremos morir" ("We Do Not Wish to Die") explains the two existential moments of man—life and death. Lovers do not want to die as they dream of a happy old age with both love and life. They wish to live each day, "the slow daily minute become a drop which unites us," secure in the knowledge of a future beauty and togetherness. In following poems his loved one is surrounded by others who cannot know love, for they are dead, but the poet knows that both love and the knowledge of death are difficult. He worries that in tragic human destiny love may be a shadow, "Comemos sombra" ("We Eat Shadow"), in spite of the glory and effort he has experienced. In the face of the difficulty of living and a demand for eternity, man refuses resignation, unsatisfied with the shadows and the substance of temporal reality in which he finds no solution in his search for immortality. Man is "Like a dog who with the crumb in his mouth is silent and obstinate"

(p. 772), as God distributes the bread of life which is but a shadow. But "when, in the teeth the shadow vanishes, starving we again continue our journey" (p. 772). José Olivio Jiménez considers this poem the most significant of all.[16]

The poet increasingly becomes aware of the presence of death, refuting in "Entre dos oscuridades, un relámpago" ("Between Two Obscurities, a Lightning Flash") Rubén Darío's "And not to know whither we go, nor whence we come." Aleixandre admits that we are but a flash of lightning between two darknesses, and that the light of life is easily extinguished, but since he accepts it in its beauty and brevity, he accepts death also. Under the large sad-faced moon of life and beyond on the long sands, perhaps the poet's travels will once more commence, alone or with his love. But for the moment the poet is resigned, seeing in love, ". . . my only security, my instantaneous repose,/ my express recognition where I feel myself and am myself/ . . . while the instantaneous long moon looks at us and with compassionate light closes our eyes" (p. 774). And so he views himself and his loved one, in "Ante el espejo" ("Before the Mirror"), tired and old, his life lived, her hair no longer shining. Life is like a steep mountain, difficult to climb, he says in "Ascensión del vivir" ("Ascent of Life"), a hard task, as he has already said in "Ten esperanza," "Difícil," and other poems, but one of brief duration. The lovers ascend to the top, resigned to their life. In the snowy silence which surrounds their white, pure heads still illuminated by the eternal sun, they contemplate human existence from the heights, laid out before them like a vast landscape. But if life is an eternal ascent, one must face the inevitable descent to death also, the final dissolution of what we were, the other side of the coin of reality, as we see in "Mirada final" ("Final Glance"), subtitled "Death and Recognition." One critic exclaims that this poem is "worthy to stand with his best . . . is a deeply felt acknowledgment of the poet's ultimate solitude."[17] Aleixandre recognizes his solitude and death, but accepts it in stoic fashion, for to live, one must die, even though life is but an instant.

> Here on the edge of life, after having projected all my life
>   as an instant, I look at myself.
> This land, was it you, love of my life? Shall I ask myself
>   thusly when at the end I know myself, when I recognize
>   myself and awake,

recently lifted from the land, and I feel myself, and seated
in the lowland, at the end, see a sky
compassionately shine?   (p. 782)

*(Aquí, en el borde del vivir, después de haber rodado toda la
vida como un instante, me miro.*
*¿Esta tierra fuiste tú, amor de mi vida? ¿Me preguntaré así
cuando en el fin me conozca, cuando me reconozca y
despierte,*
*recién levantado de la tierra, y me tiente, y sentado en la
hondonada, en el fin, mire un cielo
piadosamente brillar?)*

He cannot see his loved one as only earth and dust. She has
been the soul through whom life has been possible, and his
consolation is that he has lived. Although neither Heaven nor
Hell may exist, one may yet have salvation, as he contemplates,
"at the end . . . a sky compassionately shine" (p. 782).

II   In a Vast Dominion

Aleixandre's poetry of the thirties stressed the idea of cosmic
fusion with the material universe through love, for nature was
as one in its loving. Man was both present and absent from
that world. Next the poet examined humans, their fleeting
existence, and the individual's identification with the many,
especially in *History of the Heart*. Both humanity as a whole
and the individual soul in its relationship to the universe and
in its social responsibilities and desires concerned Aleixandre.
A fellow poet, and one of the best-known poets of the sixties,
José Angel Valente, views *History of the Heart* as "a step or
transition to a superior evolutionary phase, in which the idea
of human solidarity reaches its final limits: man only exists
with all men, and, at the same time, within a gigantic process
of struggle and unification of all the forces of the world. . . .
In a Vast Dominion unifies the total work of Vicente Aleixandre
in a powerful song of reconciliation of man and matter."[18]

History of the Heart ended with a somewhat sad and stoic
acceptance of death. *In a Vast Dominion* also sorrows at that
thought and at man's inhumanity to man, viewing him in his
historical aspects as an entity limited by time, but nevertheless
seeing the common destiny of all material which will be eternal.
In his first period man fused with the cosmos as a limited being
on earth. Now man is a historical and spatial being within a

temporal framework but still material of the cosmos in flux. Aleixandre finally has come full circle but to an expanded universe where man and nature are parts of a larger whole. José Olivio Jiménez views *In a Vast Dominion* as the second part of a two-part existential history. *History of the Heart* sought salvation through man's history and knowledge of his historical and temporal existence. Man, involved in the problem of salvation, inquired into the meaning of it all. *In a Vast Dominion* calmly seeks and finds the answer in "the vastest of dominions," that of man and his spirit, ". . . the poetical metaphysics of temporal existence of man understood as the condensation and expression . . . of a single material in which everything is integrated irrevocably . . ."[19]

The vast dominion of which the poet speaks is the world of human and cosmic matter, in its various forms as objects, animals, or men. Creation itself is a formless, shapeless mass, awaiting fruition in the flux of time. To shape a significant place for itself within eternal existence, it waits for an infusion of order through love. Some of the volume's headings are labeled "Incorporations" because the poet seeks to incorporate the material in its historical and social aspects, an unanguished but existential story of man and his circumstances, constantly becoming and evolving. Since it is a story he has to tell, the poet uses a narrative technique and thus calls the divisions of his book of poetry "Chapters." Optimistically *In a Vast Dominion* affirms things both in their temporality and physical aspects as part of one vast reality or material, both in their superficial attributes and in their profound philosophical and metaphysical meaning. One can compare the warrior of the past to a contemporary poet, see a historical prince in the body of a laborer, a past gentleman lawyer in an engineer of the present. Man is constantly evolving, becoming, so that the past, more than a prologue to the present, is the present. Lope de Vega moves and acts in the seventeenth century, but he also exists before the eyes of the poet. Velázquez comes to life, projected through the idle youths of the town square. Humanity, a single multiple unity which strives to perform its tasks of realization, and the individual man, are simple fragmented parts of an original universal matter.

In *History of the Heart*, in poems such as "Mano entregada," Aleixandre had already examined parts of the human body. He carries the process to extremes in his new poetry, and sees each human, himself a part, as composed of further fragments of matter, each striving to become a functional part of the whole. Eyes, ears, the stomach, lips, the digestive and the reproductive systems are in constant movement. As Bousoño points out, patience, will, and hope enter into the formation, and Aleixandre "converts . . . the evolution itself of the material into a moral question with which he tends to spiritualize the purely cosmic. Spiritualized man and nature are but a pulse beat of this material, a momentary incarnation of the flowing substance."[20]

In a Vast Dominion thus fuses substances and time. Things themselves are made of time which will not destroy, so man must have faith, for both he and time are but aspects of the one totality. According to José Olivio Jiménez, *In a Vast Dominion* is "the (work) which most systematically incorporates as a theme the temporal dimension of existence."[21] As Wordsworth so succinctly expressed it:

> Our birth is but a sleep and a forgetting;
> The soul that rises with us, our life's star
> Hath had elsewhere its setting
> And cometh from afar.

Man appears as an atom in a vast cosmos, but if the universe is curved about itself, man daring the vastness of space and time would then return on himself, perhaps from the route of the infinitesimally small. Finally, if the world is created by the effort of arms and hands, and the earth itself, in a sense, is a product, a town also becomes a living unit, as do its citizens, a part of the landscape as they perform their daily tasks. Since things, life, man, love, history, spirit, and flesh are all material, the poet describes people, society, dwellings, man's art, man's organs, and even the dead. Everything is part of the equation. Unfortunately, man can be unjust, and even nature makes mistakes, as it creates feeble-minded children, but wise men and fools both belong to the struggle for existence.

The minute realistic description, with close-ups of fragments, involves a camera technique. Leopoldo de Luis states, ". . . the technique now employed by Aleixandre, which we would call cinematographic, becomes quite obvious."[22] The book itself is arranged in fragments. After the dedication, "Para quien escribo" ("For Whom I Write"), the author divides his work into six chapters and an epilogue. Chapter I contains seventeen poems, and the following chapters contain twelve, six, six with an Intermission, seven, and five pairs of poems plus an isolated eleventh one, respectively. The Epilogue is a single poem. Chapter I, "Primera incorporación" ("First Incorporation"), views the physical reality of the human body in its truth. Parts of the body are the fragments of the total dignity of man, aspects of his essential life, and more than corporal divisions, they imply ethical values indispensable to the total picture. Aleixandre stresses the need for collective participation in the process of salvation. Human life is still an effort, but with the aid of men, both present and past, we may achieve continuity. After the "First Incorporation," the poet will examine other scenes. The next two chapters, "El pueblo está en la ladera" ("The Town Is On the Slope") and "Ciudad viva, ciudad muerta" ("City Live, City Dead"), contemplate places and human beings, large cities and small, shepherds, a young mother, and a fool, each with his simple history. The author includes two temporal "incorporations" separated by an Intermezzo, followed by anonymous portraits of segments of the single substance of reality. Finally, the poet in his epilogue recapitulates that historical man, history, and time itself belong to this "Materia única" ("Single Material").

The opening quotation from Goethe with which the poet begins his volume, "Only all men live humanity," gives us the key which unlocks the door of the poet's vision of totality. "Para quien escribo" starts to answer the question negatively. He does not write for somber-clothed gentlemen, nor for his angry moustache, nor for the carriage nor the hidden lady. More affirmatively he says that perhaps he writes for those who do not read him, a running lady, an old man asleep on a bench under the setting sun, a passing girl, an old lady in her doorway. Finally, completely affirmative now, he writes for the lover, for one who passes with anguish in his eyes, for the one who shared his sorrow, for the one who ignored it, for everybody. "One by one, and for the crowd. And for their breasts, and for the mouths and for the ears where, without hearing me, my word is."[23]

In the second part of this first poem he writes also for the assassin, man nourished and maddened by death, for agonizing women and children, for the predators, for the victims, for the infinite and finite sea. All are joined. Aleixandre arranges each stanza so that the final word of one leads into the next thought.

The predators, victimizing the innocent girl, lead to the next stanza, the water into which they sink, then the waters to the infinite sea to which they go, and so on. The poet finally concludes that he writes for man, "For thee and all that lives in thee" (p. 16). José Angel Valente sees the poem as a

catalogue of opposites, a vigorous and emotional enumeration of those forces, of whose violent unification, are born perpetually the new forms of life: the old man, the girl, the lover, the murderer. . . . That enumeration of opposites, perhaps, gives us the point of relation, and at the same time, the ultimate difference between . . . *Destruction or Love* and the recent extreme of Aleixandre's evolution. Opposition and unification of opposites in that book . . . protagonist . . . the force of Nature . . . "Para quien escribo" makes us see from the first lines . . . that it is the human protagonist who has now assumed the central role in the process of transformation and unification of matter.[24]

"Primera incorporación" ("First Incorporation") is the title of Chapter I. Bousoño sees these poems as "dedicated to narrating . . . fearful deed of successive matter in the process of becoming human flesh."[25] In "Materia humana" ("Human Matter") the poet addresses himself. On a dark night he had looked out into the city and found it "a single wave in which all exist, through which all is, and in which all are; arrive, pulsate, are created" (p. 20). The poet is a part of this immense corpus of united material, a young girl, an old lady, a warrior, an emperor, a monk, a pale courtesan, in short, everybody, for it is "A single wave in extension which begins in time, and follows and has no age./ Or it has it, yes, like Man" (p. 21). "El vientre" ("The Abdomen") is viewed as a depth of earth in which the body nurtures itself like a tree, "The earth-like condition of man never,/ never more clear" (p. 22).

Man is a creature of the earth, planted, watered, nurtured there to mature slowly. The bowels of man like the roots of the tree send life, which ascending as sap, becomes the breast and spinning air, sound and voice, rising to become light in the eyes and ending finally at one's crown. But this life has differing aspects such as "El brazo" ("The Arm"). It is the adventure of the trunk, and so Aleixandre examines its different physiological characteristics from shoulder to fingernails. It invented fire, wove clothes, forged iron, planted crops, and with its hand met that of another from the ends of the earth with which they "circled the entire roundness of the planet" (p. 28). He examines the composition of the foot and its parts in "Pisada humana" ("Human Tread"). Using his technique of negation he explains that it is not a kiss, nor sigh, nor moan, but yet a flower, foot or foam, representing an irretrievable moment of the passing human body.

The sixth poem of the first chapter, "La sangre" ("Blood"), is a specially unifying fragment. Blood is an irrigating fluid which brings life to the hand which wields the hoe. Thus blood is the substance of human knowledge and science. It flows through all parts of the body, and after bringing wisdom to the heart, arises again, curiously searching, surprised in its daily hope, and becoming an occasional truth, sparkling in the human mouth as "it becomes/ a human word" (p. 33). Part of its flow is to "La pierna" ("The Leg"). Man's thought seems far away, but bent under a work load, sorrow or age, he discovers that its material is the same and that in the final analysis, it and the head extended, "sleep on the same level" (p. 36). In "El sexo" ("Sex") he finds the reproductive organ basically part of the same material. He returns here to an earlier imagery where the light of day in its masculine attributes enters like a caress the voracious feminine chasm to become night, "a perfect night of the two lovers" (p. 40).

In his eighth poem, "Vientre creador" ("Creative Womb"), the poet once more returns to the abdomen, the birthplace of man and, in the act of creation, but a point of corporal light. Yet, within it, there already exist the eye, the mouth, the voice, and man. "La cabeza" ("The Head") examines its features, still material, even the mouth, "Highest sign of human life,/ most certain treasure of his endless task" (p. 45). In "El pelo" ("The Hair") he uses one of his favorite images of fire and smoke, converted into energy to be integrated into cosmic reality. Hair is the final station of man, a symbol of his upward striving, and thus in the burning cosmos both the fire of birth and the ashes of death. "El ojo: pestaña, visión" ("The Eye, the Eyelash, Vision") continues the fire image. For him the eye is "Thread or ray of shade/ within that eyelid thou art trace,/ ash of that fire" (p. 48). Reality cannot exist without limits, and hesitant truth without borders is reflected like a sad stain. Light constantly struggles against shadow, a marriage in which the eye accepts, separates and integrates. "La oreja-la palabra" ("The Ear—The Word") is a noble part of the total material. The ear must accept the sound and fury of life, and through it one encounters the invisible transubstantiation to which the world ascends. The poet can see himself here, and the cartilage, both animal and mineral, erupts through the opening to await and enjoy the world to which it listens, as men translate with their words the answer to Life. And the word, replying for the world, is many things. It moans, listens, spits, apostrophizes, clamors, as the voice of a mother, child or father, and, at times reduced to man, becomes man, "And is a burning coal./ And is a hearth, which shining, burns wills,/ and new man is born" (p. 54). Aleixandre uses his by now somewhat familiar imagery, in an almost pedestrian syntax, as boys reveal "words like dawns,/ like round kisses" (p. 54).

The final poems of the first section continue the catalogue. "Amarga boca" ("Bitter Mouth") defines it as the universe which one is ready to kiss and die, but the living mouth must also die. "El interior del brazo" ("The Interior of the Arm"), through which the nerves and veins run, is material which crushes and obtains, eager to perform its task, the formation of the world. It serves as an instrument of truth and human will, and the world, in a sense, is its product and its truth. "La mano" ("The Hand") builds on land and sea, lifts the world, builds and destroys human works, loves and works tenaciously in the earth. It is the showcase of human effort, a symbol of the brotherhood of man. Through its action material reaches a higher level, yet it is a part of the reality which impels man to determine at each moment what he is going to be in the next. "Mano del poeta viejo" ("Hand of the Old Poet") evokes Lope de Vega as a spreader of light. The final poem, "Estar del cuerpo" ("To Be of the Body"), views the human body as an earthy heaven. When man is born and emerges into the light, already in the doctor's hand he is a total being and a part of the material of the world.

Chapter II, "El pueblo está en la ladera" ("The Town is on the Mountainside"), evokes the recurring image of fire and smoke, integrity and continuity. Creation is fire, which affords the poet a sensation of infinity and permanence. "Pastor hacia el puerto" ("Shepherd Toward the Port") portrays a shepherd of indeterminate age, dressed in a hat more earth than cloth, who, his foot on the gray granite rock, urges his sheep on. But this solitary man is a total being under the heavens. As day is done and night falls, the sheep sleep, and the tired shepherd surrenders to the earth. "Felix" describes a village boy, again conceived in his relationship to the earth but full of human values. This small, blue-eyed boy lived in a village of the hills. When he grew up, the hoe and harvest substituted for a pen in his horny hands. On yearly feast days he wore a clean shirt and an eternally preserved jacket, but his hands, stained with earth, almost earth, sought heaven or the grave. He searched for light, and hoped to find it in the earth, digging furiously to reach the other side as though hearing another digger, also aspiring and hoping, there, "until finding each other, to rest their tools/ and clasp their hands from the ends of the world" (p. 80).

The title poem, "El pueblo está en la ladera," shows the stone houses built by the daily efforts of knotty hands in a town sleeping for centuries. This particular town was once visited by a queen, who, seeing the wild flowers growing among the grey grouping of hovels, exclaimed, "Mira: flores" ("Look, Flowers"), and for evermore the town was no longer Porquerizas but Miraflores. Each object has within it another. In "La madre joven" ("The Young Mother"), she visualizes the child, his legs, his arms, shoulders, and the light of his face (although he does not yet exist except in her mind) as she looks at herself in the fountain. And a real young boy, in his fragment of reality, in "En la era" ("On the Threshing Floor"), sleeps after a long hard day. At work he assumed almost mythical proportions, but asleep he is just a tired boy under the stars.

One of Aleixandre's most effective poems is "Tabla y mano" ("Board and Hand"), a lyrical exaltation of a humble moment. We see the hand leaning on the table board, each with its history. The worker's gnarled hand had killed the little infant's hand it once was much as the board destroyed its previous tree existence. Their history has a hidden origin, but at rest and together they present a joined communion. The hand and knotted fist have a vegetable appearance; the table board, constantly used, is covered with life, one it did not have as a beech tree near the vine fields. Now, as the tired hand, holding a wine glass, reposes on the stained table, we see that time and matter are one. "Yes, it rests on the table. The glass, dry/ now. And the material sleeps. It is night. A/ single confused truth. And solidarity" (p. 94).

Man suffers injustice or deprivation, as we see in "El álamo"

("The Poplar"). The large old tree overflows the tiny town square filled with houses like tired sleeping animals. Occasionally, men will aspire upward to its green heaven, and in its shadow they live, fight, work, return to rest, and die. In this little town on the folds of a mountain over an abyss, "there is naught but the poplar, which is the only heaven of these men" (p. 97). Nature, too, can be unfair as it creates an incomplete or deficient man, material by mistake. So "El tonto" ("The Fool") lives by the poplar, immobile in his chair. The poet views his twisted feet, thin clothes, face, neck, and hair. The abandoned boy's eyes contain "unmoving time" and there "light becomes animal and falls. And he sleeps" (p. 99). The first movement, occurring in December, is matched by the second one in June when the light of the countryside strikes the inert eyes of the feeble-minded Manuel, age thirty-two.

The poet is equally tender and sad in the remaining poems of this section. "En el cementerio" ("In the Cemetery") takes us through the small iron gate to see the unmoving sea of crosses, the tombs, etched by the wind, the wild flowers springing from the fertile earth beneath a perpetual sky. The succession of stones and names reveals that collective memory survives, although changed, for matter endures through time: "Mortal memory! It lasts, but never in themselves" (p. 100). And so material is material, living or dead.

> Closed walls watch, equal. All alive.
> Village of the living, of those who never die.
> Of the hopeful beneath the earth, in it.
> Genesic matter, equal, which covers man, the world.
> And is born and grows and dies. Dies not. Nobody dies.
>   (p. 106)

> *(Cerrados muros velan, iguales. Todos vivos.*
> *Aldea de los vivos, de los que nunca mueren.*
> *De los esperanzados bajo la tierra, en ella.*
> *Materia genesíaca, igual, que cubre al hombre, al mundo.*
> *Y nace y crece y muere. No muere. Nadie muere.)*

And in the faces of the children one can already see the grandfather dying as "El sol duro" ("Harsh Sun") lies on their shoulders, for they are burning coals, which while they breathe are already ash. The woodman, too, in "Figura del leñador" ("Figure of the Woodman"), leaves the town without seeing flowers or gardens, ascending the dusty path toward the blue height. As his foot and leg advance, Aleixandre discovers and describes the various parts of his body, and when he reaches the top of the hill, we discover that woodman and earth are the same. From his feet to his bronzed hair and naked chest, as a part of nature he resembles the very trees which he destroys, but "The woodman is a man, not a tree. He has a face,/ . . . He works. The tree never works" (p. 114). Nevertheless, only when he has cut his allotted number and the dead trunks lie on the ground does he assume his human form, his conscience again alive as he wipes his sweaty skin. Finally, "Cabeza dormida" ("Sleeping Head") recalls some canvases by Velázquez, as Aleixandre describes the tired young and old resting on the village bench beneath the rays of the sun.

Chapter III begins with a poem which recalls "El vals" of *Swords Like Lips*. "Bomba en la ópera" ("Bomb at the Opera") somewhat sarcastically describes an anachronistic social event at the end of the century. The poet, in a mixture of realism and fantasy, evokes the grotesque members of a lying society. But after the bomb, they are but broken dolls in their boxes, flesh on railings, and heads with frightened eyes. With their almost ridiculous deaths, the music sounds on, with nobody to hear: "It continues sounding along . . . Nobody hears it,/ and an immense coffin swims through the darkness" (p. 123). In following poems Aleixandre examines love, sex, the dance, and uninformed, pretentious professors. In the final two poems he finds life a slow burning "midst a creaking of extinguished bones" (p. 132). Although in this "Ciudad viva, ciudad muerta" it is beautiful to live and love, death comes alike for old and young, rich and poor. And when man dies, as in "El entierro" ("The Burial"), the poet asks of the funeral followers, "Are ye all now that dead man. Perhaps" (p. 135). But it takes time to die, as poor mortal man must know, and those who accompany the entourage, with their stereotyped smiles, unknowing, are also dead.

Chapter IV is "Incorporación temporal" ("Temporal Incorportation"). "Antigua casa madrileña" ("Ancient Madrid House"), the first poem, contains three sections. In the first the poet describes the façade of the old house built in 1607 on a humble Madrid street. He seeks out like a slow camera the details of the wall, windows, door, stairway and flowerpots. In the second section, since past and present both are contained within the walls, he shows us the iron gratings on the window and four red flowers in humble flowerpots. The colors and smells symbolize life, for the will to create life cannot die, as green, reddish, yellowish flowers climb and fuse with the grates. Formerly, human eyes peered out, witnesses to human existence; eyes still peer out in this reflection of temporal human history, and the house is a reality in time. In the third section, for material is never exclusive, hands expose the flowers to the light and water their daily humble lives. They are no longer the hands of a noble lady but the active hands of a young girl who works and sews, not the products of idle silks, but life seeking expression through morning flowers which breathe and seek to be free. The poet has gone from the present to the past and then once more to the present, but actually we see only one single continuous reality, an eternity, a present historical past, whose unity in time, history and humanity are symbolized by the fragmentary details of eyes, hands, flowers, and iron gratings.

In the second poem, "Castillo de Manzanares el Real" ("Castle of Manzanares the Royal"), two men and a woman visit a centenary construction, a tower, with earth at its base, which aspires to heaven and the flames of eternity: "All are live flames toward the heavens" (p. 149). José Olivio Jiménez finds Aleixandre's use of flame imagery among the most "revealing of the intuitional vision of Aleixandre and . . . perfectly worked out. . . . A material single reality, indissoluble, solitary in its parts, but worked, living, seeing itself transfused of itself."[26] So the visitors walk through the stone towers where famous authors wrote and kings spoke, and as they leave, the old doorkeeper asks them for his tip. Things belong to time, not as the destroyer, but in affirmation of its presence.

In other poems of this part, the poet paints a life full of color, and life in simple blacks and whites. We see women of the village washing clothes, a recreation of a painting by Velázquez, Lope's house and children. Lope exists both in the present and the past, representing liberty, which is more than love, and thus perpetually free to help make others so. The poet also describes the twisted houses, of various shades and hues, fountains in a dry town, a bar where sleepy oldsters play at dominoes, and returning village workers, who as they come from the field, laughing and swearing, bring both life and death, and a possible hope for the morrow.

"Intermedio" ("Intermezzo") contains one poem, "La pareja" ("The Couple"), a condensation of all lovers, past and present. Eternal, they must be unmoving as they sit laughing in the window while below them, in furious activity, young and old work and play, sleep and wake, kiss or wound, are born and die. But love is lasting and always the same against the background of a fleeting universe of which this couple is a part much as the universe is only a tear on a divine cheek.

Chapter V, "Incorporación temporal" (the second poem with this title) includes "El engañado" ("The Deceived One"), which states that to be deceived is to be a bit more dead like a handful of flowers the lover holds, a bouquet of letters which promised loyalty and love. "A una ciudad resistente" ("To a Resisting City") is an evocation of Numancia, a city of the past but also of the here and now, still a "Fierce city on a perpetual hill" (p. 181); "Hijo de la mar" ("Son of the Sea") concerns a Roman statue, buried for two thousand years in "an ancient timeless silence beneath the waves" (p. 183), and emphasizes the constancy and eternal qualities of the sea.

The statue, washed ashore, is still young, half sea, half time. Meanwhile on the same beach dark-haired Andalusians work and wonder as they pass the eternal symbol. "La vieja señora" ("The Old Lady") retains a shadowy substance of the life and hopes of a young girl within the group of finished shadows going to the grave. "Las meninas" ("The Young Ladies-in-Waiting") stresses the light and shadow, the reality and truth, the eternal qualities of Velázquez' famous painting of that title, its people perpetually surprised and fixed in time. "Historia de la literatura" ("History of Literature") affirms the poetic conscience and knowledge that man is born to die. Aleixandre evokes the poets of Spain, the Romantics, Rivas and Espronceda, the former long-lived, the latter not. But Espronceda's breast, arm, hand, and fingers created new material, a flame which still burns, for a poet is more than his verses. Espronceda fought for liberty in his active, frenzied life. A man of flesh and blood, he was a tangible historical man whose light others managed to inherit. Finally "Idea del árbol" ("Idea of the Tree") recreates one of Aleixandre's favorite subjects. Wood is not flesh, although it can be wounded and killed. It is not water, although its sap may flow in transparent drops, nor is it blood, although it may, a running river, stain the sea. The tree is really an idea, a concentric idea evolving from a geometrical nucleus like a delayed thought, material, in short, which can be expressed and defined as "tree."

Chapter VI, "Retratos anónimos" ("Anonymous Portraits"), compares the past and the present, both parts of a struggle for life. In Aleixandre's opinion time destroys nothing, ". . . it is not a destructive element of reality, but integrating. Nevertheless, the historistic conscience of the poet."[27] Each person is his own unique historical reality. The poet compares past paintings and present humans. The material of the past lives on, not as the same individual, but as part of the human species. "Primer par" ("First Pair") contrasts life and death, dusty fountains and naked statues of a seventeenth-century painting with a current being; the second pair compares the blond shadow of a woman on canvas, a girl before she was a shadow, a woman before she became light, with a young mother and wife; the third pair, the canvas of a young Spanish lad in black silk, sword in hand, with a tired face and fatigued eyes, and his counterpart, a blond who does not frequent palaces and somber corridors but works and sweats in the open sun. The fourth pair contrasts old Celestina, the procuress of the past, with a little old laundry lady on the river banks. The fifth pair shows an austere lawyer, clad in black robes, with grave and tranquil eyes and thin black hair, as the canvas portrait. The live current material has the same black hair and a light beard. Not a dreamer, he is a doer, a builder of roads to bridge water, of high apartments where the living light strikes us all. Both are the material of which all men are made. Finally, the last poem, "Impar" ("Odd"), is the canvas of a famous Velázquez painting, "Niño de Vallecas." The poet describes the dead sweet forehead, the mute, horribly sweet and tearless eyes, the heavy head which looks but sees nothing, and the dead face. Yet he exists today, wrapped in a truth which is love, voicelessly offering a supplication for salvation through trust in mankind.

The "Epílogo" ("Epilogue") is called "Materia única" ("Single Material"). The poet sums up his central idea of the duration of time and material, history and flesh. One may find this unity of material in the smile of a boy, the flesh of a leg, a harsh mountain, cities, history, famous authors or warriors, for

All is material: time,
space; flesh and work.

Material alone, immense,
it pants or sighs, and beats
here on the shore. Wet
your hand, feel, feel
there the single origin,
there in infinity
which gives still, here in thee, its foams.

(p. 244)

(Todo es materia: tiempo,
espacio; carne y obra.
Materia sola, inmensa,
jadea o suspira, y late
aquí en la orilla. Moja
tu mano, tienta, tienta
allí el origen único,
allí en la infinitud
que da aquí, en ti aún espumas.)

Carlos Bousoño considers this volume Aleixandre's greatest work. "I would dare, moreover, to say that we are before the most important work of the poet: one of the maximum creations of the poetry of our century."[28] Many will not agree, but it is apparent that this work gives new significance and understanding to Aleixandre's previous poetry in its cosmic and natural as well as human and historical aspects. Leopoldo de Luis finds it the product "of long meditations, as if born from a serene and noble contemplation of life. All its pages project that comprehensive halo, that noble approach to things and beings. And that conviction of the totality of the world in creative matter . . . which mysteriously gathers human trembling and is, . . . companions of the same and radically tragic adventure."[29] For José Olivio Jiménez, who with Bousoño has written most penetratingly about *In a Vast Dominion,* the volume has a double interest. First it offers a means of saving knowledge, intuitions "which a particular man discovered when his cries and imprecations . . . resounded falsely and kept changing into an echo of itself. Secondly, it has the virtue of incorporating itself coherently into the history of the poetic vision of its author, since the entire vision of the world is somewhat historical, always 'becoming' like the very external data of existence."[30]

CHAPTER 8

Miscellaneous Poetry and Prose

I Miscellaneous Poetry and Anthologies

IN the *Complete Poems*, published in 1960, the final section includes a variety of poems, written between 1927 and 1957, which were not published as part of any collection. Many were announced, before publication in book form, as belonging to certain works, but their appearance in literary magazines and reviews was not matched by a corresponding volume publication. The first section of the three into which these poems are divided recapitulates themes we have already examined. "Más allá" ("Beyond") evokes the beloved and the sad, grave night; "Al sol sobre los hombres" ("To the Sun Above Men") strives toward light and life; other poems evoke the moon, birds, dreams, the sleeping sea. In "La muerte del abuelo" ("The Death of the Grandfather") Aleixandre equates a real historical death experienced by the poet with a dreamed one. He inserts one dream within another in the silence of his room. "La navidad preferida" ("Preferred Christmas") recalls a Christmas in Málaga. "Consumación" evokes childhood, creation, reality, the longing for life, and the final consummation.

The second section, "Poemas amorosos" ("Amorous Poems"), predates a complete anthology published in 1960 with the same title. "Primera aparición" ("First Appearance") evokes the perfidious magical creature in the afternoon; "Visita a la ciudad" ("Visit to the City") shows us a waiting young girl in the city of Granada; "No te conozco" ("I Know Thee Not") is a sad remembrance of amorous experiences, as the moaning girl, a shadow, conveys real emotion under her lover's breast. The beloved is a river which sustains in its waters the body of the lover, a musical instrument which the poet strums. Still other poems create other images of love, such as sick, pale hands, the destructive yet creative forces love controls, the waiting, the objective presence of the loved one, the poet's dreams, the good-byes of love, and its limits and absorption. The final section "Nuevos retratos y dedi-

142

catorias" ("New Portraits and Dedications"), some of which were
to appear in a later volume, contains poems to García Lorca,
Julio Maruri, Joan Miró, San Juan de la Cruz, and Málaga's own
Salvador Rueda. In many reviews Aleixandre had previously
dedicated poetry to García Lorca, in 1937; and to Miguel Hernández, "En la muerte de Miguel Hernández" ("On the Death
of Miguel Hernández"), 1948, evoking the total vision of the
poet and lamenting his loss.

Among other anthologies are his *Mis poemas mejores* (*My
Best Poems*), selected by the poet himself, which appeared in
1956 and then in a second edition in 1961. Aleixandre constantly
extracts selections from his own poetry to create new volumes,
as we have seen in *Poemas paradisiacos* (*Paradise Poems*), from
Shadow of Paradise. In 1955 he published *Ocho poemas* (*Eight
Poems*). Often, reversing the process, before publishing a work
in its definitive edition, the poet would publish a section of a
volume, such as *Antigua casa madrileña* (*Ancient Madrid
House*), 1961, later a part of *In a Vast Dominion*. In 1965
Aleixandre published still another anthology, *Presencias* (*Presences*), his most extensive, containing almost one hundred poems.
Approximately half of these poems come from his first period
of cosmic poetry, but the volume shows the continuity of Aleixandre's work from *Ambit* through his *Retratos con nombre* (*Portraits with a Name*). *Presences,* published in a limited edition
of twenty-five hundred copies, has a preliminary note by the
poet in which he states that he "has observed the continuity
with which my poetry shows—at least a good part of it and from
the very beginning—a certain tendency to objectivity."[1] He
thought it might be significant and interesting to give a cross
section of this continuous aspect of his work based on that
constant. The anthology is divided into eight parts. He rearranges the chronology of some sections and makes some minor
changes in some of the poems.

Finally, aside from the dozens of uncatalogued and perhaps
lost poems, Aleixandre has shown a special interest in art,
writing poetry for Daniel Díaz Vásquez' collection and for Francisco Satadell López' as well. His most famous artistic excursion,
however, is *Picasso,* an edition of two hundred copies printed
in Málaga in 1961. Accompanied by paintings from the walls
of the Nerja Cave, the poem evokes both Málaga and Picasso,
born near the blue sea, amid the black, yellow, and red colors

and the unique light. The word was a line in the hand of a
child, or in his fist, a seeker of reality and truth. The painter then,

> The Malagan Pablo, wrapped in reds,
> in greens, whites, or in the pure line,
> or in the clay, kaolin, mud, moves,
> beneath a cloak of color, swings.
>
> .   .   .   .
>
> His large hand
> which for an instant seized the orb, stretches open,
> live road for human beings.[2]

II *Retratos con nombre*

Retratos con nombre (*Portraits with a Name*) is a poetic continuation of the theme of man as a social being. Aleixandre's
emotional tone in this collection, however, often verges on the
sentimental. In his evocation he seeks human truth, and the
six sections attempt to convey the essence of loved figures,
known and unknown, living and dead. In keeping with his title,
he paints his figures as a painter might evolve them from his
paints. He deals with the eternal poetic themes of hate and
love, life and death, man's existential condition, and the role
of the individual in society. Stylistically, Aleixandre uses long
lists of verbs and nouns in some of his poems, continues his
special use of "or" as "equals," uses many literary references,
adopts a narrative descriptive tone, and generally treats his
portraits with tenderness and affection. The themes and imagery
are not new, and one must disagree with Leopoldo de Luis who
sees Aleixandre in this work as one who "does not repeat himself
ineffectively; he is a poet-river, not a poet-lake, nor, much less,
a poet-basin."[3]

The first poem, "Diversidad temporal" ("Temporal Diversity"),
shows that movements give us a background against which
memories evolve. The poet seeks a common denominator in
diversity which he views, not as a goddess, but as a continuous
reality. One finds here the elements we have previously examined
of sea, light, and material of the world.

> Liberty of man might shorten his forms.
> He speaks with history and conclusion awaits.
> Man deifies the beach, and the divine?
> Human, yes. Infinite? Real. Light to its limits![4]

"El abuelo" ("The Grandfather") recalls a clean-shaven, blue-eyed, adventurous man whom Aleixandre once knew at the sea of Málaga. "Mírame bien. Tuoio soi hasta morir" ("Look Well At Me. Thine Until Death") reintroduces the theme of eternal love. A nineteenth-century lover sends his portrait to his sweetheart pledging undying love, and thus preserving it fresh and immortal for future generations. "En la meseta" ("On the Plateau") evokes his friend Jorge Guillén, still erect and thin.

> Composition harmony, the tongue
> human here I graze a zenith, corresponding
> to midday, in the sphere unafflicted and rolling
> over the eyes where completely is copied the profound sound.
>
> (p. 18)

In other poems of the first section, Aleixandre describes a sculptor, Angel Ferrant, at work in ardent dialogue with the material on which he creates. "Allende el mar" ("Beyond the Sea") evokes the poet Rafael Alberti as a youth, his painter's eye, his voice for the dead (Spanish Civil War), and his exile in America which Aleixandre views as a kind of death. Now, the poet says, the sea unites them, and common blood beats on the shore, and he adds his voice to the chorus of his praise. In continuing poems he recalls a town crier, sad and solitary, and in a self-portrait, views his years as ascending stages in his life, notes the rebellion of his body but the continuing force of his heart. The second part of the book turns to the circus to paint a tight rope walker, a juggler, an equestrienne, and a clown.

Part Three begins with "En el viento" ("In the Wind"). Passing humanity, students, workers, sailors, are mixed by destiny in their hours or lives through their communion and their tears. "En verdad" ("In Truth") recalls Dámaso Alonso as an adolescent, wide of forehead, pale of cheek, against the background of Madrid at night and the countryside by day. In the adult he sees the same light and inspiration he found in the youth. Other poems tell of a mason who fell to his death; a fat woman who wanted to be a dancer; Max Aub, poet, dramatist, critic, whom Aleixandre calls a magician who carries with him in his breast the remembered love of a city of humanity; his sister who died at birth; an elementary school teacher who taught geography and whose lessons on the Visigothic kings evoked dreams in the sleeping class; Gabriel Celaya, the poet, and his wife;

and a childhood friend who returns to his country after an absence in order to die.

Part Four dedicates portraits to Paul Eluard, the French Surrealist, to Gustavo Adolfo Bécquer, and to Gerardo Diego, whose *Manual de espumas (Manual of Foams)* was one of the important works of Aleixandre's generation. The latter recalls the "winged language sudden-/ ly brusque and white,/ which extends its pure wing through a satiny sky" (p. 75). He recalls Manuel Altolaguirre, the youngest member of his generation, as "The angel is the man and he has lived" (p. 78). Again he speaks of Jorge Guillén, his second collection of poetry, *Clamor*, in "Clamor o voz" ("Clamor or Voice"), seeing in his poetry flowers, water, light and life. The life, light, and poet burned, and the flower fled, but as time passed he became aware of life and man, history and reality, and the truth that the world moves on. The former poet still remains in the current one. "The man appeared. His face grew old . . ./ But his voice sounded. It clamored or was buried./ It lived. It died" (p. 80).

Aleixandre's first poem here is called "Sin nombre" ("Without Name"). History at times does not signal out people; a young girl dies in a deserted city; an old man lives a fruitless life; a young boy and girl are in love; all anonymous:

> Pure anonymous
> who on dying one would say
> become reintegrated in the breast
> of the rest, who follow.
>
> (p. 85)

Other poems, some of them appearing previously, concern a tired prostitute whose face and voice cannot mask the emptiness of life; the working hands of a mason who builds houses and walls, and thus truly is a basic member of civilization; an evocation of the human eyes of Gregorio Marañón; a girl who looks through her window at the mountain slope outside; a scattering of houses clustered nearby; and Camilo José Cela and his island, with its light and water.

The last section is dedicated to his dog, Sirius, of large, deep eyes, who truly understands the poet.

> Your long soft ears, your body, sovereign and forceful
> your coarse hairless paw which touches the material of the world,
> the arch of your appearance and those deep peaceful eyes
> where Creation never erupted as a surprise.   (p. 108)

The poet understands the dog, much as the dog understands him, and wherever and whenever he goes, he can see always something like the dog's eyes, mercifully upon him at the boundary.

III Prose Works

Aleixandre has a great number of prologues, critical letters, articles of remembrance, evaluations of his own poetry, and evocations of friends and literary figures, many of them later included or rewritten for his major prose work *Los encuentros* (*The Encounters*). Aleixandre also made a number of speeches on poetry and poets, later published as pamphlets or in book form. Some of his most touching prose concerns dedications to his fellow poets, especially to departed ones. In 1947, commenting in an essay reprinted in *The Encounters* on his beloved José Luis Hidalgo, a professor of painting and poet from Santander who had just died, he recalls a poetic reading he gave, the tenderness of his voice, its quality of joy. For Aleixandre, "Silvered and tranquil his name is here. His definitive material sleeps elsewhere. A mixed heaven, with turbid blue, with indecipherable gray . . . watches over the earth where he is not hidden, where he surrenders himself, where he calmly rests."[5] In a number of other reviews Aleixandre wrote a series of evocations of other friends, later also included in *The Encounters*. Of José Luis Cano he comments on his birth at the coast where two seas meet without truce, charge and fuse. He evokes the bay in winter and in spring, the radiant sky, the happy blue of Málaga. Important for him is the sovereignty of light in its marvelous harmony and almost unsupportable beauty. All this he sees as a part of Cano's poetry, along with old cultures broken on Andalusian beaches and the ancient deep sea, for that poet is an Andalusian "raised with bare feet on the vivid sands of the coast."[6]

Aleixandre is a proficient letter writer, and he has written a number of them to his friend Gregorio Prieto, to the founders of *Cántico*, to José Suárez Carreño, and to Eulalia Galvarriato. The letter to the last named, fairly typical, concerns her novel *Cinco sombras* (*Five Shadows*), which he found "round, finished, and very personal," filled with melancholy, a knowledge of the human heart, and "the work of most difficult tenderness which I have read, perhaps, since many years ago I discovered the one

which seems to me a masterpiece in the literature of fiction,
[*Adiós Cordera (Good-by Cordera)*, of Leopoldo Alas (Clarín)]."[7]
Aleixandre further comments on her femininity, the double time
planes of the novel, with its characters living in the present and
the past, the plot concerning the lives of five girls who become
women, suffer, love, and die. He is especially fascinated by the
novel because he considers the central protagonist to be time,
and its world suspended in time, which makes of it a book for
young and old alike.

Aleixandre also wrote a number of prologues, for example, to
Primavera de la muerte (*Spring of Death*) of Carlos Bousoño.
Of special interest is his prologue to volumes 100 and 101 of
the "Adonais" poetic series, reproduced in *Insula*.[8] Aleixandre
comments on an early discussion he and José Luis Cano had
about founding the "Adonais" collection in 1943. He recalls the
first poetry after 1939 in its formal, almost precious obedience
to empty formulas, and that he agreed with José Luis Cano on
the need for change and the new strivings. It is Cano who
deserves the credit for giving them form in "Adonais," the only
criteria demanded being those of authenticity and honesty. The
collection justified the faith of its founder. Aleixandre recalls
the first volume which appeared in the series, one by Rafael
Morales, *Poemas del toro* (*Poems of the Bull*), with a special
vocabulary, new concepts and sensations, so much so that the
appearance was almost a revelation, "a symbol of what the new
series was trying to be." Aleixandre comments briefly on other
poetic collections such as *Litoral* of Prados and Altolaguirre and
Héroe of Altolaguirre, both of which died in untimely fashion,
smothered by the indifference of the public. Perhaps the most
significant aspect of the publication of the one-hundredth volume
of "Adonais" is that it symbolizes the acceptance of poetry and
the new literary climate, not only by the initiated few, but by
the greatest number of people possible. That poetry can reach
the heart of fellow men, that it obtained a receptive hearing,
bodes well for a future in which poets will achieve a maximum
audience, which, in the ideal of the new poets, "will have no
limit other than that of the human condition itself."

From time to time Aleixandre wrote critical comments on
what poetry meant for him, fragments in a sense of a developing
Ars Poetica. Earlier we examined his belief that poetry means
communication. He also was constantly concerned with the

moral and ethical principles of poetry.[9] Since the secret of poetry consists of its communication with the human community, it must offer profound meaning for the soul of men. A poet who seeks exclusively for beauty will lose it, for a poet may not write for himself, a kind of suicide. Poetry means men, and although it has flexible boundaries, there can be no solitary poets. Poetry may be exquisite or pessimistic, but it may not take precedence over life. A poet is an intensified man who can communicate more easily with the wise and the innocent, as he seeks truth and knowledge. A poet will recognize himself in the young people around him, for time has two dimensions, that of the passing years and that of day-to-day living. The poet lives with natural elements and seems one of them. He loves and hopes until he dies, but the one thing he may not do is lie. His anxiety for immortality is legitimate, but he must always remember that even the tongue in which he speaks is not everlasting. Poetry, then, lives only insofar as it serves man, and although the poet's universe is infinite, it is also limited by the possibility of its human communication.

When Aleixandre was admitted to the Academy on January 22, 1950, his entrance speech departed somewhat from the formal, academic, literary analyses. His "Vida del poeta: el amor" ("Life of the Poet: Love") examined love as a theme in poets through the ages, and in analyzing them, revealed the happy ecstasy, the sad solitude, the glory, torture, liberty, and humanity of his own treatment of the theme. Baquero Goyanes found the speech to be a kind of poetry, for "the fact that the prose of Aleixandre always turns out poetic is because its author is essentially a poet."[10] In his speech Aleixandre quoted from Rodrigo de Cota, Francisco de Quevedo, and Lope de Vega in order to approach a definition of love. The verses of Juan del Encina showed ingenuous, innocent young love, and Quevedo, in his baroque flavor, revealed bitterness and disillusion. In the nineteenth century Bécquer represented renunciation. In the seventeenth, Lope represented hope. Machado made love a communion with the absolute, which for Aleixandre is his own definition of love as the face of the absolute and the destruction of time.

In 1955 Aleixandre read a speech at the opening of the academic year at the Instituto de España. Later it was printed as a twenty-page booklet.[11] Aleixandre examines poetry as an expression of the new spirit of the times in its originality, temporal explorations, existential anguish and optimism. He finds that the literature of a generation always forms an artistic unity such as that of Rosales, Vivanco and Panero. Aleixandre largely limits himself to a discussion of a decade of poetry between 1945 and 1955, and states that its essential theme is that of "human life in its historical dimension; that is man localized in time."[12] Time passes irreversibly, but it is also localized in a definite space and society with its specific problems. Man is not viewed as an invariable substance, but as a fluid becoming. Like history he is something placed within the coordinates of a geographical place and an instant of time. Campoamor recognized the problem, and if that post-Romantic and transition poet of the nineteenth century had had more talent, he would have been the guide and idol of the generation under discussion, each member of which focused his vision of the central problem in a different way and created thus a rich, complex, and varied poetic production rivaling that of Spain's Golden Age. Conscious of the theme of time, many of the poets evoke the past, their youth, or infancy, using memory (in the case of Rosales) to replace the fantasy of immediately preceding periods. The new poets, using fewer figurative metaphors, invent less and sing of human life as a historical reality limited by time and the final barrier of death.

To notice the temporal is to become anguished or to have faith and hope. Man and the poet must face their problem of destiny on earth, death, and the beyond; in the measure that the poet resolves these questions, he shows the sentimental substance which saturates his work. Some take refuge in inspired faith. Others, less happy, seek salvation and consolation, but rebel and suffer. Still others concentrate their human vision on the solidarity of the suffering fraternity of mankind. In these problems, both despair and hope as well as social and religious faith occur. The anguish is both poetic and philosophical, a phenomenon of which the World War was not the cause but a symptom. Religiosity, always a factor in Spain, naturally became a part of the theme of the temporality of human life. Aleixandre examines this religious note in Rosales, Panero and others, as he had previously examined the existential and social note in Hierro and Blas de Otero respectively.

To be a man means to be associated with daily objects in an

antiheroic existence, a theme which enters frequently in the song of the young poets, who may write of a woman marketing, or other aspects of humble human lives in their daily insignificance and social dimension. Quoting from Rafael Morales, he finds poets to be essentially moral; thus the common destiny of man, justice and injustice in human relations, and communication among them become legitimate poetic themes for Nora, Celaya and others. Since these poets are preoccupied by social concerns, they recreate the concept of Spain and its soul, somewhat neglected since the poetry of the Generation of '98, and combine it with the other themes of hope, anguish, religiosity, and return to infancy. Thus the intent of contemporary poetry is to express human and social reality as it is lived. Since it tells the story of man, it has revived a narrative form and clarified the language. In seeking identity with humanity, the new poets write for the masses with maximum simplicity and familiar language not far removed from that of daily communication. The poet has finally learned that the lyrical world is not divisible by classes nor by concepts, for all objects, Spring and Winter, the rose and the thorn, are alike. In their desire for communication and a maximum audience limited only by the human condition, the poets have purified their language and developed their poetry of anguish, hope, religion, and country in a daily context of present or immediately past life, evoked through memory and a sense of man as a historical being.

The Encounters, Aleixandre's major prose work, is a series of portraits of poets and writers, living and dead, with whom he had some kind of personal contact. More interested in their human condition, personalities, and existence than in their literary reputation, Aleixandre does not write literary criticism in the ordinary sense, but in evoking his experience, memory, imagination at the moment of meeting, the physical appearance and psychology of the writers, he analyzes their literary production. Ventura Doreste finds that "each portrait is a poem, and being thus, what matters is the powerful recreating synthesis; the judgment always remains subordinated to the poetic intuition."[13] Leopoldo de Luis says that the principal value of *The Encounters* is rooted, therefore, "in the radically human countenance with which the author presents his evocations."[14] Concha Zardoya finds that his attitude, "his manner of seeing, is almost always visionary: past, present and future are fused in a depth

of poetry; the imagery of the vital cycles are superimposed on
or face each other in the background, in which one also per-
ceives the land which gave birth to the evoked figure, the
peculiarity of the native countryside, transferred to the work
of the person."[15] Each encounter has the impact of a lyric poem.
In these thirty-seven vignettes, Aleixandre claims he wishes to
reveal "some of the Spanish poets I have known throughout
my life . . . the work is just begun and continues open."[16]

Included in *The Encounters,* which the author implies he will
elaborate upon some day, are five prose writers, two older authors
whom Aleixandre knew in his youth, and three masters of his
generation. By examining various generations temporally, he
joins more than one time period and "encounters" his writers
in the present. Since these are people he knows himself, with
the exception of the final selection dedicated to an unknown
"poet," he offers a somewhat flattering account, but one cannot
find him untruthful in his effort to give us a unity and evoke a
total personality. Political and psychological penetration accompany empathy, tenderness, and love. Aleixandre divides his
sketches into two groups, those he knew before the Spanish
Civil War, and those who began writing largely after that tragic
conflict. He uses as interludes his evocation of Hernández, a
bridge between the generations, and those of Pérez Galdós and
Pardo Bazán, two master novelists of the nineteenth century.

Students of Aleixandre's works will receive a fairly good idea
of his own longings, likes and dislikes, and his ideas about poetry
from his pictures of others. Among these are his early meeting
with Galdós, his 1916 meeting with Azorín, his 1917 encounter
with Dámaso Alonso, and his encounter with Altolaguirre and
others of his generation. He meets his models in beer halls, on
the street, in the theater, and in his home. His encounters constitute a Who's Who of Spanish literature of the twentieth
century. Young poets visit him at home. Older figures such as
Pérez de Ayala flit through his pages. The fleeting or recurring
appearance of some of his figures helps create a kind of timeless background against which he operates.

Aleixandre usually starts with a superficial physical trait of
his study and then, in a kind of moral evaluation, seeks to
penetrate his spiritual depths. With the eye of a psychologist
painter he uses delicate shades and plastic and objective treat-
ments to set off his subjective evocation. Thus he often uses

sketches of the countryside and exterior circumstances to reveal inward feeling and spirit. Nature through the forest and sea or the cafe and parlor helps project the poetic image of country or city person, Andalusian or Castilian type. As any good painter would, Aleixandre concentrates on the degree of light, and emphasizes a variety of colors. In addition to his physical description of the hair, eyes, body size, or head, which especially attracted him as a personality indicator, Aleixandre describes the way his encounters dress, laugh or smile, the quality of their voices, in short, the moral and psychological imperatives which constitute their human quality.

In "El silencio de Pío Baroja" ("The Silence of Pío Baroja"), Aleixandre recalls a visit to that famous novelist in October, 1956, five days before his death. A painful peace exudes from the half-closed eyes. Aleixandre recalls how years before he had bought Baroja's trilogy, *La lucha por la vida* (*The Struggle for Life*), and other volumes. He remembers his first encounter with Pío Baroja, a fleeting one in the park, and then, once more in the present, views his repose and serenity. "Paseo con don Miguel de Unamuno" ("Walk with Don Miguel de Unamuno") portrays the latter's constantly worn black suit and hat. Unamuno spoke to Aleixandre, a young university student, of politics. The poet wishes, looking back, that he had listened more closely. "Azorín en dos tiempos" ("Azorín in Two Times") shows us an old man with a soft walk, thin smile and clear eyes, in a small room, who remembers a literary gathering of Juan Valera.

Aleixandre returns to 1916 and his encounter with Azorín in a bookstore, and once more comes back to the small room and the old man with the marvelous blue eyes. In other portraits we see Aleixandre's barber Eduardo who told him of another client who wrote verses. The other customer, in an unprepossessing stained suit, turns out to be Antonio Machado. Aleixandre meets Ortega y Gasset in Lope de Vega's house in 1953. The poet remembers another occasion in 1918 when he heard Ortega speak. In this selection, "José Ortega y Gasset en el jardín de Lope" ("José Ortega y Gasset in Lope's Garden"), he recreates the garden, submerged in silence, the light, the movement in front of the paintings in the house, and the physical changes time has made, but he also shows us that spiritual contributions endure. In "José Moreno Villa en muchas partes" ("José Moreno Villa in Many Places"), he paints his fellow Malagan whom he met at a beer parlor in 1929. As with most of his encounters, he gives physical descriptions of the poet, the light and shadows of the afternoon, the multifaceted experience of Moreno Villa, whose "painting would give him room, the essay would be his window, to the scattered garden, and in poetry (perhaps his most secret mistress) he would once more raise his palm . . . " (p. 61). Continuing his temporal encounters, Aleixandre sees Guillén in both his youth and maturity, but the meetings seem to occur at the same instant. Although historical circumstances change, Guillén has always been faithful to himself and the joyful absorption of the world around him. This description, "Jorge Guillén, en lo ciudad" ("Jorge Guillén, in the City"), again gives us a description of the size of his head, constantly a fascinating subject to Aleixandre, and their first meeting in a Madrid cafe when Guillén was thirty-four. At the time Guillén had friends along, namely, Federico García Lorca, Pedro Salinas, Rafael Alberti, and Manual Altolaguirre. Years later, all of these friends except Alberti are dead. As Aleixandre sees Guillén, whom he always associates with light, in the shadows of the setting sun, he pictures him again pointing to a wild flower which has survived in the winter garden. "Agitating, although slowly, a positive electricity zigzagged, in bursts of light which revealed a heaven made more than ever of proximity to the human measure" (p. 68).

The two factors which recur constantly are the double temporal vision and the physical description, involving almost always some mention of size. In his selection on Pedro Salinas, he finds the latter at home with his son on one knee and his daughter on the other. For him Carlos Riba, whom he met twice, dominated fire, had lyric force fused with thought, and special spiritual and physical qualities. He remembers Riba's words that "Each poem in which we recognize our soul before divinity, removes us from destruction; thus poems are made and not completely ours now, those which we need; not the future ones among which . . . is liberty, perhaps renunciation, perhaps death" (p. 83). Gerardo Diego was slender and silent. Dámaso Alonso meant walks and literary conversation in the countryside. Less well-known writers such as Clementina Arderiu interested Aleixandre. In "Clementina Arderiu, de cerca" ("Clementina Arderiu, Close Up"), Aleixandre comments that different poets convey different impressions. Clementina's is serenity. He describes her rosy complexion, her clear eyes and gray hair. No other poet created in him such a sensation of a calm climate, a room where existence is a long understanding experience. He describes her as kind and natural. Her daily acts take on a special illumination. Her Catalan poetry talks of happy love along destroyed streets, and time appears frozen in youth.

In "Evocación de Federico García Lorca" ("Evocation of Federico García Lorca"), printed several times in other journals, Aleixandre states that different people saw Lorca in different ways, but those who loved him saw him always as the same and yet ever changing. He was really an undefinable poet, tender, innocent, burning, inspiration, " . . . in Federico, one saw especially the powerful enchanter, dissipater of sadnesses, magician of merriment, conjurer of the joy of life, master of shadows, which he exiled with his presence" (p. 111). But Lorca was also a poet of sad solitudes and sudden silences, with a great capacity for love and suffering, especially in his "Sonetos del amor oscuro" ("Sonnets of Dark Love"), passionate, enthusiastic, happy, tormented, pure and burning love poems written in 1936 but never published. In his next vignette, "Emilio Prados niño de Málaga" ("Emilio Prados Child of Málaga"), he remembers him as a child with a strong sense of justice, and at a later meeting in 1929 as a pure adult. For Aleixandre, Rafael Alberti, pale of face and grim of forehead, was a painter. Aleixandre discusses Alberti's illness, his poetic birth, and his use of colors. He devotes three time sequences to his next "encounter," José María Salgarra, but only two to Luis Cernuda, who accepted and rejected life in his search for identity, and two fairly close encounters with Manuel Altolaguirre.

Galdós had always been a favorite of Aleixandre. He read his *Episodios nacionales* as one bewitched. Compassion and mercy, says Aleixandre, were the keys to his novels, second only to those of Cervantes. In his "Intermedio mayor" ("Major Intermezzo"), Don Benito Pérez Galdós appears at a Madrid theater to receive applause at a performance of his drama, *Sor Simona* (*Sister Simona*), in 1915. Overcome with emotion, Aleixandre, a youth of seventeen, has his first physical encounter with the great novelist. In the same Intermezzo he also remembers Emilia Pardo Bazán, whom he met in 1920, a few months before her death. Following his Intermezzo, Aleixandre includes another kind of intelude about the saddest moments of his life, "Evocación de Miguel Hernández" ("Evocation of Miguel Hernández") and "Una visita" ("A Visit") to that unhappy poet's grave. Aleixandre remembers an Hernández letter asking him for a copy of *Destruction or Love*, Hernández' eternal Spring-like force, his human quality, his poverty, his shirt sleeves and sandals. "He was trusting and expected no harm. He believed in men and held hope in them. That light which above every-thing, tragically, made him die with his eyes open, was never extinguished, no, not even in his last moment" (p. 178). The visit to his burial place in Alicante took place beneath a terrible but yet innocent wind, evoking for Aleixandre the pure and truthful Hernández, more real than the living and still present.

Aleixandre follows a roughly chronological plan. After the Hernández section come portraits of Luis Felipe Vivanco, nephew of the critic, essayist and poet, José Bergamín, a great architect who seems to move in time; José Antonio Muñoz Rojas, Andalusian gentleman, distinguished, skeptical and charitable; and Gabriel Celaya, who abandoned his career as industrial engineer for poetry. In Aleixandre's encounter with Celaya and his wife, as with most of his evocations, the time of day and the quality of the light are all-important. "The final rays of the setting sun caught the shadow of Gabriel and stretched it softly on the ground" (p. 211). He remembers seeing in José Luis Cano, in his city suit with the inappropriate light imprisoned between walls, the barefoot boy on the sunny sands of Andalusia, because the summer sovereignty of the light and the sea remain as permanent elements of that poet. Blas de Otero, in "Blas de Otero entre los demás" ("Blas de Otero Among the Others"), reminds him of "those ephemeral insects flying, a minute of whose existence is crammed with a complete life" (p. 222). The spiritual search of this solitary poet involves a floodtide of love and humanity, and Blas is the poet "with the greatest vocation for brotherhood among the poets of this time" (p. 222).

Aleixandre includes several encounters with women. In "En pie, Carmen Conde" ("Carmen Conde, On Foot"), he evokes her childhood in Melilla and remembers various meetings with her through the years. He finds in her a quality of worked stone, expressive rather than beautiful. "I thought of some image of old lost civilizations, of some Easter Island silent or imperious or molds" (p. 203). He views Concha Zarodoya in "La cabeza which might have very little to do with books, a Press, boxes de Concha Zardoya" ("The Head of Concha Zardoya") as a poetess of tranquil, gesturing hands and a head excavated from a rock. "Set off against the blue of the sky her forehead is a vast plain . . . where her brows are a rocky eminence from which at times the solitary puma peers, advancing slowly along the cornice of the lid, open to the abyss" (p. 264). Susana March's voice reflects her wisdom and maturity, but it does not fit her young, fresh face. Her grave, lightly hoarse voice combines both "a voice of ancient science and admonition and . . . the fresh water of today called Susan . . . " (p. 288).

The "encounters" seem to come in a never-ending stream of names, dates, places. Rafael Morales, who wrote his first verses at the age of fourteen, testified that the "child is father to the man." The years put weight on him, making him as much father and good story teller as poet. Vicente Gaos, thin and wiry, is the least Mediterranean Valencian Aleixandre ever met. If Vicente Gaos is a "thin eagle," José Hierro, whom Aleixandre evokes at twilight, when "a melancholy light of the setting sun had reached his afternoon eyes" (p. 241), has a knowing mouth which spreads sweet or bitter honey on the paper. José Luis Hidalgo is a living synthesis of innocence and wisdom, although the dead poet's body may sleep elsewhere. Carlos Bousoño is the eternal student of poetry, discovering Rubén Darío at sixteen, Machado and others at nineteen. Julio Maruri exudes a kind of mysterious innocence; Leopoldo de Luis, a man of hidden depths, is always affable, courteous, delicate, and a patient identifier with the people. The youngest poet, José María Valverde, reminds him of a Latin American of Indian extraction. No other poet of his generation gives Aleixandre "this sensation of tranquil security" (p. 293) in his love of things and God.

Aleixandre ends his work with "El poeta desconocido" ("The Unknown Poet"), about an insignificant soldier who wrote two poems, and found it worth while to write them, but not to show them. When Aleixandre replied negatively to the soldier's question about writing night and day, the latter exclaimed, "You, then, are like anybody else" (p. 300), and departed, disappointed that Aleixandre, like him, was a man who wrote through human effort. The soldier, then, is an unknown poet whose faith suffices to move mountains.

Aleixandre is a poet who manages to master his material in a style which does not stifle it. He has created no new revolution, but he speaks, from his time of cosmic love through that of human suffering and final identification and salvation, with freshness and authenticity. His poetry, a constant dialogue between himself and his circumstance, is a spiritual voyage, at times verging on the commonplace but usually permeated with the beauty of the profound. Curious, he speaks of love, of life and death, of nature, humanity, and fleeting time. Vigorous or gentle, as the occasion demanded, he failed to invent a new poetic language, but his ardent and opaque imagery added a new dimension to the poetry of his day, as did his provocative Paradise, a precipitate of pure time, destructive love, and human material in universal communion.

Notes and References

Chapter One

1. Dámaso Alonso, *Poetas españoles contemporáneos* (Madrid, 1952), p. 7.
2. As read in Gerardo Diego, *Poesía española* (Madrid, 1934), pp. 152-53.
3. Alonso, *op. cit.*, p. 174.
4. Francisco Olmos García, "Una antología de poetas españoles de hoy," *Cuadernos Americanos,* XXIII (1964), 194.
5. Claude Couffon, "Recontre avec un gran poète . . . Jorge Guillén," *Les Lettres Nouvelles,* nouvelle série, No. 19 (July 8, 1959), 28.
6. Alonso, *op. cit.*, pp. 190-91.
7. José Olivio Jiménez, *Cinco poetas del tiempo* (Madrid, 1964).
8. Luis Cernuda, *Estudios sobre poesía española contemporánea* (Madrid, 1957), p. 184.
9. As recalled by Gerardo Diego, *op. cit.*, p. 318.
10. *Ibid.*, pp. 397-98.
11. *Ibid.*, p. 364.
12. *Ibid.*, p. 423.
13. For a recent book on Lorca, see Carl Cobb, *Federico García Lorca* (New York: Twayne Publishers, 1967).
14. Luis Cernuda, *Estudios,* pp. 105-6.
15. Rafael Bosch, "The New Nonconformist Spanish Poetry," *Odyssey,* II (1962), 223.
16. José María Castellet, *Viente años de poesía española. Antología (1939-1959)* (Barcelona, 1960), p. 77.

Chapter Two

1. Max Aub, *La poesía española contemporánea* (Mexico, 1954), p. 154.
2. Concha Zardoya, "Los tres mundos de Vicente Aleixandre," *Revista Hispánica Moderna,* XX (1954), 69.
3. Enrique Canito, "Diálogo con Vicente Aleixandre," *Insula,* V, No. 50 (February, 1950), 3.
4. As reported by Fernando Charry Lara, *Cuatro poetas del siglo veinte* (Bogotá, 1947), p. 14.

5. Vicente Aleixandre, "Rubén Darío en un pueblo castellano," *Revista de Occidente*, I, No. 3 (June, 1963), 293-94.

6. Vicente Gaos, "Fray Luis de León, 'fuente' de Aleixandre," *Papeles de Son Armadans*, XI, Nos. 32-33 (1958), 348.

7. Carlos Bousoño, *La poesía de Vicente Aleixandre* (Madrid, 1950), pp. 16-26.

8. Aub, p. 154.

9. Jorge Blajot, "Más allá de la palabra," *Razón y Fe* (May 1, 1950), 532.

10. Leopoldo de Luis, "La obra completa de Vicente Aleixandre," *Papeles de Son Armadans*, XVIII (1960), 191-92.

11. Jorge Guillén, *Language and Poetry* (Cambridge, Mass., 1961), p. 216.

12. Jorge Guillén, "Algunos poetas amigos," *Papeles de Son Armadans*, XI, Nos. 32-33 (1958), 156.

13. Canito, *Insula*, p. 3.

14. José Luis Cano, *Poesía española del siglo XX* (Madrid, 1960), p. 268.

15. *Ibid.*, p. 264.

16. Charry Lara, *op., cit.*, p. 12.

17. *Ibid.*, p. 29.

18. *Ibid.*, pp. 31-32.

19. Federico Carlos Sáinz de Robles, *Historia y antología de la poesía española* (Madrid, 1964), p. 215.

20. Guillermo Díaz Plaja, *Historia de la poesía lírica española* (Barcelona, 1948), p. 426.

21. Rodrigo Fernández Carvajal, "El tiempo en la poesía de Vicente Aleixandre," *Corcel*, Nos. 5-6 (1944), 105.

22. Alejandro Busuioceanu, "El epifanismo de Vicente Aleixandre," *Insula*, IV, No. 39 (1949), 8.

23. Charry Lara, *op. cit.*, p. 15.

24. *Ibid.*

25. Carlos Bousoño, prologue to *Poesías completas de Vicente Aleixandre* (Madrid, 1960), p. 17.

26. *Ibid.*, p. 21

27. Gabrel Celaya, "Notas para una cantata en Aleixandre," *Papeles de Son Armandans*, XI, Nos. 32-33 (1958), 377.

28. *Ibid.*, p. 378.

29. *Ibid.*, p. 382

30. José Olivio Jiménez, *Cinco poetas del tiempo*, p. 52. Also see Castellet, *Veinte años de poesía española*, p. 70. Castellet, while accepting Dámaso Alonso's contention that Aleixandre follows a general evolution of Spanish poetry toward human emotion, finds, rather than a radical change, a humanization that is progressive.

31. Vicente Aleixandre, *La destrucción o el amor* (Madrid, 1945), p. 15.

32. Francisco Olmos García, p. 197.

33. Carlos Bousoño, "Dos ensayos," *Papeles de Son Armadans*, XI, Nos. 32-33 (1958), pp. 250-51.

34. Gerardo Diego, *Poesía española*, p. 494.

35. *Ibid.*, p. 495.

36. *Ibid.*, p. 494.

37. Canito, *Insula*, pp. 3, 6.

38. *Ibid.*, p. 6.

39. Aleixandre, "Poesía, comunicación," *Correo Literario*, I (June 1, 1950), 3.

40. Aleixandre, "Cumpleaños," *Papeles de Son Armadans*, XI, Nos. 32-33 (1958), 123.

41. Jorge Mañach, "Visitas españolas: Vicente Aleixandre," *Insula*, XV, No. 162 (1960), 3.

42. Aleixandre, *Mis poemas mejores* (Madrid, 1961), p. 9.

43. Dámaso Alonso, "Vicente Aleixandre," *Insula*, V, No. 50 (February, 1950), 1. See also: *Diccionario Enciclopédico*, Mexico: "UTE-HA," I (1953), p. 1149, which defines him as "one of the most discussed lyric values of the modern literary generation."

44. Charles David Ley, *Spanish Poetry Since 1939* (Washington, D. C., 1962), p. 73.

45. Juan Ramón Jiménez, "Vicente Aleixandre," *Corcel*, Nos. 5-6 (1944), 77.

46. Dámaso Alonso, "El Nilo," *Corcel*, Nos. 5-6 (1944), 80.

47. José Suárez Carreño, *Corcel*, Nos. 4-5 (1944), 94.

48. Carlos Bousoño, *Corcel*, Nos. 4-5 (1944), 100.

49. Jorge Campos, "Nuestro amigo, Vicente," *Corcel*, Nos. 4-5 (1944), 101.

50. Claudio Rodríguez, "Fuerte olor a existencia," *Papeles de Son Armadans*, XI, Nos. 32-33 (1958), 430.

51. Jaime Ferrán, "De Velintonia 3 recuerdo sobre todo los domingos," *Papeles de Son Armadans*, XI, Nos. 32-33 (1958), 370.

52. José Hierro, "Testimonio de Aleixandre," *Papeles de Son Armadans*, XI, Nos. 32-33 (1958), 240-44.

53. Juan José Domenchina, *Antología de la poesía española contemporánea* (Mexico, 1947), p. 390.

54. Gonzalo Torrente Ballester, *Literatura española contemporánea* (Madrid, 1949), p. 440.

55. Federico Carlos Sáinz de Robles, *Panorama Literario, 1954*, II (Madrid, 1955), 170.

56. Jorge Mañach, *Insula*, p. 3.

57. José Mariá Castellet, p. 70.

58. Dámaso Alonso, "Vicente Aleixandre," *Insula*, V, No. 50 (February, 1950), 7.

59. Eugenio de Nora, "Aleixandre, renovador," *Corcel*, Nos. 5-6 (1944), 96.

60. Roque Esteban Scarpa, *Poetas españoles contemporáneos* (Santiago de Chile, 1953), p. 316; Guillermo Díaz-Plaja, *Literatura hispánica contemporánea* (Barcelona, 1963), p. 302; Ramón Castelltort, *La poesiá lírica española del siglo xx* (Barcelona, 1957), p. 185; José Luis Cano, "Vicente Aleixandre en la Academia," *Insula*, IV, No. 43 (1949), 2.

61. José Luis Cano, *Antología de la nueva poesía española* (Madrid, 1958), p. 15.

62. "Aleixandre y el corazón," *ABC* (October 29, 1955), 35.

63. Leopoldo de Luis, "Actualidad de Ambito," *Insula*, V, No. 52 (1950), 2.

64. "Poetry of the Dispersion," *Times Literary Supplement* (London, December 23, 1955), 776; Ventura Doreste, "Ponderación de Aleixandre," *Insula*, XII, No. 124 (1957), 4; Ramón Castelltort, p. 188; Gabriel Celaya, "Notas para una 'Cantata en Aleixandre,' " *Papeles de Son Armadans*, XI Nos. 32-33 (1958), 375; Eugenio de Nora, "Aleixandre, renovador," *Corcel*, Nos. 5-6 (1944), 95-96.

65. Ramón Gómez de la Serna, "Gemelismo: Gerardo Diego y Vicente Aleixandre," *Revista Nacional de Cultura*, No. 104 (May-June, 1954), 19; Carlos Bousoño, *La Poesía de Vicente Aleixandre*, pp. 105-6; Javier Alfaya, "Dos cantatas de Gabriel Ceyala," *Insula*, XX, No. 221 (April, 1965), 7.

Chapter Three

1. Sigmund Freud, *The Standard Edition of the Complete Psychological Works of Freud* (London, 1961), XIX, 42.

2. *Psychoanalysis Today*, ed. by Sandor Lorenz (New York, 1944), p. 66.

3. C. G. Jung, *Modern Man in Search of a Soul*, tr. by W. S. Dell and Cary F. Barnes (London, 1945), pp. 194-95.

4. Sigmund Freud, "Formulations on the Two Principles of Mental Functioning," in *The Standard Edition* (London, 1958), XII, 224.

5. Sigmund Freud, *Delusion and Dream—An Interpretation in the Light of Psychoanalysis of Gradiva*, tr. Helen Downey (London, 1921).

6. Sigmund Freud, *Leonardo da Vinci, A Study in Sexuality*, tr. A. A. Brill (New York, 1947).

7. Lawrence Kubie, *Neurotic Distortion of the Creative Process* (Lawrence, Kansas, 1958).

8. *Ibid.*, p. 143.

9. *Psychoanalysis Today*, p. 38.

10. Juan José Domenchina, *Antología de la poesía española contemporánea* (Mexico, 1947), p. 391.

11. Max Aub, *La poesía española contemporánea* (Mexico, 1954), pp. 156-59.

12. Dámaso Alonso, *Poetas españoles contemporáneos* (Madrid, 1952), p. 323.

13. Luis Cernuda, *Como quien espera el alba* (Buenos Aires, 1947), p. 44.

14. Aleixandre, *La destrucción o el amor* (Madrid, 1945), p. 17.

15. Carlos Bousoño, *La poesía de Vicente Aleixandre* (Madrid, 1950), p. 10.

16. Eleanor Turnbull, *Contemporary Spanish Poetry* (Baltimore, 1945), quotes Pedro Salinas on Aleixandre on pp. 17, 299.

17. Gerardo Diego, *Poesía española contemporánea* (Madrid, 1962), p. 649.

18. Federico Carlos Sáinz de Robles, *Panorama Literario, 1954* (Madrid, 1955), II, 170.

19. Carlos Bousoño, p. 11.

20. Vicente Aleixandre, *La destrucción*, pp. 17-18.

21. Vicente Aleixandre, *Poesías completas* (Madrid, 1960), pp. 99-100. All future citations from Aleixandre's poetry, unless otherwise noted, are from this edition.

22. Carl Jung, *Psychology of the Unconscious* (New York, 1944), p. 237.

23. Karl Abraham, in *Selected Papers on Psychoanalysis* (London, 1948), p. 203, relates darkness to womb fantasies. As the symbol of the mother it signifies both birth and death.

24. Bertram D. Lewin, *The Psychoanalysis of Elation* (New York, 1950), p. 111.

25. *Psychoanalysis Today*, p. 317.

26. Bertram D. Lewin, "Phobic Symptoms and Dream Interpretation," *The Psychoanalytic Quarterly*, XXI, No. 3 (July, 1952), 313.

27. Lewin, *The Psychoanalysis of Elation*, pp. 107-8.

28. Abraham, p. 176.

29. Other sea poems in this collection which relate the sensual to death and decay, and show the sea as both love and death, involving a continuing symbolism of "round mouths," "rotten fish," "a sweet passion of water of death," and the like are "La muerte o antesala de consulta" (pp. 153-54), "Víspera de mí" (pp. 163-64), "El mar no es una hoja de papel" (pp. 182-83), and "Sobre tu pecho unas letras" (pp. 184-85).

30. Melanie Klein, *The Psychoanalysis of the Child* (London, 1949), p. 211. Fish attacks represent an attack on the father's penis. Carl Jung, *Psychology of the Unconscious*, p. 223, equates the fish with a libido symbol. The fish may be a phallic symbol or may, at times, represent the woman.

31. Dámaso Alonso, *Poetas españoles*, p. 298.

32. Similar themes may be found in other poems of the collection such as "Circuito" (p. 224), where he seeks the love of "sirens of

the sea"; "Nacimiento último" (pp. 230-31), where he views the sea as eternal life and death; "Toro" (p. 240), which emphasizes auto-eroticism and narcissistic enjoyment of self, for his need for love is not easily fulfilled by women; "Muñecas" (pp. 247-48), about the pleasant-unpleasant aspects of physical love and girls at whose breasts bronze beetles bite; "Madre, Madre" (pp. 257-58); "Palabras" (p. 260); "Tempestad arriba" (pp. 267-68); and "Donde ni una gota de tristeza es pecado" (pp. 289-90), on destructive death imagery and the pleasure-pain involved in love.

33. Lewin, *op. cit.*, p. 104.

34. *Ibid.*, p. 48.

35. *Ibid.*, p. 111.

36. Freud, *Standard Edition* (1959), XX, 67. The forest, like the tree, mythologically has been portrayed as a maternal symbol. The juxtaposition of the sea and forest symbols seem significant.

37. Otto Rank, *The Trauma of Birth* (New York, 1962), p. 149.

38. *Psychoanalysis Today*, p. 160.

39. Freud, *The Basic Writings of Sigmund Freud* (New York, 1938), pp. 394-96. See also: *Standard Edition* (1953), IV and V, 227, 399-401, 403n., 406.

40. The remaining poems in *Destruction or Love* which contain sea symbolism continue to identify it with sexual force and the love-death relationship. Among these are "Unidad en ella" (pp. 307-8); "El mar ligero" (pp. 309-10); "Sin luz" (pp. 311-12); "Junio" (pp. 319-20); "A ti viva" (pp. 331-32); "Orillos del mar" (pp. 333-34); "Quiero saber" (pp. 335-36); "El frío" (pp. 370-71), where he becomes the sea, "absolute ocean that I am," but continues to seek life, light and love; "Soy el destino" (pp. 375-76), "only sea to which all loving limits come"; "Que así invade" (pp. 389-90); "Cuerpo de piedra" (pp. 393-94); and "Total amor" (pp. 407-8).

41. Aleixandre reveals a desire to fuse with the ocean coupled with a resistance to rejoining it. The sea *no es* a bed, a shroud. The regressively attractive mother symbol, the sea, is said not to be the very thing he holds it to be, a mechanism of denial or negation.

42. Bousoño, *La poesía de Vicente Aleixandre*, p. 7.

43. Alonso, *Poetas españoles*, p. 309.

44. Aleixandre, *Algunos caracteres de la nueva poesía española* (Madrid, 1955), p. 11.

45. Other poems which recall the sea as eternal, a far-off love, sexual passion, earlier paradise, and yet a continuing sea of both life and death, are "El río" (pp. 475-76), "Plenitud del amor" (pp. 519-21), "Mensaje" (pp. 529-30), "El aire" (p. 538), "El mar" (p. 539), "Cuerpo sin amor" (p. 550), "Adiós a los campos" (pp. 560-61), "Ciudad del paraíso" (pp. 546-65), and "Hijos de los campos" (pp. 566-67).

46. J. C. Flugel, *The Psychoanalytic Study of the Family* (London, 1935), pp. 67-69.

47. Patrick Mullahy, *Oedipus, Myth and Complex* (New York, 1948), p. 163.

48. Lewin, "Phobic Symptoms and Dream Interpretation." Aleixandre uses the sea as an archetypal motif. For archetypal motifs see: C. G. Jung, *The Integration of the Personality* (New York, 1939), pp. 52 ff.

49. Flugel, p. 66.

50. Northrop Frye also examines archetypal motifs in *Anatomy of Criticism* (Princeton, 1957), p. 99. Water (hence sea, ocean, etc.) in a dream has the symbolic meaning of mother. It is constantly used with this meaning in Aleixandre's poetry.

51. Frederick Clark Prescott, *The Poetic Mind* (New York, 1926), p. 276.

52. Lewin, "Reconsiderations of the Dream Screen," *The Psychoanalytic Quarterly*, XXII, No. 2 (1953), 174-98.

53. As recounted by Fernando Charry Lara, *Cuatro poetas de hoy*, p. 31.

54. *Ibid.*, p. 18.

55. Alonso, *Poetas españoles contemporáneos*, p. 287.

56. Bousoño, *La poesía de Vicente Aleixandre*, pp. 46-47.

57. *Ibid.*, p. 103.

58. Gullón, "Itinerario poético de Vicente Aleixandre," *Papeles de Son Armadans*, XI, Nos. 32-33 (1958), 197.

59. Guillén, "Algunos poetas amigos," *Papeles de Son Armadans*, XI, Nos. 32-33 (1958), 154.

60. Monterde, *La poesía pura en la lírica española* (Mexico, 1953), pp. 105-13.

61. Díaz-Plaja, *Historia de la poesía lírica española* (Barcelona, 1948), p. 426.

62. Cernuda, *Estudios sobre poesía española contemporánea* (Madrid, 1957), pp. 195-96.

63. Angel del Río, "La poesía surrealista de Aleixandre," *Revista Hispánica Moderna*, II (1935), 21.

64. Other critics who find Aleixandre a Surrealistic poet include José María Souvirón, *La nueva poesía española* (Santiago de Chile, 1938), p. 51, and Luis Felipe Vivanco, *Introducción a la poesía española contemporánea* (Madrid, 1957), p. 354. José Olivio Jiménez suggests that the Spanish critics who deny the influence of Surrealism are "perhaps influenced by a nationalism which tries to denigrate all trans-Pyrenean relationship . . ." (*Hispania*, L, No. 4 [1967], 936).

Chapter Four

1. Aleixandre, *Mis poemas mejores* (Madrid, 1956), p. 15.

2. Gullón, "Itinerario poético de Vicente Aleixandre," pp. 195-96.

3. Doreste, "La unidad poética de Aleixandre," *Insula*, V, No. 50 (February, 1950), 6.

4. Aleixandre, *Poesías completas* (Madrid, 1950), p. 52. Further citations in the text are to this edition.

5. Gerardo Diego, "Pasión de la tierra," *Corcel*, Nos. 5-6 (1944), 81. "Today these other poems are perhaps definitely lost with other papers of the poet, and I would regret it because their quality was as great as that of those chosen."

6. Aleixandre, *Mis poemas mejores*, p. 31. "It is my work closest to surrealism, although . . . never felt . . . surrealistic poet . . . not believed in the strictly oneiric . . . nor in the consequent abolition of the artistic conscience."

7. Gullón, p. 204.

8. José Luis Cano, *Poesía española del siglo veinte* (Madrid, 1960), p. 299.

9. Luis Felipe Vivanco, *Introducción a la poesía española contemporánea* (Madrid, 1957), p. 342.

10. Aleixandre, *Mis poemas mejores*, p. 10.

11. Bousoño, *La poesía de Vicente Aleixandre*, p. 100.

12. Diego, *Corcel*, p. 81.

13. Gullón, pp. 198-201.

14. Bleiberg, "Vicente Aleixandre y sus poemas difíciles," *Insula*, V, No. 50 (February, 1950), 6.

15. *Ibid.*, p. 6.

16. Diego, *Corcel*, p. 81.

17. Rank, *The Trauma of Birth*, p. 149. See also: Geza Roheim, *Gates of the Dream* (New York, 1952), p. 347. Roheim points out that these water beings devour their victims: ". . . the possible interpretation of these man-eating beings as the infant's oral aggression in talion form . . ."

18. Lewin, "Phobic Symptoms and Dream Interpretation," *The Psychoanalytic Quarterly*, XXII, No. 3 (July, 1952), 313.

19. Lewin, "Reconsiderations of the Dream Screen," *The Psychoanalytic Quarterly*, XXII, No. 2 (1953), 187. ". . .the inside of a hollow space or concavity may represent the breast . . ." Also Freud, *The Basic Writings of Sigmund Freud* (New York, 1938), p. 372. ". . . 'wood,' generally speaking, seems, in accordance with its linguistic relations, to represent feminine matter."

20. Alonso, "Espadas como labios," *Revista de Occidente*, CXIV (December, 1932), 329.

21. Charry Lara, pp. 20, 31.

22. Bousoño, *La poesía de Vicente Aleixandre*, p. 48.

23. Alonso, *Poetas españoles contemporáneos*, p. 292.

24. Rodrigo Fernández Carvajal, *Corcel*, p. 107.

25. Leopoldo de Luis, "El sentido social en la poesía de Vicente Aleixandre," *Papeles de Son Armadans*, XI, Nos. 32-33 (1958), 418.

26. Gullón, "Itinerario . . .," p. 206.

27. Alonso, *Poetas españoles contemporáneos*, p. 293.

28. *Ibid.*, p. 327.

29. De Nora, "Aleixandre, renovador," *Corcel*, Nos. 5-6 (1944), 95.

30. Barral, "Memoria de un poema," *Papeles de Son Armadans,* XI, Nos. 32-33 (1958), p. 394.

31. Rodrigo Fernández Carvajal, p. 105.

Chapter Five

1. Alonso, *Poetas españoles contemporáneos*, p. 327.

2. Concha Zardoya, "Los tres mundos de Vicente Aleixandre," *Revista Hispánica Moderna*, XX (1954), p. 67.

3. Alonso, *Corcel*, Nos. 5-6, p. 88.

4. Concha Zardoya, *Poesía española contemporánea* (Madrid, 1961), p. 411.

5. Salinas, *Literatura española del siglo XX* (Mexico, 1949), p. 213.

6. Aleixandre, *Mis poemas mejores*, p. 57.

7. Cano, "El amor en la poesía de Vicente Aleixandre," *Corcel,* Nos. 5-6 (1944), p. 97.

8. Charry Lara, p. 28.

9. Juan Chabás, *Literatura española contemporánea* (Havana, 1952), p. 543.

10. Salinas, *Literatura española del siglo XX*, p. 211.

11. *Ibid.*, p. 219.

12. Cano, *Corcel*, p. 86.

13. *Times Literary Supplement*, "Poetry of the Dispersion," 776.

14. Nora, "Forma poética y cosmovisión en la obra de Vicente Aleixandre," *Cuadernos Hispanoamericanos*, No. 7 (January, 1949), 117.

15. Alonso, *Poetas españoles contemporáneos*, p. 294.

16. Eugenio Frutos, "Las poesías completas de Vicente Aleixandre," *Indice*, XV, Nos. 150-51 (1961), 30.

17. Angel del Río, "La poesía surrealista de Vicente Aleixandre," *Revista Hispánica Moderna*, II (1935), 22.

18. Alonso, "La destrucción o el amor," *Revista de Occidente,* CXLIV (June, 1935), 331.

19. Alonso, *Poetas españoles contemporáneos*, p. 303.

20. Carlos Bousoño, *La poesía de Vicente Aleixandre*, p. 234.

21. Lewin, "Phobic Symptoms and Dream Interpretation," p. 313.

22. Lewin, "Reconsiderations of the Dream Screen," p. 187.

23. Bousoño, *La poesía de Vicente Aleixandre*, p. 23.

24. Cano, *Corcel*, p. 86.

25. Aleixandre, *Mis poemas mejores*, p. 93.

26. Ventura Doreste, "Aspectos de Aleixandre," *Insula*, XV, No. 167 (October, 1960), 1.

27. Concha Zardoya, "Los tres mundos de Vicente Aleixandre," p. 70.

28. Doreste, "Aspectos de Aleixandre," p. 6.

29. Bousoño, "Un nuevo libro de Aleixandre," *Insula*, V, No. 53 (1950), 2, 7.

30. Melchor Fernández Almagro, "Mundo a solas," *ABC* (May 14, 1950), 27.

31. Concha Zardoya, *Poesía española contemporánea*, p. 452.

Chapter Six

1. José Luis Cano, "Málaga en Vicente Aleixandre," *Papeles de Son Armadans*, XI, Nos. 32-33 (1958), 332.

2. Aleixandre, *Poemas paradisíacos* (Málaga, 1952), prologue.

3. José Luis Cano, *De Machado a Bousoño* (Madrid, 1955), p. 97.

4. Aleixandre, *Mis poemas mejores*, p. 107.

5. Aleixandre, "De una carta a Dámaso Alonso," *Corcel*, Nos. 5-6 (1955), 110-11.

6. Fernández Carvajal, *Corcel*, p. 107

7. Bousoño, *La poesía de Vicente Aleixandre*, p. 128.

8. Rafael Benítez Claros, "Vicente Aleixandre: *Sombra del paraíso*," *Cuadernos de Literatura Contemporánea*, 15 (1944), 264.

9. Bousoño, *op. cit.*, p. 27.

10. Cano, *Corcel*, p. 86.

11. Alonso, *Ensayos sobre poesía española* (Buenos Aires, 1946), p. 377.

12. Charry Lara, pp. 31-32.

13. Bousoño, "Sobre *Historia del corazón* de Vicente Aleixandre," *Insula*, IX, No. 102 (June, 1954), 10.

14. Concha Zardoya, "La presencia femenina en *Sombra del paraíso*," *Revista de las Indias*, 107 (Jan.-Feb., 1949), 147-53.

15. Concha Zardoya, *Poesía española contemporánea*, pp. 444, 453.

16. Gil, "Vanguardia y complemento de *Sombra del paraíso* en el último libro de Vicente Aleixandre," *Cuadernos Hispanoamericanos*, No. 15 (May-June, 1950), 597.

17. Alonso, *Ensayos sobre poesía española*, p. 390.

18. Vivanco, *Introducción a la poesía española contemporánea* (Madrid, 1957), pp. 372-80.

19. Aub, *La poesía española contemporánea* (Mexico, 1954), p. 157.

20. Benítez Claros, p. 273.

21. Bousoño, *La poesía de Vicente Aleixandre*, p. 175.

22. *Ibid.*, p. 19.

23. Cano, *Poesía española del siglo veinte*, p. 271.

24. Lewin, "Reconsiderations . . .," p. 191.

25. Cano, "Vicente Aleixandre: *Nacimiento último,*" *Insula*, VIII, No. 90 (June, 1953), 6.

26. Aleixandre, *Mis poemas mejores*, p. 153.

27. Gullón, "Itinerario . . .," p. 234.

28. Cano, *De Machado a Bousoño*, p. 112.

29. Aub, p. 155.

30. Alvarez Villar, "El panteísmo en la obra poética de Vicente Aleixandre," *Cuadernos Hispanoamericanos*, LIX, No. 175 (1964), 183.

31. Diego, "Curva ascendente," *Insula*, V, No. 50 (February, 1950), 1.

Chapter Seven

1. Aleixandre, *Mis poemas mejores*, p. 173.

2. Frutos, *Indice*, XV, 30.

3. Leopoldo de Luis, "El sentido social en la poesía de Vicente Aleixandre," *Papeles de Son Armadans*, XI, Nos. 32-33 (1968), 415-16.

4. Souvirón, "Humano y excelente," *Cuadernos Hispanoamericanos* (July, 1954), 133-34.

5. Aleixandre, *op. cit.*, p. 11

6. Concha Zardoya, "*Historia del corazón,*" *Cuadernos Hispanoamericanos*, XIV, No. 4 (July-August, 1955), 237.

7. José Olivio Jiménez, *Cinco poetas del tiempo*, p. 57.

8. Concha Zardoya, *Poesía española contemporánea*, p. 483.

9. J. M. Cohen, "Exile from Paradise," *Times Literary Supplement* (May 17, 1957), 306.

10. Gullón, "Itinerario . . .," p. 231.

11. Bousoño, "Sobre *Historia del corazón* de Vicente Aleixandre," *Insula*, IX, No. 102 (June, 1954), 10.

12. Leopoldo de Luis, "El sentido social . . .," p. 427.

13. *Ibid.*, p. 422.

14. Sáinz de Robles, *Panorama Literario, 1954* (Madrid, 1955), II, 171.

15. Cano, *De Machado a Bousoño*, p. 119.

16. Jiménez, *Cinco poetas del tiempo*, p. 66.

17. "Poetry of the Dispersion," *Times Literary Supplement* (London, December 23, 1955), 776.

18. Valente, "Vicente Aleixandre: la visión de la totalidad," *Indice*, XVII (1963), 29.

19. Jiménez, *op. cit.*, p. 71.

20. Bousoño, "Materia como historia. El nuevo Aleixandre," *Insula*, XVIII, No. 194 (January, 1963), 12.

21. Jiménez, "Vicente Aleixandre en dos tiempos," *Revista Hispánica Moderna*, XXIX (1963), 275.

22. Leopoldo de Luis, "En un vasto dominio," *Papeles de Son Armadans*, XXVIII, No. 83 (1963), 165.

23. Aleixandre, *En un vasto dominio* (Madrid, 1962), p. 13. Further quotations in the text are from this edition.

24. Valente, p. 29.

25. Bousoño, *Insula*, No. 194, 1.

26. Jiménez, *Cinco poetas del tiempo*, pp. 86-87.

27. *Ibid.*, pp. 93-94.

28. Bousoño, *Insula*, No. 194, 12.

29. Leopoldo de Luis, *Papeles de Son Armadans*, No. 83, 169.

30. Jiménez, *op. cit.*, p. 72.

Chapter Eight

1. Aleixandre, *Presencias* (Barcelona, 1965), p. 7.

2. Aleixandre, *Picasso* (Málaga, 1961), pp. 18-19.

3. Leopoldo de Luis, "Un nuevo libro de Aleixandre," *Papeles de Son Armadans*, XXXIX, No. 115 (1965), 98.

4. Aleixandre, *Retratos con nombre* (Barcelona, 1965), p. 10. Page references in the text are to this edition.

5. Aleixandre, "Recuerdo y homenaje," *Corcel*, Nos. 13-15 (1947), 336.

6. Aleixandre, "José Luis Cano en su fondo andaluz," *Insula*, IV, No. 37 (1949), 1.

7. Aleixandre, "Carta a Eulalia Galvarriato," *Insula*, II, No. 23 (November, 1947), 1.

8. Aleixandre, "Cien volúmenes de poesía," *Insula*, IX, No. 97 (January, 1954), 1, 2.

9. Aleixandre, "Poesía, moral, público," *Insula*, V, No. 59 (November, 1950), 1-2.

10. Mariano Baquero Goyanes, "Vicente Aleixandre: Fidelidad a la poesía," *Arbor* (April, 1950), 593.

11. Aleixandre, *Algunos caracteres de la nueva poesía española* (Madrid, 1955).

12. *Ibid.*, p. 8.

13. Doreste, "La prosa de Vicente Aleixandre," *Insula*, XIII, No. 141 (August, 1958), 1.

14. Leopoldo de Luis, "El sentido social . . .," p. 434.

15. Concha Zardoya, *Poesía española contemporánea*, p. 528.

16. Aleixandre, *Los encuentros* (Madrid, 1958), pp. 15-16. Further page references in the text are to this edition.

Selected Bibliography

PRIMARY SOURCES

I. Books by Vicente Aleixandre

Ambito (Málaga: Litoral, 1928; Madrid: Raiz, 1950).

Espadas como labios (Madrid: Espasa Calpe, 1932; Buenos Aires: Losada, 1957).

Pasión de la tierra (Mexico: Fábula, 1935; Madrid: Adonais, XXXII, 1946; Buenos Aires: Losada, 1957).

La destrucción o el amor (Madrid: Signo, 1935; Madrid: Alhambra, 1945; Buenos Aires: Losada, 1954).

Sombra del paraíso (Madrid: Adán, 1944; Buenos Aires: Losada, 1947).

Mundo a solas (Madrid: Clan, 1950).

Poemas paradisíacos (Málaga: El Arroyo de los Angeles, IV, 1952).

Nacimiento último (Madrid: Insula, 1953).

Historia del corazón (Madrid: Espasa Calpe, 1954; Madrid. Espasa Calpe, 1960).

Algunos caracteres de la nueva poesía española (Madrid: Góngora, 1955).

Mis poemas mejores (Madrid: Gredos, 1956; Madrid: Gredos, 1961).

Los encuentros (Madrid: Guadarrama, 1958).

Poemas amorosos. Antología (Buenos Aires: Losada, 1960).

Poesías completas (Madrid. Aguilar, 1960).

Antigua casa madrileña (Santander: Hnos. Bedia, 1961).

En un vasto dominio (Madrid: Revista de Occidente, 1962).

Presencias (Barcelona: Ed. Seix Barral, 1965).

Retratos con nombre (Barcelona: El Bardo, 1965).

II. Pamphlets, Articles, Letters, Essays, Scattered Poetry

"Noche: onda y síntesis," *Verso y Prosa,* 5 (Murcia, May, 1927).

"Mundo Poético," *Verso y Prosa,* 12 (Murcia, October, 1928).

"Federico" (semblanza de Federico García Lorca), *Hora de España* (Valencia, June, 1937).

"Poética," *Corcel,* 5-6 (Valencia, 1944).

"Autocrítica del poeta sobre *Sombra del paraíso,*" *Espadaña,* 3 (León, June, 1944).

171

"Confidencia literaria," *Entregas de poesía*, 67 (Barcelona, 1944).

"Adolescencia y muerte," prologue to *Primavera de la muerte* of Carlos Bousoño, *Adonais*, XXIX (Madrid, 1946), 9-29.

Letter to Eulalia Galvarriato, *Insula*, 23 (Madrid, Nov. 15, 1947).

"José Luis" (semblanza de José Luis Hidalgo), *Corcel*, 13-15 (Valencia, 1947), 335-36.

Letter from the Spanish poet Vicente Aleixandre, *Atenea*, 277 (Concepción, Chile, April, 1948).

Letter to Gregorio Prieto, *Cobalto*, Vol. D. No. 1 (Barcelona, July 1, 1948).

Letter to Gregorio Prieto (prologue to *Poesía en línea* of Prieto), *Colección Adonais*, LIII (Madrid, 1948).

"En la muerte de Miguel Hernández," *Cuadernos de las Horas Situadas* (Zaragoza, 1948).

Letter to the founders of *Cántico*, *Cántico*, 3 (Córdoba, 1948).

"Un saludo," *La Isla de los Ratones*, I (Santander, 1948).

Prologue to *Nocturnos y otros sueños* by Fernando Charry Lara (Bogotá, 1948).

"José Luis Cano en su fondo andaluz," *Insula*, 37 (Madrid, January 15, 1949).

"Poesía, comunicación," *Correo Literario*, I (Madrid, June 1, 1950).

"Vida del Poeta: el Amor y la Poesía," entrance speech to the Royal Spanish Academy, Madrid, 1950.

Letter from Vicente Aleixandre, *Almenara*, I (Zaragoza, 1950).

"Poesía, moral, público," *Insula*, V, No. 59 (Nov., 1950), 1-2.

Letter from Vicente Aleixandre to José Suárez Carreño on his novel, *Las últimas horas*, Destino (Barcelona, June 1, 1950).

"Revisión de Galdós," *Insula*, VII, No. 82 (Oct., 1952), 3.

A la salida del pueblo (Las Palmas de Gran Canaria, 1953).

"Clementina Arderiu de cerca," *Insula*, VIII, No. 95 (Nov., 1953), 1, 3.

"El niño ciego de Vázquez Díaz" by Daniel Vázquez Díaz, Ateneo (Madrid, 1954). A brief prose essay.

"Cien volúmenes de poesía," *Insula*, IX, No. 97 (Jan., 1954), 1, 2.

Ocho poemas, seleccionados por su autor in *Cuadernos Julio Herrera y Reissig*, No. 39 (Montevideo, 1955).

"Cumpleaños," *Papeles de Son Armadans*, XI, Nos. 32-33 (1958), 121-23.

Picasso, Cuadernos de María Cristina, 13, El Guadalhorce (Málaga, 1961).

A poem in *Desnudos*, libro de estampas, by Francisco Satadell López (Valladolid, 1961).

Homenaje a Luis Cernuda, *La Caña Gris*, 6 (Valencia, 1962), pp. 11-13.

Prologue by Aleixandre, "Cien volúmenes de poesía," in *Adonais.*
Segunda Antología. (Madrid: Ed. Rialp, 1962).

"José Antonio Muñoz Rojas entre corte y cortijo," *Revista de Occidente,* I, No. 3 (June, 1963), 296-300.

"Rubén Darío en un pueblo castellano," *Revista de Occidente,* I, No. 3 (June, 1963), 291-96.

SECONDARY SOURCES

1. Books

Adonais. Segunda Antología. (Madrid: Ed. Rialp, 1962). A continuation, with new poets, of the famous poetry collection. Prologue by Aleixandre.

ALONSO, DÁMASO. *Ensayos sobre poesía española* (Buenos Aires: Revista de Occidente, 1946). Poetry studies from the *Poema del Cid* through Luis de León, Góngora, Bécquer and others. Contains a forty-page discussion of Aleixandre.

————. *Poetas españoles contemporáneos* (Madrid: Gredos, 1962). Studies on Bécquer and members of the Guillén-Lorca generation.

AUB, MAX. *La poesía española contemporánea* (Mexico: Impta. universitaria, 1964). Brief examinations of Modernism and its poets, post-Modernists, the Guillén-Lorca generation, and Spanish poets outside of Spain.

BOUSOÑO, CARLOS. *La poesía de Vicente Aleixandre* (Madrid: Ediciones Insula, 1950; 2. ed. Madrid: Gredos, 1955). The most complete study of Aleixandre's works, especially useful for its study of structural elements in his works.

CANO, JOSÉ LUIS. *Antología de la nueva poesía española* (Madrid: Ed. Cultura Hispánica, 1958). Anthology of poets from Miguel Hernández (1910-1942) through Claudio Rodríguez (b. 1934).

————. *De Machado a Bousoño* (Madrid: Insula, 1955). A series of notes rather than critical studies on the poetry of Antonio Machado, Unamuno, Guillén, and others. A reprint of articles in *Insula,* it has essays on Aleixandre.

————. *Poesía española del siglo XX* (Madrid: Ediciones Guadarrama, 1960). Examines various poetic generations from '98 through the post-war period. The Aleixandre material is reprinted from earlier articles and deals with him as a romantic, mystic pantheist, etc.

————. *El tema España en la poesía española contemporánea* (Madrid: Revista de Occidente, 1964). An anthology which studies Spain as a theme from the eighteenth century through the Generation of 1950, including poets in exile.

CASTELLET, JOSÉ MARÍA. *Veinte años de poesía española. Antología (1939-1959)* (Barcelona: Editorial Seix Barral, 1960). Anthology with an historical introduction of the principal trends of twentieth-century Spanish poetry from Rubén Darío through Luis Cernuda.

CASTELLTORT, RAMÓN. *La poesía lírica española del siglo xx* (Barcelona: Librería Spica, 1957). Excellent discussion of the development of the varying poetic movements of twentieth-century Spain.

CERNUDA, LUIS. *Estudios sobre poesía española contemporánea* (Madrid: Ediciones Guadarrama, 1957). Clearly expressed and perceptive, though severe, historical criticism of twentieth-century Spanish poets.

CHABÁS, JUAN. *Literatura española contemporánea (1988-1950)* (Havana: Cultural, 1952). A good history of contemporary Spanish literature containing interesting information on Aleixandre as a Romantic poet.

CHARRY LARA, FERNANDO. "La poesía neo-romántica de Vicente Aleixandre," in *Cuatro poetas del siglo veinte* (Bogota: Universidad Nacional, 1947). Contains correspondence from Aleixandre and a good discussion of Surrealism. Contains studies on Rilke and other poets by other authors.

COBB, CARL. *Federico García Lorca* (New York: Twayne, 1967).

DÍAZ PLAJA, GUILLERMO. *Historia de la poesía lírica española* (Barcelona: Labor, 1948). A history of Spanish poetry with good analyses of many poets. Finds Aleixandre a Romantic poet.

DIEGO, GERARDO. *Poesía española* (Madrid: Signo, 1934). One of the two best early anthologies of twentieth-century Spanish poetry.

———. *Poesía española contemporánea* (Madrid: Taurus, 1959). A reprint which unites the two earliest complete anthologies of twentieth-century Spanish poetry (1932 and 1934). Contains valuable statements by the poets on their poetic creeds.

DOMENCHINA, JUAN JOSÉ. *Antología de la poesía española contemporánea* (Mexico: "UTEHA," 1947). Third edition of one of the good early anthologies with generous selections and bio-bibliographical notes from Juan Ramón Jiménez through Miguel Hernández.

FLUGEL, JOHN CARL. *The Psychoanalytic Study of the Family.* 5th ed. (London: Hogarth Press, 1935). Marriage, parents, children, and their relationships are studied.

FREUD, SIGMUND. *The Basic Writings of Sigmund Freud,* tr. and ed. by A. A. Brill (New York: The Modern Library, 1938). A standard reference which contains, among other things, *The*

Psychopathology of Everyday Life and *The Interpretation of Dreams.*

————. *Delusion and Dream,* tr. by Helen Downey (New York: Moffat, Yard and Co., 1917). An interpretation of literature through psychoanalytic examination of *Gradiva,* a novel by Wilhelm Jensen.

————. *Leonardo da Vinci, A Study in Sexuality,* tr. by A. A. Brill (New York: Random House, 1947). Artistic creation in its relationship to sexual drives examined through a psychosexual study of infantile reminiscence.

————. *The Standard Edition of the Complete Psychological Works of Freud,* tr. under the general editorship of James Strachey with the help of Anna Freud and others (London: Hogarth Press, Vols. XII, XIX, XX, 1958-1961). As the title implies, the authoritative collection of Freud's works.

FRYE, NORTHROP. *Anatomy of Criticism* (Princeton: Princeton University Press, 1957). Four perceptive critical essays. Interesting information of archetypes in poetry.

GONZÁLEZ MUELA, JOAQUÍN. *El lenguaje poético de la generación Guillén-Lorca* (Madrid: Insula, 1954). A kind of grammar of poetry which studies the differences between prose and poetic language, poetry and non-poetry, in that generation.

GUILLÉN, JORGE. *Language and Poetry* (Cambridge: Harvard University Press, 1961). In addition to his comments on Berceo, Góngora, and kinds of poetic language, interesting for discussion of poets he knew in Spain.

JIMÉNEZ, JOSÉ OLIVIO. *Cinco poetas del tiempo* (Madrid: Insula, 1964). Examines the organic theme of time in the poetry of Aleixandre, Cernuda, Hierro, Bousoño and Brines.

JUNG, CARL GUSTAV. *The Integration of the Personality* (New York: Farrar & Rinehart, 1939). Useful for its discussion of archetypal motifs of the collective unconscious and dream symbols.

————. *Psychology of the Unconscious,* tr. by Beatrice Hinkle (New York: Dodd, Mead & Co., 1944). A study of the symbolisms of the libido and the evolution of thought.

KLEIN, MELANIE. *The Psychoanalysis of Children* (London: Hogarth Press, 1949). A classic work, first published in 1932, by one of the pioneers in the field of child behavior and analysis.

KUBIE, LAWRENCE. *Neurotic Distortion of the Creative Process* (Lawrence, Kansas: Noonday Press, 1961). Examines interactions between creative and neurotogenic processes and the psychodynamics of neurosis and creativity.

LEWIN, BERTRAM D. *The Psychoanalysis of Elation* (New York: Norton, 1950). A study of manic states, denial, defense mech-

anisms, dreams and the like, along with a review of the literature
on the subject.

LEY, CHARLES DAVID. *Spanish Poetry Since 1939* (Washington, D. C.:
The Catholic University Press, 1962). Contains good biblio-
graphies and insights by the poets of the last twenty-five years
into their own works. Evaluates Aleixandre's role as mentor.

MONTERDE, ALBERTO. *La poesía en la lírica española* (Mexico: Impta.
Universitaria, 1953). A short study of the Brémond·Valéry
polemic and its relationship to pure and surrealistic poetry in
Spain.

MULLAHY, PATRICK. *Oedipus, Myth and Complex* (New York: Her-
mitage Press, 1948). Reviews psychoanalytic theory and studies
the Oedipus trilogy of Sophocles.

PRESCOTT, FREDERICK CLARK. *The Poetic Mind* (New York: Mac-
millan, 1922). Examines the psychological factors involved in
the poetic process, such as abnormal states, imagination, and
dreams.

Psychoanalysis Today, ed. by Sandor Lorenz (New York: International University Press, 1944). A series of studies on various
aspects of psychoanalysis and its relation to psychosomatic problems, social work, ego-psychology, hysteria and phobias, etc.,
by experts such as Ferenczi, Marianne Kris, Melanie Klein, Franz
Alexander, Bertram D. Lewin, and A. A. Brill.

RANK, OTTO. *The Trauma of Birth* (New York: R. Brunner, 1952).
A somewhat disputed text by a well-known psychoanalyst whose
theory is that the intrauterine state and its termination is a
rebirth or kind of biological repetition.

ROHEIM, GEZA. *Gates of the Dream* (New York: International University Press, 1952). An evaluation of dreams and animism by
a well-known anthropologist.

SÁINZ DE ROBLES, FEDERICO CARLOS. *Historia y antología de la poesía
lírica española* (Madrid: Aguilar, 1964). A general anthology
of Spanish poetry. Sáinz finds Aleixandre original, romantic,
surrealistic, and existential.

SALINAS, PEDRO. *Literatura española siglo XX* (Mexico: Antigua
Librería Robredo, 1949). The first edition is Mexico: Séneca,
1941. Contains studies on the Generation of '98, Modernism,
Unamuno, Valle Inclán, and Aleixandre's generation.

TORRENTE BALLESTER, GONZALO. *Literatura española contemporánea*
(Madrid: Afrodisio Aguado, 1949). Perhaps the best general
study of contemporary Spanish literature. He comments on
Aleixandre's authenticity and excellent formal qualities.

TURNBULL, ELEANOR. *Contemporary Spanish Poetry* (Baltimore:
Johns Hopkins Press, 1945). Translations of many of the Guillén-

Lorca generation of poets with short introductions. Valuable for Pedro Salinas' evaluations cited by Miss Turnbull.

VIVANCO, LUIS FELIPE. *Introducción a la poesía española contemporánea* (Madrid: Ediciones Guadarrama, 1957). Some interesting photographs. Somewhat incoherent studies on a variety of poets from Juan Ramón Jiménez through Leopoldo Panero.

ZARDOYA, CONCHA. *Poesía española contemporánea* (Madrid: Ediciones Guadarrama, 1961). Not intended as complete studies on the poets but as an examination of special aspects of their work. She examines Bécquer in a new light, the mirror and crystal in Machado, God in the works of Juan Ramón Jiménez, and the sea in Rafael Alberti. One of the most valuable studies on Aleixandre.

2. Articles

"Aleixandre y El Corazón," *ABC*, October 29, 1955, p. 35. Anonymous review, probably by Gerardo Diego, of *History of the Heart*.

ALFAYA, JAVIER. "Dos Cantatas de Gabriel Celaya," *Insula*, XX, No. 221 (April, 1965), 7. Considers Aleixandre perhaps the greatest living Spanish poet.

————. "Dos nuevos libros de Vicente Aleixandre," *Insula*, XX, No. 227 (October, 1965), 5. Comments on *Portraits with Name and Presences*.

ALONSO, DAMASO. "La destrucción o el amor," *Revista de Occidente*, No. 144 (June, 1935), 331-40. Notes on Aleixandre's volume, showing its burning romanticism and pantheism.

————. "Espadas como labios," *Revista de Occidente*, CXIV (December, 1932), 323-33. Finds the poetry deliberately irrational.

————. "El Nilo," *Corcel*, 5-6 (1944), 80. Views Aleixandre as a father of the Nile surrounded by the younger poets, his currents.

————. "Vicente Aleixandre," *Insula*, V, No. 50 (February 1950), 1, 7. The answering lecture to Aleixandre's Academy speech. Comments on wide critical acclaim achieved by Aleixandre and his poetic following.

ALVAREZ VILLAR, ALFONSO. "El panteísmo en la obra poética de Vicente Aleixandre," *Cuadernos Hispanoamericanos*, LIX, No. 175 (1964), 178-84. Examines pantheistic elements in his works. Considers "El enterrado" of *Final Birth* one of the greatest poems on death.

ANDERSON IMBERT, ENRIQUE. "Aleixandre, Rubén Darío y Unamuno," *Sur*, Buenos Aires, No. 230 (September-October, 1964). A brief examination of the relationship of Rubén Darío and the Spanish poets, especially Unamuno.

ARTECHE, MIGUEL. "Sombra del paraíso," *Atenea*, XCVI, No. 297 (March, 1950), 309-12. Review of *Shadow of Paradise*.

BAQUERO GOYANES, MARIANO. "Vicente Aleixandre: Fidelidad a la poesía," *Arbor* (April, 1950), 593-94. Discussion of his Academy entrance speech; Baquero views the speech itself as a kind of poetry.

BARRAL, CARLOS. "Memoria de un poema," *Papeles de Son Armadans*, XI, Nos. 32-33 (1958), 394-400. An analysis of "The Waltz" which he finds rhythmically almost perfect and whose social implications he reinforces.

BENÍTEZ CLAROS, RAFAEL. "Vicente Aleixandre: *Sombra del paraíso*," *Cuadernos de Literatura Contemporánea*, 15 (1944), 261-73. Use of language, melody and rhythm by Aleixandre and the uniqueness of his poetic world.

"Bibliografía sobre Vicente Aleixandre," *Papeles de Son Armadans*, XI, Nos. 32-33 (1958), 443-63. Based largely on Bousoño's 1950 bibliography.

BLAJOT, JORGE. "Más allá de la palabra," *Razón y Fe* (May 1, 1950), 632. Agrees with Aleixandre that neither verse form nor words are important in themselves.

BLEIBERG, GERMÁN. "Vicente Aleixandre y sus poemas difíciles," *Insula*, V, No. 50 (February, 1950), 6. Finds *Passion of the Earth* his most anguished book and terribly sincere, if obscure.

BOSCH, RAFAEL. "The New Nonconformist Spanish Poetry," *Odyssey*, II (1962), 222-34. Examines the beginnings of "realistic and historical" poetry from 1950 on.

BOUSOÑO, CARLOS. "Dos ensayos," *Papeles de Son Armadans*, XI, Nos. 32-33 (1958), 245-55. Examines the term "great poetry" and gives a rapid survey of Aleixandre's poetry and his unity of vision.

————. "Materia como historia. El nuevo Aleixandre," *Insula*, XVIII, No. 194 (January, 1963), 1, 12. Sees *In a Vast Dominion* as his greatest work and basic to an understanding of all his poetry.

————. Prologue to *Poesías completas de Vicente Aleixandre* (Madrid: Aguilar, 1960), pp. 11-44. Views Aleixandre's work as falling into two main groups, cosmic love and human love. An excellent summary of Aleixandre's work through *History of the Heart*.

————. "Sobre *Historia del corazón* de Vicente Aleixandre," *Insula*, IX, No. 102 (June, 1954), 3, 10. A review of that work and its place in his total production. Sees it as a high point of his second phase and as a hopeful message.

————. "Un nuevo libro de Aleixandre," *Insula*, V, No. 53 (1950), 2, 7. A review of *World Alone* which he finds the link between *Destruction or Love* and *Shadow of Paradise*.

BUSUIOCEANU, ALEJANDRO. "El epifanismo de Vicente Aleixandre," *Insula*, IV, No. 39 (March, 1949), 7, 8. Denies the term neo-Romantic and coins Epiphanism for Aleixandre's poetry of the unreal, inaccessible to rational knowledge.

CAMPOS, JORGE. "Nuestro amigo Vicente," *Corcel*, 5-6 (1944), 101. Popular possibilities of Aleixandre's poetry and his human value.

CANITO, ENRIQUE. "Diálogo con Vicente Aleixandre," *Insula*, V, No. 50 (February, 1950), 3, 6. Discusses the poet's love of nineteenth-century novels, his feeling that poetry is communication, that his is, and has been, clear, etc.

CANO, JOSÉ LUIS. "El amor en la poesía de Vicente Aleixandre," *Corcel*, 5-6 (1944). The universality of love in Aleixandre's poetry and his identification with natural forces.

————. "El tema de España en la poesía española contemporánea," *La Torre*, IX, No. 33 (1961), 51-80. Spain as a preoccupation from the eighteenth century on and the love and anguish felt by her poets, including the current generation.

————. "Málaga en Vicente Aleixandre," *Papeles de Son Armadans*, XI, Nos. 32-33 (1958), 332-40. Aleixandre's visit to *Litoral*, the effect of the sea in his works, its identification with Paradise.

————. "Vicente Aleixandre en la Academia," *Insula*, IV, 43 (July, 1949), 2. Stresses his influence through personal contact as well as through his works.

————. "Vicente Aleixandre: *Nacimiento último*," *Insula*, VIII, No. 90 (June 15, 1953), 6-7. A review, stressing the poem's pantheistic elements.

CELAYA, GABRIEL. "Notas para una 'Cantata en Aleixandre,' " *Papeles de Son Armadans*, XI, Nos. 32-33 (1958), 375-85. Views him as the most continuing poet of his generation, sees the four stages in his work, comments briefly on some of them.

COHEN, J. M. "Exile from Paradise," *Times Literary Supplement*, London, May 17, 1957, p. 306. Shapes and textures in Aleixandre's free verse and its negative and positive qualities.

————. "Recent Poets of Spain," *Times Literary Supplement*, London, November 2, 1956, p. 650. Review of Cano's *From Machado to Bousoño* and Bousoño's *The Poetry of Vicente Aleixandre*.

COUFFON, CLAUDE. "Recontre avec un gran poète: Jorge Guillén," *Les Lettres Nouvelles*, Novelle Serie, No. 19 (July 8, 1959), 28-30. Interview with Guillén and his remarks on the dehumanized poetry of his generation.

DIEGO, GERARDO. "Curva ascendente," *Insula*, V, No. 50 (February, 1950), 1-2. Recollection of early poems, especially those up to Fray Luis de León.

————. *"Pasión de la tierra,"* Corcel, 5-6 (1944). Comments on some lost poems of Aleixandre. Views *Passion of the Earth* as a book without limits and of dark instincts.

DORESTE, VENTURA. "Aspectos de Aleixandre," *Insula,* XV, No. 167 (1960), 6. Approach of the poet to human life which he also finds evil.

————. "Ponderación de Aleixandre," *Insula,* XII, No. 124 (1957), 4. Finds Aleixandre a liberating force and one who innovates but also has lasting value.

————. "La prosa de Vicente Aleixandre," *Insula,* XIII, No. 141 (1958), 1, 2. Examines *The Encounters* and finds his prose essentially poetry.

————. "La unidad poética de Aleixandre," *Insula,* V, No. 50 (February, 1950), 6. Finds the germs of all his poetry in *Ambit.*

DUQUE, AQUILINO. "Una victoria sobre el tiempo," *Cuadernos Hispanoamericanos,* No. 133 (June, 1961), 125-34. Review of the Aguilar *Complete poems.* Citing Angel Valente and José María Castellet among others, he sees Aleixandre's poetry as a way of stopping time and a revolution in expression.

FERNÁNDEZ ALMAGRO, MELCHOR. *"Mundo a solas,"* ABC, May 14, 1950, pp. 27-28. A review.

FERNÁNDEZ CARVAJAL, RODRIGO. "El tiempo en lo poesía de Vicente Aleixandre," *Corcel,* Nos. 5-6 (Homenaje a Vicente Aleixandre, Valencia, 1944). States that Aleixandre's books were constructed according to a specific concept of time with a varying formula for each.

FERRARÁS, RAFAEL. "Sobre la generación poética de 1927," *Papeles de Son Armadans,* XI, Nos. 32-33 (1958), 301-14. A brief examination of the Guillén-Lorca generation of poets.

FRUTOS, EUGENIO. "Las poesías completas de Vicente Aleixandre," *Indice,* XV, Nos. 150-151 (1961), 30. A review of the 1960 Aguilar edition, in which he finds *Destruction or Love* Aleixandre's first achievement of real authenticity, and comments on the metaphysical and human aspects of *History of the Heart.*

GAOS, VICENTE. "Fray Luis de León, 'fuente' de Aleixandre," *Papeles de Son Armadans,* XI, Nos. 32-33 (1958), 344-63. Compares the poetry of Luis de León to that of Aleixandre and shows great similarities in imagery, structure, etc.

GARCIASOL, RAMÓN. "Notas sobre la nueva poesía española (1939-1955)," *Revista Nacional de Cultura,* XIX, No. 119 (1956), 48-64. Defines the "realism" of contemporary poetry as too narrow a definition, preferring the term "historicity." The themes are traditional but the tone has changed.

GIL, ILDEFONSO M. "Vanguardia y complemento de *Sombra del paraíso* en el último libro de Vicente Aleixandre," *Cuadernos*

Hispanoamericanos, No. 15 (May-June, 1950), 587-90. Claims *Shadow of Paradise* is the book of Aleixandre's maturity.

GIL DE BIEDMA, JAIME. "Encuentro con Vicente, al modo de Aleixandre," *Papeles de Son Armadans*, XI, Nos. 32-33 (1958), 388-91. His meeting in Barcelona with Aleixandre at his hotel, and Aleixandre's ability as a good listener.

GÓMEZ DE LA SERNA, RAMÓN. "Gemelismo: Gerardo Diego y Vicente Aleixandre," *Revista Nacional de Cultura*, No. 104 (May-June, 1954), 19-27. Considers Aleixandre and Diego the head of the whole contemporary poetic movement.

GUILLÉN, JORGE. "Algunos poetas amigos," *Papeles de Son Armadans*, XI, Nos. 32-33 (1958), 151-65. Remarks about Spanish poetry in general, the meaning of poetry, the themes of his poetic generation, love, universe, destiny, death, and their devotion to poetry.

GULLÓN, RICARDO. "La generación española de 1936," *Insula*, XX, Nos. 224-25 (1965), 1, 24. Aspects of the poets Rosales, Leopoldo Panero, and others of this generation.

———. "Itinerario poético de Vicente Aleixandre," *Papeles de Son Armadans*, XI, Nos. 32-33 (1958), 195-234. Traces his entire poetic work, the darkness of *Passion of the Earth*, its chaos and sincerity, the hope of *Swords Like Lips*, etc.

HIERRO, JOSÉ. "Testimonio de Vicente Aleixandre," *Papeles de Son Armadans*, XI, Nos. 32-33 (1958), 240-44. His introduction to Aleixandre's poetry, his initial dislike, and his growing affection for the poet and his work through the years.

JIMÉNEZ, JOSÉ OLIVIO. "El tiempo en la poesía actual," *Insula*, XX, No. 218 (1965), 1, 10, 12. A resumé of the final pages of the introduction to *Five Contemporary Poets*. He considers the 1927 and the 1936 generations to be the principal exponents of the central theme of time.

———. "Medio siglo de poesía española," *Hispania*, L, No. 4 (1967), 931-46. An excellent short survey of twentieth-century Spanish poetry.

———. "Vicente Aleixandre en dos tiempos," *Revista Hispánica Moderna*, XXIX (1963), 263-89. States that *In a Vast Dominion* is the work which most systematically incorporates the temporal dimension of existence as a theme.

JIMÉNEZ, JUAN RAMÓN. "Vicente Aleixandre," *Corcel*, Nos. 5-6 (1944), 77. A reprinting of a much earlier evaluation by Jiménez of Aleixandre as a reflector of nature.

LEWIN, BERTRAM D. "Phobic Symptoms and Dream Interpretation," *The Psychoanalytic Quarterly*, XXI, No. 3 (July, 1952), 295-322. Application of dream psychology concepts to the neuroses, study of phobias and theory of anxiety.

————. "Reconsiderations of the Dream Screen," *The Psychoanalytic Quarterly*, XXII, No. 2 (1953), 174-99. Elaboration of his 1946 paper that dreams contain special structures which serve as a projection drop for the dream picture, genetically a segment of the baby's view of the breasts.

LUIS, LEOPOLDO DE. "Actualidad de Ambito," *Insula*, V, No. 52 (April, 1950), 2. Views Aleixandre as one of the most significant Spanish poets of all time.

————. "El sentido social en la poesía de Vicente Aleixandre," *Papeles de Son Armadans*, XI, Nos. 32-33 (1958), 415-28. Comments on the continuity of Aleixandre's work and finds social meaning in works even before *History of the Heart*. Sees pseudo-existentialism in his poetry.

————. "El tema de España en la poesía contemporánea," *Papeles de Son Armadans*, XXXV (1964), 192-200. A review of Cano's work in which he disputes the latter's use of the words "generation of 1950."

————. "En un vasto dominio," *Papeles de Son Armadans*, XXVIII, No. 83 (1963), 157-69. Comments on the movie camera technique of Aleixandre and the totality of the world in creative matter.

————. "La obra completa de Vicente Aleixandre," *Papeles de Son Armadans*, XVIII (1960), 191-96. Discusses the syntactic aspects of his imagery in this review of the Aguilar edition.

————. "Un nuevo libro de Aleixandre," *Papeles de Son Armadans*, XXXIX (1965), 95-102. An analysis of *Portraits with Name* which he views as a new contribution to the poetic evolution of Aleixandre.

MAÑACH, JORGE. "Visitas españolas: Vicente Aleixandre," *Insula*, XV, No. 162 (1960), 3, 5. Comments on Aleixandre's illness, his timidity, his desire to unify in his poetry, his increasing simplicity as a mature poet, and his human preoccupations.

MORALES, RAFAEL. "*La poesía de Vicente Aleixandre*," *Cuadernos Hispanoamericanos*, No. 28 (April, 1952), 115-16. A review of Bousoño's work on Aleixandre.

————. "Un nuevo libro de Vicente Aleixandre," *Cuadernos Hispanoamericanos*, No. 43 (July, 1953), 119-21. Finds *Final Birth* full of dazzling imagery.

MUÑOZ ROJAS, JOSÉ A. "A cielo raso," *Cruz y Raya*, No. 25 (1935), 135-47. Discussion of *Destruction or Love*.

————. "*Sombra del paraíso*," *Escorial*, No. 43 (May, 1944), 458-63. A review of that work.

————. "Vicente Aleixandre a treinta años vista," *Papeles de Son Armadans*, XI, Nos. 32-33 (1958), 322-23. Recalls first meeting with Aleixandre in 1929 and a visit to his house at Velintonia, 3.

NORA, EUGENIO. "Aleixandre, renovador," *Corcel*, Nos. 5-6 (1944), 95-96. Sees Aleixandre as the poet with the greatest influence on younger poetic generations and as the innovator of a new poetic world.

————. "Forma poética y cosmovisión en la poesía de Vicente Aleixandre," *Cuadernos Hispanoamericonas*, No. 7 (January, 1949), 115-21. Sees Aleixandre's poetry as a radical departure from classic form and logical meanings.

————. "Hacia una revisión de libros capitales," *Cisneros*, No. 6 (1943), 97-102. Analyzes *Destruction or Love* as one of the important works, praising it for its sincerity, richness, and grandeur, almost unmatched in Spanish poetry.

OLMOS GARCÍA, FRANCISCO. "Una antología de poetas españoles de hoy," *Cuadernos Americanos*, XXIII, No. 133 (1964), 191-233. Examines various Catalan poets, their realistic poetry, and their belief in art as at the service of history.

RICA, CARLOS DE LA. "Vanguardismo en los años cincuenta," *Papeles de Son Armadans*, XXXVII (1965), No. 109, iii-xvi; No. 110, xxv-xlviii. Studies poets belonging to *The Bird of Straw* and *Deucalión* groups from about 1950 on, their irony, tenderness, and new poetic horizons.

RÍO, ANGEL DEL. "La poesía surrealista de Aleixandre," *Revista Hispánica Moderna*, II (1935), 21-23. Views *Destruction or Love* as a desperate desire on Aleixandre's part to pierce the mystery of the universe.

SOUVIRÓN, JOSÉ MARÍA. "Con los debidos respetos," *Papeles de Son Armadans*, XI, Nos. 32-33 (1958), 315-19. Affectionate recall of his friendship with Aleixandre, whom he visualizes always against a Malagan background, and with Dámaso Alonso on Aleixandre's sixtieth birthday.

————. "Humano y excelente," *Cuadernos Hispanoamericanos*, No. 55 (July, 1954), 133-35. Feels the real continuity of Aleixandre's work depends on his human passion.

Times Literary Supplement. "Poetry of the Dispersion," London (December 23, 1955), p. 776. States that Aleixandre's generation constitutes a little Golden Age and that the poet's principal value lies in his vigor and imagery.

TORRE, GUILLERMO DE. "Contemporary Spanish Poetry," *Texas Quarterly*, IV, Part I (1961), 55-78. Studies briefly movements such as Modernism, Ultraism, and Surrealism. Finds the principal guide of the Generation of 1927 to have been Juan Ramón Jiménez. Examines the Generation of 1936 and beyond.

VALENTE, JOSÉ ANGEL. "Vicente Aleixandre: la visión de la totalidad," *Indice de Artes y Letras*, XVII (1963), 29-30. Sees *History of the Heart* as a transition to the stage where human solidarity reaches its final limits, and *In a Vast Dominion* as the reconciliation of man and matter and as the unifying force of all Aleixandre's work.

VALVERDE, JOSÉ MARÍA. "De la disyunción a la negación en la poesía de Vicente Aleixandre," *Escorial,* No. 52 (1945), 447-57. Discusses Aleixandre's syntax in relation to his vision of the world.

————. "Dos visitas," *Papeles de Son Armadans,* XI, Nos. 32-33 (1958), 328-31. Describes briefly a visit to Aleixandre and to Dámaso Alonso and recalls their mutual poet friends.

WHITMORE, KATHERINE R. "A Lyrical Decade: Spain, 1940-1950," *Hispania,* XXXVI, No. 2 (May, 1953), 170-76. Comments on the prolific production of lyric poetry, the reviews of the day, and some of the poetic trends, along with brief comments on the melodic sweep of Aleixandre's poetry and his effect on young writers.

ZARDOYA, CONCHA. "*Historia del corazón,*" *Cuadernos Americans,* XIV, No. 4 (July-August, 1955), 237-79. Views the volume as the history of the poet's life and through his the history of human life.

————. "La presencia femenina en *Sombra del paraíso,*" *Revista de las Indias,* 107 (January-February, 1949), 147-74. The search for beauty beneath the improbable and an optimistic approach to time and love mark Aleixandre's poetry.

————. "La técnica metafórica en la poesía contemporánea," *Cuadernos Americanos,* XX, No. 116 (1961), 258-81. Examines metaphoric peculiarities from Unamuno through Miguel Hernández.

————. "Los tres mundos de Vicente Aleixandre," *Revista Hispánica Moderna,* XX (1954), 67-73. The interaction of love and destruction, the need for fusion, and the place of man in the cosmos as revealed in Aleixandre's poetry.

Index